Capital Rambles:

Exploring the National Capital Region

Katharine Fletcher

Maps by Eric Fletcher

Fitzhenry & Whiteside

Published in Canada by Fitzhenry & Whiteside, 195 Allstate Parkway, Markham, Ontario L3R 4T8

Published in the United States by Fitzhenry & Whiteside, 121 Harvard Avenue, Suite 2, Allston, Massachusetts 02134

www.fitzhenry.ca godwit@fitzhenry.ca

10 9 8 7 6 5 4 3 2 1

National Library of Canada Cataloguing in Publication

Fletcher, Katharine, 1952-
Capital rambles : exploring the National Capital Region / Katharine Fletcher ;
maps by Eric Fletcher.
Includes index.
ISBN 1-55041-770-3
1. National Capital Region (Ont. and Quebec)—Guidebooks. 2. Ottawa (Ont.)—
Guidebooks. 3. Gatineau (Quebec)—Guidebooks.
I. Fletcher, Eric, 1951- II. Title.
FC2783.F57 2004 917.13'84044 C2003-900909-2

Publisher Cataloging-in-Publication Data (U.S.)
(Library of Congress Standards)

Fletcher, Katharine.
Capital rambles : exploring the National Capital Region / Katharine Fletcher ; maps by Eric Fletcher. —1st ed.
[346] p. : ill., photos., maps ; cm.
Includes index.
Summary: A walking tour guide highlighting Canada's National Capital region.
ISBN 1-55041-770-3 (pbk.)
1. National Capital Region (Ont. and Québec)—Guidebooks. 2. Ottawa (Ont.)—Guidebooks. 3. Outdoor recreation—Ontario, Eastern—Guidebooks. I. Title.
917.13/ 7044 dc22 GV191.46.O6.F61 2004

Fitzhenry & Whiteside acknowledges with thanks the Canada Council for the Arts, the Government of Canada through the Book Publishing Industry Development Program (BPIDP), and the Ontario Arts Council for their support of our publishing program.

Cover / Interior book design by Karen Petherick
All maps were designed by Eric Fletcher
Cover Image Credits: See back cover
Printed and bound in Canada

Dedication

Where would we be without the keepers of the past? *Capital Rambles* is dedicated to the memory of a mentor and friend, author and historian Diane Aldred. Diane's legacy of books inspires us to cherish our past, so we can better understand our future and our place in this world.

Contents

Contents

Contents

Contents

Preface

For years writing Capital Rambles has lingered on my mind, haunting me while I've explored Canada's National Capital Region (NCR). I've hiked, snowshoed, cross-country skied, ridden bicycles and horses, kayaked, and canoed through its many landscapes, moods, and seasons. After living in Ottawa from 1974 to 1989, my husband Eric and I moved to the West Québec countryside we cherish so much.

Since May 1989, home has been a heritage farmhouse sheltered from the north wind by the Eardley Escarpment, the sinuous ridge describing the southern boundary of Gatineau Park. We telecommute with editors throughout the world from this landscape of elemental Canadian Shield, mixed hardwood and softwood forests, picturesque farmland, and dramatic riverscapes. It's a spectacular region to call home — but I did not grow up in the NCR.

I was born in England, spending my happiest years as a young girl exploring a ridge called Alderley Edge, which overlooks the Cheshire Plain. Fast-forward to Toronto, where my parents emigrated in 1958. I first visited the National Capital Region in the late sixties, on a grade ten physical geography expedition. We Toronto schoolgirls were variously impressed — or not — with the trip. But my geography teacher, Miss Prestwich, claimed my rapt attention as she spun her tales. After passing Peterborough's drumlins and eskers we motored north, entering the glacially scoured landscape of gouged rocks and ribbon lakes alongside Highway 7 near Madoc.

What followed is a bit of a blur, until we crossed the Ottawa River at those boiling rapids known as the Chaudière Falls. That's when memory kicks in once more. Surely we were told to look to the right to the spires of Parliament Hill as we rolled through downtown Hull, now Gatineau. Miss Prestwich hummed along, telling us how Jacques Gréber, the Parisian urban planner hired by Prime Minister Mackenzie King, create a living master plan for the capital. She told us about some of the plan's outstanding features, such as the "emerald necklace" of the Greenbelt, with its park-like roadways, and the creation of a federal district.

My most vivid recollection was hiking Gatineau Park's King Mountain Trail. I recall ascending through mysterious, dark hemlock woods along its north face, then emerging into another world where heat and sunshine blasted exposed, ancient Precambrian rock of the Eardley Escarpment. Here, stunted oak clung to thin topsoil and blue harebells nodded on the May breeze. Then and there, while I gazed over the flat plain below, I lost my heart to the Ottawa Valley.

My impressionable young mind drank in the view of the flat valley floor stretching as far as my eyes could see. In the near distance, the Ottawa River twinkled, coursing through fields, woods, and alongside hamlets toward Ottawa. Miss Prestwich spun stories of Samuel de Champlain, who paddled upriver in 1609, 1613, and 1615 in a birch bark canoe in his historic wild goose chase for a passage to China.

I remember getting intensely still, as children do when entranced. I also recall feeling envious of the explorer. What did Champlain see? Was he ever afraid? How did this landscape differ then? Did he see many animals or birds? What did he and his native guides eat? Who did he meet?

A decade later, my boyfriend (soon to be husband) Eric Fletcher took me cycling, hiking, and skiing in Gatineau Park. And, from 1985 to 1988 while researching my first book *Historical Walks: The Gatineau Park Story*, I discovered Champlain's journal. In it, he chronicles the answers to my schoolgirl questions; in it I still find the thrill of adventure though it was penned almost four hundred years ago.

Fast forward to the present. The mighty Ottawa River still sounds its siren call to me. Eric and I have paddled *Windigo*, our home-made cedar-strip canoe, alongside Rideau Falls, and have ventured close to the Chats Falls' dam west of Quyon, in Champlain's paddle strokes. We will never tire of this river's story, changing moods — or its denizens.

Water defines the sprawling National Capital Region that encompasses almost 5,000 square kilometres of Eastern Ontario and West Québec. The three sister rivers — Ottawa, Rideau, and Gatineau — meet here at the capital. The Ottawa River connected early peoples with a trade route from the Great Lakes (and beyond) down the French, Mattawa, Ottawa, and St. Lawrence rivers to the Atlantic. Water also has its way with the land, carving physical features deep into the earth, gouging caves like the Laflèche and Lusk caverns that we can explore, and creating ancient terraces or beachheads that lie like a memory upon the valley.

I know and love this land. It is a pleasure to reveal just a few of its stories while we ramble along together, exploring our National Capital Region by car, on foot, in canoe or kayak, on horseback, bicycle, cross-country skis, or snowshoes. Whatever the season, different moods await you in our world-class capital that perhaps fortunately remains one of our crowded, busy world's best-kept secrets.

Finally — why did I call this book "*Capital Rambles*"? Because according to the *American Heritage Dictionary of the English Language*, the old-English derivation of "ramble" is "wandrian," which is where we get "wander." With my love of adventure and gentle conveyances such as canoes, skis, and horses, I consider "rambling" a poetical description of how I like to leisurely explore our natural world. I hope you'll agree. Come, pack your curiosity and join me on my rambles!

Katharine Fletcher
Quyon, Québec
Spring 2004

Special note: As of spring 2004, the Mayor of Ottawa Bob Chiarelli announced a draconian 82 percent budget cut to the capital's heritage programs. Several sites mentioned in *Capital Rambles* may be affected and, in a worst-case scenario, might be closed. These include the Cumberland Heritage Museum, Bytown Museum, and Pinhey's Point estate. Because the sites will still exist (albeit perhaps in a different name or form) I decided to keep them on the principle that if you are keen, you may get special permission to visit them. Let's hope the Mayor has a change of plan and decides to fund these important cultural icons of the National Capital Region.

PART ONE

Introducing the National Capital Region

The Landforms

Who has seen the wind?
Neither you nor I.
But when the trees bow down their heads
The wind is passing by.

Christina Rosetti's poem aptly describes the effect of the wind's otherwise invisible presence. We cannot see the forces of nature that have bullied and cajoled our landscape into its present, ever-evolving form. Canada's capital is topographically blessed: three mighty rivers — the Ottawa, Rideau, and Gatineau — tumble their way through broad valley floors and outcrops of Canadian Shield. To the north of the Ottawa River, in Québec, the Eardley Escarpment juts above the valley floor. To the south, in Ontario, undulating farmland, wetlands, and outcrops of moraine tease us into wondering how today's National Capital Region was formed over the eons of time.

We human beings dwell in the present and fret about the future. Few of us share the geologist's indulgence of appreciating time as a broad continuum, during which massive forces shape our present and future realities. Instead, we worry about the here and now. We concern ourselves with the potability of our water, for instance, oblivious to the geophysical realities that created "natural pollutants" such as traces of salt in our water. Who among us recognizes that saline water in some wells is the result of the Champlain Sea, which flooded this part of North America 12,000 years ago?

The present is the legacy of the past in inestimable ways. I invite you to pause and travel back in time, to appreciate the incredible natural diversity we enjoy here in the valley. Ottawa is a world-class capital in numerous ways, and its spectacular setting is, I believe, its most precious asset.

VIEW FROM THE TOP

There's no better way to appreciate the beauty and diversity of Ottawa's physical geography than from aloft. Take a hot air balloon ride some day — or rent a plane from the Carp airfield. Or, actually look out of the window as your airplane makes its descent into Ottawa's international airport. What you'll see is a landscape of water, rock, forests — and sprawling urban life.

There's another way to capture a snapshot of the valley, though, by getting your view from the top of King Mountain just like I did as a teenager. Cross the Ottawa River and drive or cycle to King Mountain in Gatineau Park, then hike to its summit. At 344 metres (1,129 feet), it is the highest point on the Eardley Escarpment. Get out your detective eyes and start to interpret the clues spread before you on the valley floor. You'll notice a variety of land uses. There is agricultural land with cattle grazing and crops growing, punctuated by farmhouses and their outbuildings. There are sand and gravel pits, limestone quarries, residential developments along with their tidy looking flower and vegetable gardens. Off to the east you'll spy the urban sprawl of Gatineau and Ottawa, but there are also villages, bush lots, wetlands, and watercourses.

Several iterations of transportation systems are visible, too. The Ottawa River was the original "Trans-Canada Highway," offering Paleo-Indian peoples through to explorers, coureur-de-bois, and Jesuits a transportation route from the Atlantic to Great Lakes and the hinterland beyond. Now the Ottawa is a recreational corridor: on a summer's day sailboats dart about while, hidden from view, white-water rafters tumble through hydraulic rapids on the Upper Ottawa. From King Mountain, we can also locate railway bridges and tracks, and a variety of road networks, from major highways to gravelled back roads.

The way we human beings use the landscape is dictated by physical geography or, more specifically, by topography, which in turn has been forged over millennia by glacial and other geophysical forces. In the late 1800s for example, the rocky Eardley Escarpment was home to approximately 200 settlers, but by 1915, the majority had abandoned their homesteads. Why? Because the topsoil was too scant upon the ridge to support anything but subsistence farms. Settlers found it too tough to eke out an existence here, and left to find an easier life elsewhere.

Eons of mountain building, ice ages, and marine deposition have created this varied landscape. Such combined forces over billions of years created the sedimentary rocks (Nepean sandstone and Grenville limestone) that are quarried today, plus the glacial till, sand, and gravel we use for many purposes, from fill to cement.

Geologists such as Dr. Alice Wilson and Dr. Donald Hogarth have written detailed descriptions of the NCR's geology. Broadly speaking, six geophysical stages created the landscape: mountain-building, marine submergence, faulting, glaciation and the Laurentide Ice Cap (also known as the Wisconsin Ice Cap), submergence under the Champlain Sea, and finally, the uplift which created the present-day Ottawa River watershed.

PRECAMBRIAN MOUNTAIN-BUILDING

The Gatineau Hills are part of a mountain range geophysicists call the Laurentian Highlands, created during the Precambrian mountain-building era, over a billion years ago. This is the rock we call the Canadian Shield, composed of metamorphic quartzites, marbles, and gneisses, as well as igneous granites and syenites, born from hundreds of millions of years of repeated sedimentation, erosion, intrusion, and volcanic activity.

Although fossils are rare, it is possible to find algae, sponges, and worm burrows here. This was the age of upheaval and, as unbelievable as it might seem today, at one time the Gatineau Hills were higher than the Rocky Mountains.

PALAEOZOIC ERA: THE GREAT SEAS

After the volcanic activity of the Precambrian era came seven great periods of submergence during which waves of oceans successively flooded and drained the land. Roughly 600 million years ago the first immense seas of the Cambrian era deposited sediments that eventually compressed, creating the local Nepean sandstone that was quarried and used in buildings such as at Parliament Hill.

Next came the Ordovician age when limestone and shale were deposited, layer upon layer. Pancake-like stacks of Ordovician limestone can easily be viewed at the Deschênes Rapids (north shore, near Aylmer), the Chaudière Falls, or in downtown Ottawa at the start of the Rideau Canal in the cliffs of Entrance Bay below the Château Laurier. Thin layers of shale are easily spotted along the south shore of the Ottawa River, particularly in the western sector of the NCR between Pinhey's Point and Shirleys Bay.

The Cleft at the Chaudière and Philemon Wright's house (1833) by P.J. Bainbrigge. NAC C-11848.

Along with the oceans' coming and going came vast periods of erosion, during which wind, water, and varied temperatures exacted their toll on the landscape.

Ordovician times saw the first vertebrates, many marine invertebrates, and the first land plants. Fossils of such creatures as trilobites, brachiopods, pelecypods, fish, and algae trapped in this stone attest to the life that once flourished in the warm Ordovician waters.

AT FAULT: CREATING THE OTTAWA VALLEY PLAIN

Between 400 million and 120 million years ago, major faults fractured the land. Geologically speaking, Ottawa resembles the hub of a wheel, with faults thrusting from it like spokes. One fault describes the base of the Eardley Escarpment; another lies to the immediate north of that ridge. Examine a map to view the "line" made by Philippe, Mousseau (Harrington), and Meech lakes in Gatineau Park. Their alignment is no coincidence: they lie along a fault.

Another fault parallels the eastern section of the Ottawa River, to the south of the shore and north of Alexandria. Running north of Vaudreuil and south of Lachute, it links the Gloucester fault to the

Lake of the Two Mountains. To the west are numerous faults: one follows the Mississippi River from Arnprior (on the Ottawa River) south to Almonte; another courses along the Carp Escarpment.

Perhaps the most famous fault in the Ottawa Valley region is the one lying at the base of the Eardley Escarpment, forming the start of the rift valley that extends southwards over 100 km to Gananoque and upper New York State. Here along the escarpment, the land slipped downward along a fault marked by today's Mountain Road. Because of thousands of years of erosion and faulting, the younger Ordovician limestone and shale lie exposed along the Ottawa River, while the more ancient Precambrian rock of the Eardley Escarpment towers above the flat valley floor.

Dr. Alice Wilson points us toward another local example of a dramatic fault. It starts in Gatineau Park, running through Ottawa and extending south of the NCR. This is the Gloucester Fault. She notes:

> One of the main faults extends down the Mines road in the Gatineau Region. In its hollow lies Fairy Lake. Its effect is visible in the tilted rocks of the islands around the [Lemieux] filtration plant. It crosses Carling Avenue at the Experimental Farm hill and the Morrisburg Road just south of Leitrim, still curving to the southeast. A little west of Russell village it breaks.[1]

What created the faults? Probably it was pressure in the earth's mantle, caused while the Appalachian Mountains started to rise first in the New England states and then into what are now the Maritime provinces. Imagine how the Earth's crust strained, buckled, and shifted as this second major era of mountain building began. The pressure caused cracks to shatter the substrata — and the earth literally shape-shifted.

ICY ENCOUNTER: LAURENTIDE ICE SHEET

Climate change is hardly a modern phenomenon. During the billions of years that have seen the creation of continents via the shifting of tectonic plates, mountain building, eons of erosion, Ordovician seas, and the emergence of mammals, reptiles, and vegetation, temperatures have frequently altered — often drastically.

It seems fantastical, but 20,000 years ago approximately a kilometre of ice covered the Ottawa Valley. The Laurentide (or sometimes, the Wisconsin) Ice Sheet covered Canada and here in the east it extended south, to what is now New York City. Over the thousands of years, the ice sheet wore the Eardley Escarpment down to more or less its current height.

As it progressed southwards in Pleistocene times, the ice scraped and gouged Precambrian rock from the Laurentian Highlands (of which Gatineau Park is a tiny fraction), carrying some of its rock in its icy mantle. When the ice sheet receded some 12,000 years ago, rocks suspended in it were left behind. Boulders called "erratics" dot the landscape from Montréal and Ottawa south into New York State. Other topographical features such as scratches and grooves on rock, as well as eskers and drumlins, indicate the direction of the ice sheet's movement. Geologists who can interpret these telltale "signposts" tell us that the ice crossed through Ottawa in a southeasterly direction through the Ottawa Valley, Manotick, and proceeded southwest to Lake Ontario.

The weight of the Laurentide Ice Sheet caused the land to sink below sea level; thus, when the sheet melted over time, it created the conditions for the next great era.

THE CHAMPLAIN SEA

As the ice receded, the salt waters of what is now the Atlantic Ocean flowed inland and created the Champlain Sea. The salt water could flood the interior because the weight of the ice sheet had pushed the land below sea level. It is difficult to think of the earth's mantle being "flexible," but it is. After the nearly kilometre-high ice melted, the land gradually started to rebound. Over time, the saline water would retreat and create our present eastern seaboard, but not before the sea made its own great changes upon our Ottawa Valley which we still can recognize today.

How far inland did this vast sea penetrate and how deep was it? Marine deposits plus fossilized sea shells and other marine life show that the Champlain Sea extended south of the St. Lawrence River (south of Ogdensburg) and into the valley now filled by Lake Champlain in New York State. In the NCR, it was approximately 150 metres or so above the present level of the Ottawa River.

Geological maps of the Ottawa Valley show a remnant of sea beach located above the Eardley Escarpment at Kingsmere Lake north of King Mountain in Gatineau Park. Does the beach's presence indicate that the Champlain Sea covered the entire escarpment, even at its highest elevation? No. So, how did it get there?

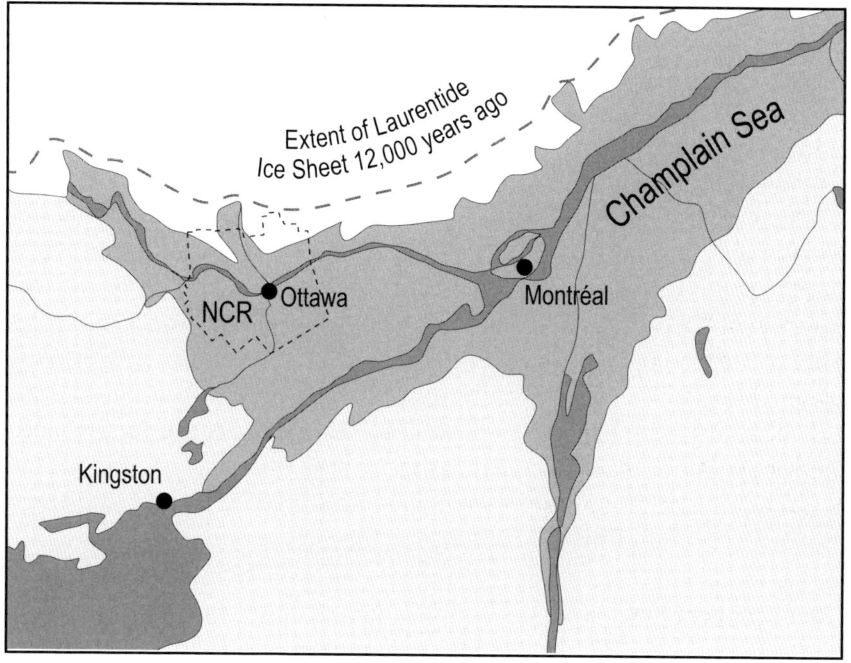

Extent of the Champlain Sea 12,000 years ago.

UPLIFTING TIMES

The answer lies in the phenomenon of uplift. After the ice sheet receded, salt water rushed inland. After the ice had gone, the process of depression, or downward force, abated and the land started to rebound. Today, if you visit Champlain Lookout in Gatineau Park (west of King Mountain), you will be standing on top of the Eardley Escarpment looking south over the flat rift valley and the Ottawa River. Now imagine the scene 10,000 years ago: you would be standing on an island whose summit would permit you to view the Champlain Sea extending westwards to Pembroke.

Along with the ocean waters came marine life. Archaeological remains unearthed near Green's Creek (east of Ottawa's downtown core) reveal that over 10,000 years ago harp seals, humpback and finback whales, and harbour porpoises lived here. A beluga whale skull was discovered in Pakenham Township by a local landowner digging a well (see Mississippi Mills ramble). You can view some of fossils and bones of these marine creatures at Ottawa's Canadian Museum of Nature. Over time, as the earth rose, the watershed of the Ottawa River receded to its current course.

As it receded, it left terraces, or beachheads, proving that the recession was gradual. Old beaches in the Ottawa Valley show themselves as raised elevations: a major one snakes along Highway 148 in the Pontiac region of West Québec. Just beyond Breckenridge, the highway veers right, coursing along a particularly level plain before abruptly rising onto a terrace. This is one of the old beachheads, created as the water drew back from lapping at the base of the Eardley Escarpment. As the land rose, new water levels were created as the mighty expanse of Champlain Sea drained back to the Atlantic. As you drive or cycle along the highway here, imagine the broad sweep of beach once visible.

Of course, the water did not simply rush in, only to subsequently recede. Water defines not only topography — hence the beachheads — but also soil type. The Champlain Sea sifted glacial moraines, tumbled rocks into gravel, and, as the waters receded, deposited swathes of different soil types throughout the Ottawa Valley.

This returns us to land use. Geomorphology defines nation building. Types of soil — whether they be the peat bogs of Ramsay Lake (west of the Eardley Road in Gatineau Park) or Mer Bleue, or the sand pits on Petrie Island — determine everything from natural biodiversity to industrial and other human activities.

Trade Along the Ottawa

Ancient peoples as well as European settlers discovered that natural watercourses provided the best transportation routes. Even the challenges of portaging several kilometre-long swathes of rapids (such as along Chats Falls near Quyon) represented a far less arduous route to First Nations people and explorers than did clearing roads through bush and swamp. So it should be no surprise that our National Capital Region's abundant rivers, streams, and lakes provided handy trade routes.

The NCR comprises 4,715 square kilometres of watercourses, wetlands, woodlands, pasture, and mountains in the provinces of Québec and Ontario. Although the twin mega-cities of Gatineau and Ottawa dominate the urban landscape, the region is rich with historic villages, tiny hamlets, and sometimes mystifying dots on a map representing settlements that otherwise have slipped from memory. All told, the population of the NCR is almost 1.1 million across twenty-seven municipalities. These are the facts, but what is the story of trade and human settlement?

EARLY TIMES

Watercourses not only define the Ottawa Valley topographically, they formed the earliest transportation routes into the hinterland. As the land rebounded from the weight of the melting ice sheet, the receding Champlain Sea was fed by a network of increasingly freshwater rivers and lakes. Paleo-Indian peoples paddled canoes along this water network, portaging around treacherous rapids to convey their precious trade items. These nomads travelled from one locale to another not solely to trade, but also to follow the seasonal migration of birds, fish, and mammals for food and shelter. They ventured from the Great Lakes to the Ottawa via the French River, then descended the St. Lawrence to the Atlantic Ocean.

Arrowheads (more properly termed "fluted projectile points") found at the Rideau Lakes and carbon dating of human bones from a site on Allumette Island indicate that people were in the Ottawa River watershed at least 5,000 years ago. Other artifacts discovered in Debert, Nova Scotia, and at various places on Prince Edward Island prove that early peoples settled there around the same time. One has the sense that as the water levels receded, human activity occurred almost immediately.

Artifacts from the early archaic period of some 5,000 years ago are on permanent display in the Kichi Sibi exhibit at the Canadian Museum of Civilization (CMC), in Gatineau. Here you can view a 400 to 700 year old bird effigy pipe bowl of soapstone found in March Township and donated to the museum in 1902. Here too is a very exciting find: a native copper lance or spear point dating from 3,000 to 5,000 years ago. It was discovered at Lac des Fées (near Brewery Creek, see Brewery Creek ramble) and was given to the museum in 1914.

Quartz and chert spear points were discovered on Allumette Island (just west of the NCR in the Ottawa River, opposite Pembroke), as were copper objects such as axes, awls, and knives. Similar archaeological finds in Wisconsin, Michigan, Illinois, and New York states, along with Manitoba, appear to prove the existence of an extensive Great Lakes–Ottawa Valley–New England trade route.

At the time of first contact with Europeans in the early 1600s, several Aboriginal settlements existed along the Ottawa River. Leamy Lake (named after settler Andrew Leamy) and Jacques-Cartier parks, at the confluence of the Gatineau and Ottawa rivers, were sites of a summer settlement where people paddling along the Ottawa would stop, rest, and trade. The shallow estuary would have provided welcome respite from some of the river's fiercest rapids, with ample opportunity to fish and hunt waterfowl (ducks and geese) as well as game in the surrounding woods.

Few traces of First Nations people exist in Gatineau Park, probably due to the imposing ridge of the Eardley Escarpment, although folk rumour has it that Ridge Road (trail #1) was an old "Indian footpath." As well, Pinecrest Cemetery features remnants of an old "Indian trail" that once connected the Ottawa and Rideau waterways.

Algonquin traders sometimes spent the winter at the Huron's Georgian Bay villages, where they learned pottery techniques and traded information and goods. After contact with the Europeans, these First Nations peoples began to travel in large flotillas of canoes laden with furs down the Ottawa River en route to the French traders living in Montréal. Control over the river route soon became critical: from 1610 to the late 1640s, the Algonquin exacted tolls from anyone paddling upriver, but their domination ended during the Iroquois attacks of 1648-49. In order to gain supremacy over the lucrative fur trade with the Europeans, the Iroquois invaded and razed the Huron settlements along Lake Superior. At that time there were over 30,000 Huron peoples living in roughly two dozen communities along Georgian Bay.

After the Iroquois war, some First Nations peoples fled west to escape further attack. In 1650, Jesuit Paul Ragueneau brought 300 Hurons down the Ottawa to live near Québec City. Thus, the mid-1600s were an unsettled time along this all-important corridor to the heart of the continent.

VOYAGEURS ALONG THE OTTAWA

The French recognized that the Algonquin, Huron, and other tribes would be crucial partners to the trade and settlement of New France. It was critical for them to gain control over the First Nations' trading route. In its totality, this route extended from the Great Lakes east along the French River, through Lake Nipissing and the Mattawa River to the Ottawa, and from there via the St. Lawrence to Montréal, culminating in Québec.

The question was how to exact control? How could the French transform a series of strategic outposts in the wilderness into a viable colony? By learning the First Nations' ways.

French explorer Étienne Brûlé seems to have been the first European to venture up the Ottawa River in 1610 and was probably the first white man to view the Great Lakes. He was only one of the many intrepid souls sent to live among the native peoples to learn their language and customs. Thus, Brûlé could act not just as a proficient guide to the country, but also as an interpreter.

Three years later, in 1613, Samuel de Champlain paddled west from Île Sainte-Hélène (Montréal) to Allumette Island (some 100 km west of Fitzroy Harbour in Ontario and Quyon in West Québec, the westernmost "boundary towns" of the NCR). His party consisted of two birch-bark canoes, two Algonquin guides, two Frenchmen, and "the boldest liar" he had ever met — Nicolas de Vignau, who claimed he had discovered a body of salt water to the west. Vignau appeared credible: he had stayed with the Algonquin from 1611 to 1612. Believing the young man had discovered *la mer du Nord* (Northern Sea), Champlain mounted the expedition, another goal of which was to encourage the natives he met to bring furs downriver to Montréal.

Champlain was the first to make maps of the Ottawa River and the first European to name the topographical features along it. His daily journal of 1613 is readily available from public libraries and his precise notations reveal many details of the journey, its hardships, and its fascinations. He dutifully records the confluence of the Gatineau River and notes the Rideau Falls to its south; he describes what we now call Gatineau Park and the Eardley Escarpment when remarking upon a ridge of mountains to the north. As well, he carefully recorded the names of the woodland Algonquin bands he encountered: Quenongebin, Oüescariny, Kinouchepirini, Kichesipirini, Otaguottouemin, Matou-oüescariny, and Charioquet. Note that the Kichesipirini gave their name to the Kitchissippi Lookout on the Ottawa River Parkway.

Artist's fanciful rendering of Champlain being paddled downriver, entitled "Samuel de Champlain — 1607." Watercolour by De Rinzey, n.d. NAC C-13320.

Possibly the most interesting passages of Champlain's diary are descriptions of events that he witnessed. One such incident was the *tabagie* conducted at the portage around the Chaudière Rapids. Here the Algonquin passed around a plate and burned tobacco while singing and making solemn speeches. The ceremony honoured and pacified the river spirit who, they hoped, would grant them safe passage upstream.

The spirits evidently permitted Champlain's group to proceed without incident. Human vanity and deceit, however, created problems. Vignau had lied to Champlain about finding a passage to the East; undoubtedly, he had heard all about Henry Hudson's explorations of Hudson's Bay in 1610–11. It was not until Champlain arrived on Allumette Island and met the Algonquin chief, Tessouat, that Vignau's deceitfulness was uncovered. Tessouat suggesting killing Vignau: Champlain offered mercy. We can only imagine with what anger and discouragement his little party of explorers would have turned back …

Champlain returned in 1615, this time venturing to Georgian Bay. Missionaries followed in the paddle strokes of the founder of New France. During the same year Recollet priest Joseph le Caron negotiated the Ottawa River's rapids, also en route to Georgian Bay. A few years later (1626–1644) Jesuit fathers Jean de Brébeuf (who is remembered by a statue in Gatineau's Parc Brébeuf (see Aylmer Road ramble), Antoine Daniel, Charles Garnier, Noël Chabanel, and Gabriel Lalemant also headed upstream en route to Ste-Marie-Among-the-Hurons and their mission stockade. These priests transported all their personal supplies and their livestock, chickens, cows, and pigs, upstream with them.

But the Black Robes were doomed. Iroquois "martyred" them all men during an attack upon the mission. Although they are long gone, their memory is recalled in the Boy Scout camp named Camp Echon, just west of Constance Bay, named in honour of Father Jean de Brébeuf whose Huron name was "Echon."

The 1600s also saw the first penetration of the *pays d'en haut* or hinterland by coureurs-de-bois who traded with First Nations peoples for the furs so popular with Europeans. Among those who paddled upstream from Montréal were Nicolas Perrot (1658), Pierre-Esprit Radisson (1661), and Nicolas d'Ailleboust, sieur de Coulonge (1694) whose name is recalled in Fort Coulonge and the Coulonge River.

Not only did these hardy folks penetrate the wetlands, forests, and mountains of Canada, some also ventured into the United States. Between 1668 and 1672, Louis Jolliet used the Ottawa River as a route to the Mississippi four times; in 1669 Cavelier de la Salle paddled west heading for Ohio; in 1690 the founder of Louisiana, Pierre le Moyne, passed through the Ottawa region; and 1694 saw Antoine de Lamothe-Cadillac on his way to founding Détroit.[2]

European demand for furs created intense competition along the waterways for control of the wilderness riches. In its heyday, the territory explored by the French extended from Hudson's Bay to the

Gulf of Mexico, from the Atlantic seaboard and St. Lawrence River west to the Great Lakes.

Frenchman Médard Chouart des Groselliers voyaged up the Ottawa in 1654, 1655, 1659, and 1660. Eight years later, he was on an English expedition founded by Prince Rupert, in Hudson's Bay. Indirectly, his employer was Britain's King Charles II who had granted a charter to a new company called "The Governor and Company of Adventurers of England trading into Hudson's Bay" — a mouthful that over the years was shortened to the "Hudson's Bay Company." By 1682 a variety of French fur trading monopolies had coalesced into the Compagnie du Nord, whose activities largely centred on the Ottawa River to Lake Temiskaming. Despite English outposts, the French dominated the fur trade for 160 years. The beginning of the end came in 1759 when the British took Québec. After the fall of Montréal a year later, the British presence grew stronger along the Ottawa. Meanwhile, the battle for the fur trade continued.

THE COMPANY MEN

One of the first British explorers to travel up the Ottawa was Alexander Henry, who portaged around the Chaudière Falls in 1761. As he voyaged westwards, Henry noted the old French trading post at Fort Coulonge. After the fall of New France, the rivalry between already established French and British traders — not to mention First Nations peoples' trade aspirations — grew increasingly intense. British Montréal merchants sent "*les canots du maîtres*" (12-metre birch-bark trade canoes) upriver with French paddlers in company of Scottish and English traders. How tempers must have flared while everyone jostled for their place, particularly after the fall of Nouvelle France.

Several traders banded together in 1779 to create the North West Company to consolidate some of the territory, and in the hopes of destroying the Hudson's Bay Company (HBC). After forty-one years of rivalry, the North West Company merged with the HBC, retaining the latter name.

Not all traders were associated with the big companies. In 1786, Joseph Mondion set up a little trading post and farm at Chats (pronounced "shaw") Falls, one of the wildest rapids on the Ottawa just upstream of today's Quyon. Mondion recognized a location of business merit, precisely where all the river traders paused and unpacked their canoes in preparation for the arduous portage around the rapids. No one knows precisely why Mondion only lasted fourteen years on the point half a kilometre downstream, though rumour indicates he sold liquor to the voyageurs. Although many traders probably sold spirits to one and all, because this practice was taboo, perhaps Mondion was "encouraged" to leave.

Incidentally, it's not known exactly how Chats Falls got its name. "Chats" means "cat" in French. One explanation suggests river rocks here at the falls badly scratched canoes, leaving gashes resembling cats' claw marks on them.

By 1822, when Scottish-born John McLean ventured west of Ottawa in the employ of the HBC, the Chats was well known — and a superb location to challenge the competition. McLean established a HBC post possibly on an island here, though other records indicate it may have been on Indian Point (also known as Mondion's Point, Julien's Point, and Hudson Point). McLean planned to go head-to-head with the rival North West Company.

Philemon Wright. COA CA-11918.

McLean documented his experiences in a book published in 1849, entitled *Notes of a Twenty-five Years' Service in the Hudson's Bay Territory*. He did not languish at the Chats; after serving the HBC in Fort Coulonge and Fort William, he had made his way to Labrador by 1839, where he was the first European to see Churchill Falls.

While we explore the mighty Ottawa by white-water raft, kayak, or canoe these days, we can easily share a spirit of adventure with those who came before us. The extreme dangers, the possibility of ambush by Iroquois, or of treachery at the hands of a rival fur trader, thankfully lie in the past.

Such is the story of the great company of adventurers who have paddled upstream before us. None of the men described here were settlers, the exception being Joseph Mondion, who operated a farm upstream of Quyon on Pontiac Bay's Indian Point for fourteen years. Mondrian's agricultural efforts were probably at a fairly subsistence level meant only to support him at his fur trading post in the wilderness. By 1800, Mondion was gone. In that pivotal year marking the turn of the century, New Englander Philemon Wright settled the north shore of the Chaudière Falls, calling his settlement Wrightsville.

What about the settlement of the Ottawa Valley? To meet the region's first settlers, we must look at two major political events: the conquest of New France in 1759 on the Plains of Abraham, and the American Revolutionary War of the late 1700s.

Settlers on the Ottawa

Any discussion of the Canadian political landscape quickly gets down to Québec. So it should come as no surprise that to get a clear picture of how the Ottawa region was settled, we need to look back to the conquest of New France, to Québec City, and to the Battle of the Plains of Abraham where, in 1759, British General James Wolfe defeated French General Montcalm. The victory witnessed the death of both generals — and delivered a mortal blow to New France. On 10 February 1763 the British and French signed the Treaty of Paris in which the French king surrendered control of thousands of acres of snow to its arch enemy. New France was no more. While France descended into a period of political and social turmoil, culminating in the French Revolution of 1789, Britain had its hands full in its new territories.

Britain had to figure out a way to appease the French in British North America, quickly. Their defeat gave the victor a vast new territory extending south from Hudson's Bay to the Gulf of Mexico, bounded by that great American river, the Mississippi, in the west (not to be confused with the Mississippi River in the Ottawa Valley). Britain urgently needed a supply of loyal citizens to populate her colony particularly because the French-speaking population vastly exceeded the British and other immigrant peoples loyal to the Crown. As well, there was increasing unrest from the colonies south of the St. Lawrence River.

Knowing this, King George III of England signed a Royal Proclamation also in 1763, in which he paved the way to pay loyal British soldiers in land grants. Brilliant strategy, wasn't it? In one fell swoop King George could populate his colonies in North America with loyal Britons who, by no coincidence, were professional soldiers. With soldiers poised to settle the new land, Britain could relax — at least a bit — when contemplating the natives, French, and the troublesome upstart elements to the south.

In their book, *The Carleton Saga*, Harry and Olive Walker note that some 115,000 non-Aboriginal people had settled in what is now Québec, compared with 2,000 in Ontario. Although Canada's first chief colonial administrator, Sir Guy Carleton, incurred English-speaking settlers' wrath for his lenient treatment of the conquered French, he was being strategically brilliant. If you think about it,

Carleton would have placed the entire colony at risk had he suppressed the French language or Catholicism.

Perhaps fortunately for British interests, conditions became increasingly ripe for emigration here on a scale hitherto unimagined. In 1783, Americans still loyal to King George III looked north to Canada after the American Revolutionary War ripped the Thirteen Colonies from Britain's empire.

THE LOYALISTS NEED LAND

One person's concept of loyalty is another's treason. Such was the case with the American Revolutionary War, during which thousands of citizens living in Britain's Thirteen Colonies became *personae non gratae*.

The Loyalists remained true to King George III and became instant exiles in the new American communities. In many instances, their homes, possessions, and livestock were confiscated or burned. Even though many Loyalists were destitute, family members and former neighbours turned upon them, making their lives intolerable. So they fled in droves to British North America, to the areas that now comprise the provinces of Nova Scotia, New Brunswick, Québec, and Ontario. More than 40,000 Loyalists made the trek into Canada at the end of the Revolutionary War in 1783.

This exodus of English-speaking colonists was a boon to the British government, which agreed to grant each Loyalist family 200 acres of land. Every son would get a similar grant when he came of age, as would daughters upon marriage. What better way to colonize the backwoods and create loyal Anglo-Saxon settlements? There remained a niggling question, though: precisely where would these people live? Land was needed, which meant two things: a survey was required and an arrangement with the native peoples was necessary!

In fact, the land had already been surveyed. In 1764, Samuel Holland had been appointed surveyor general of Québec and the northern district of North America. When Sir Frederick Haldimand succeeded Sir Guy Carleton as governor of Québec in 1778, he had instructed Holland to survey the territory from the St. Lawrence River and Lake Ontario (what is now the Bay of Quinté) north to the Ottawa River. Holland did, and defined the counties of Glengarry, Prescott, Russell, Stormont, Dundas, Carleton, Lanark, Grenville, Leeds, Frontenac, Addington, and Hastings, almost three million acres.

THE CRAWFORD PURCHASE

The land Holland had surveyed was hardly an unpopulated wasteland. For thousands of years it had been the territory of nomadic peoples. Even in Holland's time, the land lying between the two great rivers was home to the Mississauga, Algonquin, Huron, Iroquois, and other First Nations peoples. Could European settlement be safely accomplished on lands that were traditional hunting grounds? How did the British government and Governor General Haldimand convince these people to give up their ancestral territories?

It proved all too simple.

The deal came about largely because a British soldier named Captain William R. Crawford. Crawford had lived and worked with the Algonquin and Mississauga, learning their culture and language — and gaining their trust perhaps rather in the same way Étienne Brûlé had done. Crawford negotiated well for Britain's interests. The Haldimand papers in Ottawa's National Archives of Canada reveal how the land was paid for. Negotiating on behalf of the First Nations People was Chief Mynass, a Mississauguan who, in exchange for his people's vast territory requested "powder and ball for their winter hunting and such coarse red cloth as will make about a dozen coats."[3]

By 1783, the Algonquin and Mississauguans had lost their land, home, and way of life thanks to the Crawford Purchase. Effectively they were expropriated from their heritage of millions of acres lying between the two rivers, for a handful of shot, some blankets, and some whiskey. Is "expropriated" too harsh? Did the native people understand the significance of what they were trading? Perhaps their greatest mistake was to place trust in King George III and his representatives. Chief Mynass, who had actually travelled to London, evidently did. Surely the First Nations peoples couldn't have foretold the demise of their nomadic way of life, the unending waves of immigration, nor the European's inexorable demand for land.

Just because they couldn't have foretold the future and made what turned out to be a rotten deal in good faith doesn't mean First Nations people were simple dupes. They believed the English king would look after their interests. As settlers took over their hunting and fishing grounds, and as the indigenous peoples became marginalized in their former lands, First Nations' peoples repeatedly appealed to King George. It was to no avail, and today their petitions read both pitifully and shamefully.

Thanks to the Crawford Purchase, by 1783, Carleton County included Nepean, Marlborough, North Gower, Osgoode, and Gloucester. The land west of Nepean (in Carleton County) was surveyed later, between 1812 and 1814. In 1819, the British negotiated a second deal with the Mississauguan nation, purchasing lands that became Torbolton, Fitzroy, Huntley, March, and Goulbourn townships.

These two substantial land purchases coupled with the original Crawford Purchase, represent portions of the Ontario section of our modern National Capital Region.

DAWN OF THE TIMBER INDUSTRY

The story of the permanent settlement of Ottawa's twin city, Gatineau, started with New Englander Philemon Wright who settled north of the Chaudière Falls in 1800 with a handful of friends and relatives. A canny business entrepreneur, Wright knew opportunity when he saw it and he had canoed up the waterways a few times prior to 1800 to check out the prospects here. His papers in the National Archives of Canada reveal that he climbed trees to assess the lay of the land: he came, he saw, and, he conquered, for Wright became an Ottawa Valley "lumber baron," entrepreneur, and man of influence.

The tiny settlement on the banks of the Chaudière soon became known as Wrightsville. Wright recognized the surrounding forests represented valuable resources: timber was precisely what Britain required for her navy. In 1806 Napoleon had blockaded the Baltic, a region that had provided the British Navy with timber for its ships for years. Wright correctly ascertained he could make tremendous profits if only he could fell the timbers, square them, and float them down the Ottawa to Montréal and Québec City.

In 1806, he successfully sent his first raft of timber down the Ottawa River, an event that single-handedly birthed the Ottawa Valley lumber industry. Wright and his pals had already constructed a saw and grist mill at the Chaudière, so the little community prospered. Within forty years, the Chaudière Falls were powering many an American immigrant's sawmills, gristmills, and factories, as were the Rideau Falls, to the east.

Wright was neither the only New Englander nor the only immigrant interested in the shores of the Ottawa at this time. A steady trickle of American settlers had been venturing upriver from Montréal, just as his group did, heading north from upper New York State in winter on the frozen Richelieu River network, a useful highway to the north. Although he was a Republican, not a Loyalist, he and others like him left America because there was greater opportunity here in the Canadas. Many other New Englanders joined him: the Reverend Asa Meech was one, a Congregationalist minister, teacher, and farmer who eventually settled on land near the lake in Gatineau Park that now bears his name, in 1821.

The timber trade grew and settlers from the British Isles streamed into the colony. Britain needed timber, and had to settle their vast colonies. What better ballast could there possibly be than human beings, aka "settlers"? Soon British ships packed with emigrants sailed from England to Québec and Montréal, deposited their weary load, and returned home with more squared timbers. Although many emigrants looked to the developing towns for housing and a livelihood, others were given land grants and encouraged to clear farms, thus protecting British interests.

J.R. Booth's rafts of pine timber at Sharples and Dobell's Cove, Sillery, Québec, 1891. Photo: John Thomson. NAC C-6073.

Part of a panorama; ships loading lumber in Québec City harbour, ca, 1860. Photo: Ellisson & Co. NAC C-90136.

How did the first immigrants live? English artist W.H. Bartlett's prints show us what the earliest rough structures were like, though even these rude dwellings adopted a somewhat "picturesque" look under his hand that belies reality. His works depict single-room log homesteads in tiny clearings, a stone's throw from the verge of impenetrable looking forests, and on the shore of a waterway. Bartlett's prints speak volumes of how daunting a task it must have been for these settlers to clear a patch of ground and build a shelter beside the wall of the forest. After all, the woods were home to the wolf and bear, raccoon and porcupine, far more likely (and destructive) neighbours than a kindly fellow settler.

Although many of us are reasonably familiar with emigration from France and Britain, as well as from the United States, few of us realize that many Québeckers are descendants of German-speaking peoples. Because personages like George III and other English royalty were of Hanoverian stock at this point in history, Germanic-speaking peoples had a special "friendly" connection to British territories.

What was happening in Germany during the 1700s and 1800s, to cause people to seek a better life elsewhere? Alice Biehler Burich records German settlement of the Gatineau hills in *Olden Days*, her history of Mulgrave–Derry, an area just outside the eastern boundary of the NCR in West Québec.

Although feudalism had formally ended in the mid-1700s, it took considerable time before the peasants — or serfs —benefited from the change in social and political structure. Burich notes that by 1770 Denmark and some of the west German states formally abolished serfdom, although even as late as 1788 peasants were still forbidden to leave their village.[4] In some German states, such as Prussia, it would be 1807 before serfdom was abolished — the year after American settler Philemon Wright sent his first raft of squared timber from Wrightsville (Gatineau) down the Ottawa River to Québec City.

W.H. Bartlett print depicting first rudimentary shelter of homesteaders, with forest behind. NCC 172.

During the 1800s, life in what we now call Germany was rough, particularly if one was not a member of the landowning class. Burich explains:

> At the beginning of the 19th century the German lands were composed of Austria, Prussia, and a group of smaller states over which no emperor had been able to impose unity or common laws. These independent states were ruled by territorial princes. Following the final campaign against Napoleon in 1815 their number was reduced from over 300 to 38.
>
> German society was divided into three classes: the upper class consisted of the nobility; the middle class was made up of intellectuals, professionals and businessmen; the lower class, small tradesmen, peasants and serfs. A wave of pan-German nationalism swept the country following 1815 and many of the middle class agitated for reform. They were opposed by the princes who preferred to be 'a small prince rather than someone else's subject'. The clash resulted in the formation of a German Confederation, an inefficient, repressive police system that lasted for the next 30 years.[5]

German immigrants to the Ottawa Valley came predominantly from Prussia, a sprawling country comprising parts of modern Denmark, France, Germany, and Poland. Their religions were Lutheran, Catholic, and an offshoot of Presbyterian called Reformed. Burich explains that:

> the vast majority came from the rural northeast provinces of Prussia. They were agricultural workers — in reality, peasants who for generations had been bound to the large estates of wealthy landowners in a kind of hereditary serfdom, where the lords of the land decided the course of their lives. In a time when no one knew what the next year's [political] alliances might be, the only loyalty expected of peasants was to the landowner.[6]

How alluring the promise of owning one's own land must have been to these disenfranchised people. Prospects for improving one's lot is the great equalizer, the great carrot for all emigrants, whatever era we're talking about.

Emigration from Europe intensified after the revolutionary period between 1848 and 1852, when political and social upheaval swept most of that continent. Unrest deepened after the crop failures particularly of wheat and potatoes in 1848. Rural peoples migrated to the cities, but urban populations were suffering too. Emigration offered the chance of a new life, so many crossed the Atlantic to start afresh in a new land where not coincidentally, they could live without onerous religious and political persecution. Burich tells us that most German settlers of this time could read and write, most knew how to farm, and along with being able to sew and garden, many a woman was a capable midwife. The more versatile the better, for farming the stony soils east of the Gatineau River and west of it, towards Ladysmith (north of Gatineau Park) was backbreaking.

By the mid-1800s, the best land had already been allotted. Even by 1826, Levi Bigelow had already built and was operating a sawmill on the Lièvre River below Dufferin Falls, and vast tracts of rocky bush lay under the control of lumbermen such as W.C. Edwards and the Maclaren and Wright families. In order to make a go of it, the male new immigrants had little choice but to leave their wives (who were often pregnant) in late November to work in the shanties located along the Lièvre, Blanche, Coulonge, and upper Ottawa watersheds. What a time this must have been for the new settlers: clearing land, building a rough home, then living apart as their wives maintained the homesteads as best they could with young children to mind. When the men returned, it was time to clear more land and plant crops. It was a challenging, lonely life, particularly as they had to learn a new language, too. Moreover, because British emigration officials either could not or would not pronounce the Germanic names, many surnames were anglicized. Rupert John Last, an author who chronicles the history of Poltimore in his book *Know thy Neighbour*, notes this happened to the Tscheschlock family, who became the Cheslocks.

Life was so arduous here in the rocky land east of the Gatineau that many German-speaking settlers chose to leave for the west, the next territory to be perceived as the new land of opportunity. In 1872, the Dominion Lands Act was passed; on 7 November 1885 the last spike of the CPR railway was driven; and in 1896 the Klondike gold rush commenced. All three events inspired many to leave the Ottawa Valley to seek a better life in the exciting western frontier. By 1910, fifty-eight per cent of the population in the townships of Mulgrave-Derry east of the Gatineau River (and just east of the NCR boundary) were of German descent. Poltimore, on the Lièvre River watershed, was also settled by Germans and several names, such as chemin Pinkos still exist, recalling the European immigrants who settled here along with the Scots, Irish, English, and French. Today, descendents of these German-speaking settlers still live in the National Capital Region, immensely enriching our capital region's cultural heritage.

The Shanty in the Bush. (No. 1, Three views in the life of a shanty farmer. From "The Eastern Townships — Information for Intending Settlers," 1881.) NAC C-005755.

Fifteen years after settlement. (No. 2, Three views in the life of a shanty farmer. From "The Eastern Townships — Information for Intending Settlers," 1881.) NAC C-005756.

Thirty years after settlement. (No. 3, Three views in the life of a shanty farmer. From "The Eastern Townships — Information for Intending Settlers," 1881.) NAC C-005757.

DEFENCE TACTICS

While settlement grew, so did the British government's anxiety. Yes, it was a good thing to populate the countryside and burgeoning towns dotted along the Ottawa and other watersheds. But how could they defend the colonies? Sure, Loyalists had settled in the new land, as had others who pledged allegiance to the British Crown. It was perhaps an obvious strategy to give land grants to officers and soldiers, but notwithstanding these efforts, the territory was vast. Then along came the War of 1812, and the Brits realized the St. Lawrence was one long indefensible "border" between two distrustful neighbours. How could they defend their colonies against potential American invasions?

The unlikely seeming answer was to build a strategic supply route from Montréal to Kingston. Troops, munitions, and supplies could be transported along the 202 km distance. The idea took hold and Colonel John By of the Royal Engineers arrived at the little community opposite Wrightsville, to accomplish the job. In the years 1826 to 1832 he oversaw one of the greatest engineering projects of the nineteenth century.

Take a long second look at the canal. Look, for instance, at the Entrance Bay locks, sandwiched between Ottawa's fairytale castle (the Château Laurier) and Gothic spires of Parliament Hill. Walk down to stand beside the first of the eight locks there. Perhaps you'd like to remove your shoes and socks and conjure the life of the Irish navvies who worked, barefoot and with a pick-axe, chipping away at the Ordovician limestone cliffs to create the locks you see today.

Then turn south and, with the Ottawa River at your back, imagine the scene in 1826. You'd be standing in a cedar swamp, and perhaps you'd be forgiven if you thought Colonel By was nuts to think he could dig through it all to Kingston. But "nuts" he decidedly wasn't. Instead he and his Royal Engineers, his surveyors like John MacTaggart, and his legions of workers cursed, dug, blasted (with gunpowder), and some died of malaria or other afflictions, as they constructed this engineering wonder at a cost of £800,000. Cheap, you say? Sounds like it today, I agree — but sadly for By, this figure represented a cost overrun of some £300,000. Despite his amazing achievement, By died in England, both destitute and ridiculed by a public and government who blamed him for unconscionable excesses.

On a happier note, By was very much alive and well when the citizens in the raw community on the Ottawa honoured him by calling their home Bytown, a name that suited everyone from 1819 to 1854. In the early 1850s several cities had dreams of grandeur because the country required a capital and perhaps a name with the suffix "town" didn't seem, well, quite chic enough. Bytown was renamed Ottawa after a First Nations peoples who, ironically, didn't live in these parts at all. They were based on Manitoulin Island, but traded here, along the river. In another link to First Nation's peoples, Bytown's name change occurred on 1 January 1855, in honour of the two hundredth anniversary of the reopening of the Ottawa River to trade after the Indian Wars.

Strategic defence and wars. If By's Rideau Canal had not been constructed here, who knows what the capital of Canada would have been? Perhaps Montréal, Kingston, or Toronto — the other burgs then vying for the honour. Queen Victoria instead selected Ottawa as capital on 31 December 1857, for a variety of reasons that included strategic defence and the existence of the canal. If you wish, be a tourist in the capital and hop on one of the canal's summertime boat tours. As you travel to Dow's Lake, imagine you're on *The Rideau*, the steamship that first plied the canal from Kingston to Ottawa on its inaugural opening, 29 May 1832.

Becoming a Nation's Symbol: Planning the NCR

When Queen Victoria selected Ottawa as capital of Canada in 1857, the sprawling town was an industrial eyesore with a dreadfully boisterous reputation. As development of the Chaudière continued, stacks of sawn lumber covered Victoria Island, the LeBreton Flats, and Hull (today's Gatineau). Ottawa, it seemed, did not convey a fitting symbolism for the capital of the young country. Neither did the region immediately surrounding the city. Moreover, many inhabitants were known as unruly types who enjoyed tanking up on dubiously brewed liquor after a hard winter in the bush.

But a capital Ottawa was, and so the proud community started to pull up its socks. Every capital needs an impressive seat of government and well-designed neighbourhoods of homes, markets, industry, and business. By had surveyed Bytown's streets in a typical English grid pattern in 1826, laying out the Byward Market and Lowertown streets, as well as Wellington and Rideau. Now that Ottawa was capital, the citizenry and developers alike were in the mood for improvements!

When the first sod was turned at Parliament Hill on 20 December 1859, Ezra Butler Eddy's industrial complex lined the Chaudière, Thomas MacKay's mills crowded the Rideau, and water was still drawn in barrels from the Ottawa River both to Lowertown and to Uppertown residences and businesses. When the first public servants moved into their offices on Parliament Hill on 8 September 1865, they had probably spent a difficult summer being sickened by the smell of the city during summertime's heat. In her social history of Ottawa, *A Private Capital*, late author Sandra Gwyn tells of how the prime minister of the day, Sir John A. Macdonald, wrinkled his nose with disgust at the stench of the drains.

Increasingly, beginning in the 1870s, Ottawa's citizens looked north to the countryside in the Gatineau Hills for summer cottages wherein they could get away from the smells and the stifling heat of the city. William Jeffs, the most significant landholder along Kingsmere Lake (earlier known as Loon Lake, then Jeffs Lake), subdivided his property, selling lots to summer cottagers. Another landowner at the lake, St. Andrew's Church in Old Chelsea, sold its property to Levi Crannell, who subsequently built a stately mansion, sheds, stable, and boathouse in 1901 and 1902.

View on Kingsmere Lake near J.R. Booth residence (Opeongo), possibly photographed from Prime Minister Mackenzie King's cottage, Kingswood, c. 1900. NAC PA-134792.

The McKinley Crannell House at 228 Kingsmere Road. Pictured are Gertrude Crannell, Edith Crannell and Florence McPherson Crannell. Photo c. 1910. HSG 01342.

In 1900, almost three decades before he became prime minister, Mackenzie King cycled up to Kingsmere and immediately fell in love with its sylvan surroundings. Eventually King would amass 500 acres there; when he died in 1950, his bequest of Kingsmere to the people of Canada became one of the larger parcels of property in the newly created Gatineau Park. (Also in 1950, Parisian urban planner Jacques Gréber was finalizing his Master Plan for the creation of a National Capital Region.)

Subdivision for summer residences would also happen at Meech Lake, named for Asa Meech, the New England Congregationalist minister who also operated one of the first farms (some 200 acres) on the lake's southern shore.

PRIME MINISTER LAURIER'S VISION: TODAY'S LEGACY

In 1884, Sir Wilfrid Laurier visited Washington, D.C. The American capital possessed a surrounding — and planned — federal district. A comparison between the two capitals was not complimentary to Ottawa. Said Laurier, "I would not wish to say anything disparaging of the capital, but it is hard to say anything good of it. Ottawa's not a handsome city and does not appear to be destined to become one." Inspired by the American model, he resolved to create a national capital region.

After becoming prime minister, Laurier created the Ottawa Improvement Commission (OIC) in 1889. A precursor to the Federal District Commission and today's National Capital Commission, the OIC was mandated with the beautification of the capital. Not a moment too soon, some argued, particularly because in 1900 Ottawa was almost destroyed by the Great Fire. This conflagration totally consumed downtown Hull (now Gatineau) and threatened to destroy Ottawa. It was started when a chimney overheated: gusts of wind blew sparks onto surrounding rooftops as well as the piles of sawn lumber that lined both sides of the Ottawa River at the Chaudière Falls. Before the flames could be extinguished, most of Hull and much of Ottawa had been razed. Incidentally, future prime minister Mackenzie King first came to Ottawa by train after the Great Fire. His first impression of the capital was bleak to say the least. Just imagine what he must have felt as his train crept through Ottawa's blackened, fire-ravaged wasteland. Prime Minister Laurier's comments must surely have echoed in his mind.

Laurier's government gave the OIC a budget of $60,000. This would not go far, but it did facilitate the cleanup of the industrial waterfront, plus the building of the western driveway alongside the Rideau Canal. This roadway is today's Queen Elizabeth Driveway, and by 1912 it was landscaped with gardens and picturesque "stick" gazebos constructed out of twisted tree branches. Central Park and the Patterson Creek development were also started under the OIC's direction at this time. Railway tracks lined the eastern bank of the Rideau Canal and in 1912 the Grand Trunk Railway's Union Station was built across from the Château Laurier. The beautification of the downtown had begun — but World War I prevented the OIC from procuring a larger budget and realizing more regional plans.

The OIC — and the successive commissions through to the NCC of today — published numerous reports. Frederick Todd's 1903 Report was the first to recommend formally the conservation of some park lands in Québec. In 1915, the Holt Report recommended the creation of a Federal District, modelled on Washington and other international capitals. Holt noted, "The highly commendable work of the Ottawa Improvement Commission should be extended and enlarged by the development of a broad and forceful policy as to further park lands, and there should be established a National Park or Forest Reserve in the Laurentian Hills, under the control of the Dominion Government."[7]

In 1927, the Federal District Commission replaced the OIC and for the first time the beautification of the capital included lands in Québec. The FDC's budget had grown to $250,000 and instead of the OIC's committee structure, which had consisted of a chairman, three federal appointees plus the mayor of Ottawa, the FDC now had a ten-member board that worked in tandem with the mayors of Ottawa and Hull.

During the 1920s, Ottawa Ski Club members were responsible for building many of the hiking and skiing trails we still enjoy today. These people understood that development, if left unchecked, would destroy the woodlands surrounding the sylvan lakes. By the early 1930s what is now Gatineau Park resembled a patchwork quilt of clear-cut spaces, woodlots, farms, and residential properties. Jobbers clear-cut trees, particularly as the Great Depression set in, to sell in the towns and cities for firewood to heat homes, hospitals, and shops. Ski club members and other local residents were aghast to see how quickly the forests were being decimated. Stumps prevailed on increasing numbers of lots. Would the Gatineau Hills become a barren wasteland?

In 1934, ski club members and other concerned citizens organized the Federal Woodlands Preservation League. They lobbied strenuously for the conservation of the Gatineau woodlands, and they convinced two prime ministers, R.B. Bennett (who particularly enjoyed Lac Mousseau/Harrington Lake) and Mackenzie King, to become honorary presidents of the League. The League's ultimate goal? To create a park.

By 1935, King owned considerable property beside Kingsmere Lake, southwest of Old Chelsea, and he must have been an obvious choice as honorary president of the Federal Woodlands Preservation League. This was an organization of people who wanted to preserve and protect the wooded hills north of Ottawa. Their lobbying of the federal government, plus other efforts such as the publication of *The Lower Gatineau Woodland Report*, helped Todd's (if not King's) vision for a protected park of about 50,000 acres in the Gatineaus to take root and grow. By 1939, the FDC had purchased roughly 16,000 acres. Although the Second World War intervened, the park lands acquisition program was well underway by the 1950s; in 1952, a 4,500-acre property (Edwards-Herridge) was

Parliamentary Committee examines National Planning exhibit on display in Parliament Buildings, Centre Block, Ottawa, 1949. Photo: Chris Lund. NAC PA-146176.

purchased on Lac Mousseau. Today, that land is the site of the prime minister of Canada's retreat, known as "Harrington Lake."

Coincident with this period of early environmental activism, King met Parisian urban planner Jacques Gréber in Paris in 1936, while visiting the site for the Paris World Exhibition of 1937. The two men got along well and, King invited Gréber to Ottawa to help shape the development of the Canadian capital and its region. Gréber was keen, arriving in Canada in 1937 to commence his research. World War II broke out, and he returned to his homeland in 1939. Gréber came back to Ottawa in 1946 but only after stipulating that he be a part of a national committee mandated to define the capital region as a Canada-wide symbol. Gréber believed the plan for the capital region could only succeed if it was considered "a national undertaking of which each Canadian can be proud and through which national desires and aspirations can be expressed through material accomplishments."

Canadian planners John M. Kitchen and Édouard Fiset became key players in what became known as the National Capital Planning Committee, a body comprised of representatives from across Canada. During the next four years, the *Plan for the National Capital* evolved.

In 1950, Gréber's Master Plan, colloquially referred to as the "Gréber Plan," was published in 1950 (the year of King's death), and tabled in the government of Prime Minister Louis St. Laurent in 1951. Five major recommendations gave birth to the capital region as we know it today:

1. Relocation of the railway from the Rideau Canal and downtown core to the suburbs.
2. Creation of a Greenbelt system of park lands encircling the city.
3. The purchase of more properties to expand Gatineau Park.
4. Decentralization of government offices, which created the new developments of Tunney's Pasture (and set the stage for the development of Hull in the 1960s).
5. Extending the parkway system and the number of urban parks in Ottawa and Hull.

Compelling though the Gréber Plan was, politics and other priorities intervened, and the Plan lay dormant for the rest of the decade. Only with the new Conservative government of John Diefenbaker in the late 1950s was the Plan revived. In February 1959, the National Capital Commission was born.

The National Capital Region was also *re*born, expanded from the FDC's original 2,330 square kilometres as stipulated in 1945, to its present 4,715 square kilometres bounded by Buckingham, Poltimore, Wakefield, and Quyon in Québec, and Fitzroy Harbour, Almonte and the Mississippi Mills, and Russell, Embrun, and Cumberland in Ontario. The number of commissioners was expanded to twenty by the National Capital Act of 1958, to represent the people of Canada even more fully. Yet although the mayors of Ottawa and Hull had been commissioners of the FDC, they were not included in the NCC's board of directors.

Why not? Surely, this would have seemed a logical if not ideal way in which to ensure the elected political leaders of Hull (and therefore several Québec municipalities) and Ottawa (along with several Ontario municipalities) had a voice?

Installation of pre-cast, pre-stressed concrete units to form deck of Gatineau Parkway Notch Road Overpass. The 15-ton deck unit is being lifted into position by heavy cranes. February 1959. NCC 5256.

An *Ottawa Citizen* article provides a hint as to why the mayors were left off the board. "NCC brass argued that a seat on the board would conflict with the mayors' jobs as civic leaders. Area residents and some politicians complained it was a deliberate attempt to mute public criticism and avoid municipal scrutiny of the commission's work. ... NCC chairman General Samuel Findlay Clark said the mayors often broke commission confidentiality by reporting deliberations to their councils, often before the government had a chance to examine and approve them. Gen. Clark also reported that the mayors, particularly Ottawa's Charlotte Whitton, used their position to demand a voice 'rivalling the chairman's.'"[8]

In 1959, the Conservatives boosted the NCC's operating budget to $15.7 million, a figure more commensurate with this agency's expanded duties (the FDC's budget was a now modest-seeming $760,000). NCC was mandated to acquire and hold property; construct parkways, bridges and railways; create, operate and maintain parks; and perform a host of other functions. (In 1995, the number of NCC board members was reduced to fifteen; by 2002 the NCC's budget was $101.9 million.)

The face of the NCR has altered under the leadership of successive NCC chairmen — and it continues to do so. The current NCC manages Gatineau Park and many other parklands including Jacques-Cartier Park in Hull and Mer Bleue near Cumberland. It has spent $43 million to create the Greenbelt, which extends over 200 square kilometres around Ottawa and Gatineau. Residents tend to love and ardently defend their beloved Greenbelt, although a few urban planners view it differently. Some believe Gréber's well-intended vision of an "emerald green necklace" designed to define and protect precious parklands and to beautify the capital has actually become a tourniquet, constricting the logical development of the city.

Back in 1898, when the Ottawa Improvement Commission was created, Prime Minister Laurier said his goal was "to make the city of Ottawa as attractive as possibly could be; to make it the centre of the intellectual development of this country and above all, the Washington of the North."

Undoubtedly, Ottawa has become a world-class capital ... and the National Capital Region of today is an enviable federal district embracing areas of diverse cultural heritage and spectacular natural beauty.

PART TWO

The Rambles

Key to Rambles:

The Rambles

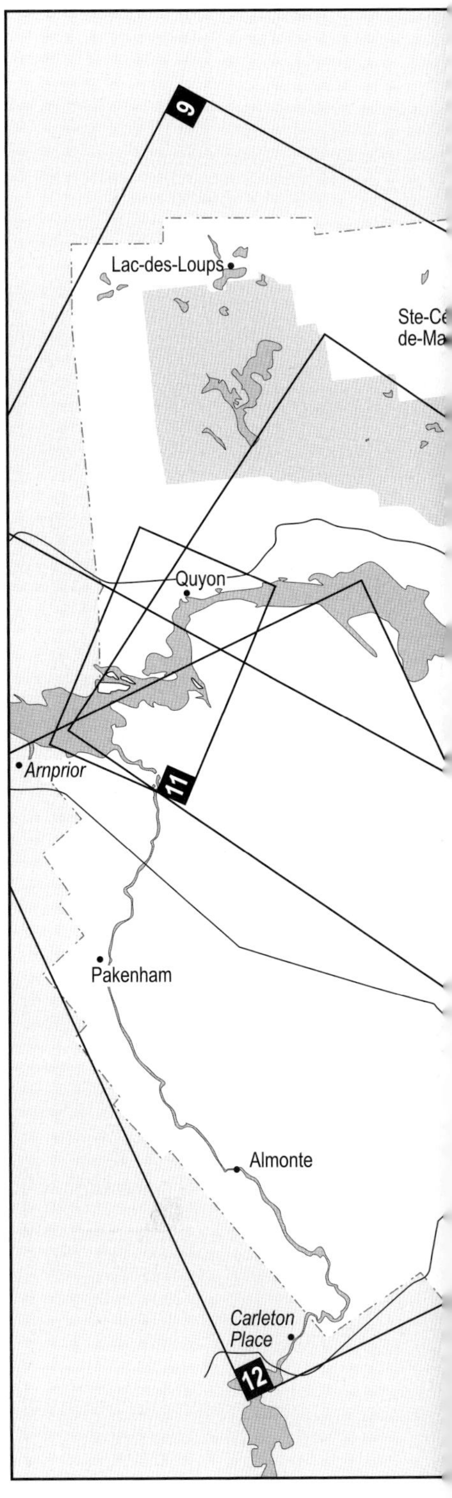

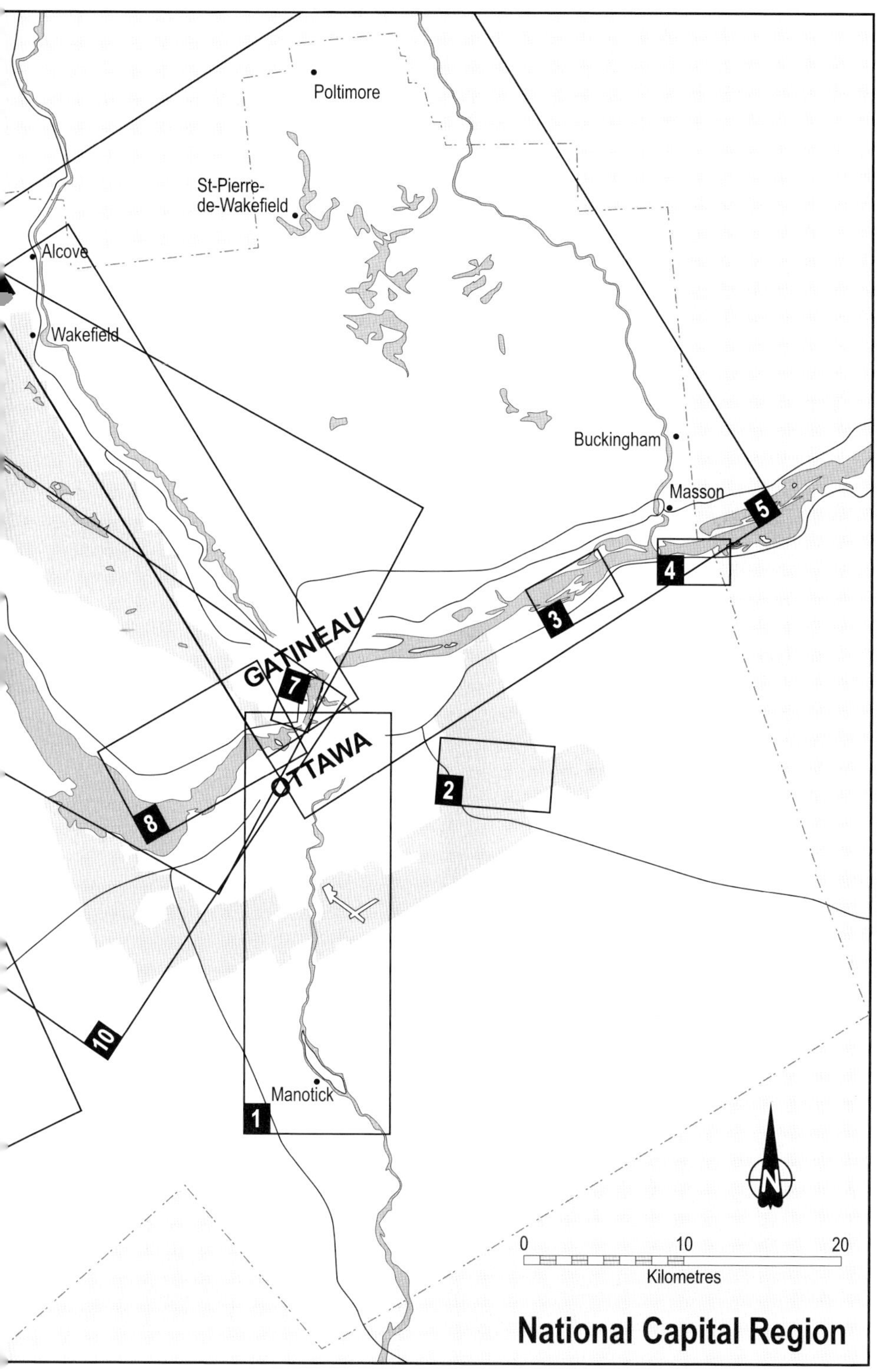
Poltimore
St-Pierre-
de-Wakefield
Alcove
Wakefield
Buckingham
Masson
GATINEAU
OTTAWA
Manotick
1
2
3
4
5
7
8
10
N
0
10
20
Kilometres
National Capital Region

FIRST THINGS FIRST: ORIENTING YOURSELF TO THE NATIONAL CAPITAL REGION

These rambles are specifically designed so that you can explore every quadrant of the National Capital Region, in both the Outaouais (West Québec) and in Ontario. Study the map of the NCR to orient yourself to the scope of the NCR as well as its major roads. Because the NCR is well defined by several major watercourses — the Ottawa, Gatineau, Lièvre, Mississippi, and Rideau rivers, not to mention the Rideau Canal — all rambles provide ample opportunity to be near bodies of water.

Using the twin cities of Ottawa/Gatineau as your "hub," the rambles splay out in a counter clockwise direction like spokes on a wheel. The rambles commence with a drive (or cycle or paddle) of the Rideau Canal. Then they proceed to describe combinations of drives, walks, bicycle, canoe or kayak trips, or even skiing and snowshoeing explorations (where these modes of conveyance are applicable) of Mer Bleue, Petrie Island, Cumberland Village, Lièvre River, Gatineau River, Brewery Creek, Aylmer Road, Gatineau Park, Ottawa River, Chats Falls (at Quyon), and the Mississippi Mills. Mer Bleue is a significant wetlands, while the Chats Falls ramble is actually an historic paddle of the Ottawa River west of Quyon, Québec.

Whether you are an armchair traveller, someone who likes to explore back roads by car, or an avid cyclist, canoeist, kayaker, or hiker, I hope you enjoy discovering our National Capital Region. I even have a suggestion or two for horseback enthusiasts!

BACKUP MATERIALS

There are many resources available should you wish to find out more information on the places you'll visit. I have not included Internet addresses in *Capital Rambles* simply because they are so volatile; still, a search on any of the rambles key place names will usually result in a host of Internet "hits."

If you want to conduct further historical research, I suggest you start by enquiring at the City of Ottawa Archives. Because of the amalgamation of several adjacent jurisdictions on 1 January 2001, the City of Ottawa is now a central repository for most museums and historical societies on the Ontario side. One call to the main city archives can connect you with all associated heritage groups you need. Québec also has several sources of information, including the Gatineau Archives, the Aylmer Heritage Association, Aylmer Museum, the Gatineau Valley Historical Society, and the Buckingham Historical Society.

If you are seeking French genealogical or other information, I suggest you again try the City of Ottawa Archives: this is where the Société franco-ontarienne d'histoire et de généalogie is based.

In terms of natural history, check the Ottawa Field Naturalists' Club, Le Club des ornithologues de l'Outaouais (Outaouais Bird Watchers' Club) for starters, and search on the web for information. Similarly, as you'd expect there are many other special interest groups, from the Friends of Petrie Island to you name it! Seek, and you will find!

LONGER EXCURSIONS: B&BS, INNS, CAMPING, AND HUT-TO-HUT

This is not a travel guide as such, so you will not find a comprehensive list of places to stay.

I have, however, listed the names of places you might like to dine in or stay at en route if they are particularly relevant in the context of each ramble. For instance, in Wakefield (see Gatineau River ramble) the heritage Wakefield Mill is now an auberge/inn, and in places like Fitzroy Harbour's nearby provincial park of the same name, along the Rideau Canal, or in Gatineau Park, you will find ample opportunities for overnight camping.

- Gatineau Park: During summer, the parkways are closed on Sunday mornings from May until the end of September. This allows cyclists, in-line skaters, and hikers to enjoy and explore the parkway road network. The parkways close for the winter, after the first snowfall or threat from freezing rain.
- When hiking, biking, skiing, snowshoeing, or otherwise exploring on land, please stay on designated trails. Places like Baxter Conservation Area, Mer Bleue, and Gatineau Park are wildlife sanctuaries for animals, birds, fish, and plants. Be a guardian of the wild.
- Plan your outing and tell someone where you are going, your destination, and estimated return time.
- Footwear is crucial: wear appropriate, comfortable, flat-soled, sturdy shoes — not a new pair if hiking. If horseback riding, you must wear shoes with a defined heel not bigger than 1 inch (athletic shoes are not acceptable) and do wear a helmet.
- Take a daypack (ensure the zippers are sound) so that your hands are free to use the binoculars and camera that you'll bring. (For longer excursions, consider a first-aid kit.)

Pointer boat on the Gatineau River at Cascades.
River men used these to help sort logs — but on leisure days they were put to good use, c. 1920. HSG 02095–072.

- In bug season (mid-May through July), pack insect repellent. Mosquitoes and black flies can be particularly vicious in spots like Mer Bleue, an open bog wetland.
- Pack a lunch and always take extra drinks; water is best. In fact, some of the rambles are fairly remote so even if you're driving, you may wish to pack a picnic.
- Take identification books for flowers, animals, birds, rocks.
- Learn to identify and avoid poison ivy. "P.I." is endemic and not fun to have. Can you identify it? If not, obey this woodland saying: "leaves of three let them be." And, avoid picking whitish-green berries for your Christmas wreath like a friend of mine did, come late November. Those are the fruit of this toxic plant. And yes, she got a bad rash. So will you.
- Be smart about clothing: layering is best; wool keeps you warm even if wet; micro fibre as in "river pants" resists both wind and water and, if soaked, dries easily. Wear a hat for warmth, to discourage bugs, to protect you from rain, sleet, or snow, and to shield you from the sun.
- Pick up your garbage! Leave nothing but your footprints on the trail, nothing but your paddle strokes in the water.
- Swimmers beware: the rivers can be extremely treacherous and you can have problems with undertows. Always ask local residents about the safety (or lack thereof) of waterways: in the summer of 2002 a father and daughter drowned at the confluence of the Quyon and Ottawa rivers, and a teenage boy drowned on the Ottawa River, near Lemieux Island. Be careful: smooth waters can hide undercurrents.
- Always wear a lifejacket if you are in a canoe or kayak.
- Dog note: Dogs are being restricted more and more. NCC regulations stipulate dogs must be kept on a leash no more than 2 metres long. A maximum of two dogs per person was the rule as of 2004 but rules change so inform yourself. That being said, there are many places in the NCR where dogs remain welcome. Again: remember that wildlife live in the region and require sanctuary. Keep your dog on a leash for the protection of the denizens of the wild spaces.
- Horses are restricted too: for example, there is only one stable currently allowed to offer rides in Gatineau Park (based in Luskville, see Gatineau Park ramble). If you want to ride, be aware of constraints: inform yourself. If you have your own horse, find out where

you are permitted to ride before you trailer your animal. Fines apply and are given in Gatineau Park. It is wise to wear a helmet: falling from a horse is just as serious as from a bike. Take care.

- Ferries are fun to use. The Cumberland to Masson and the Fitzroy Harbour to Quyon ferries are seasonal. Neither is very expensive: at the time of writing they were less than $6 per car, one way. Cyclists and walkers can also use them. Fees vary.
- Finally, the countryside is not "unowned, waste land" waiting for your personal enjoyment. Please ask a landowner *prior* to venturing onto any land for any reason: a picnic, to bird watch, or to pick those juicy red apples. And, if you are given permission, ensure you use gates (and close them), and do not climb fences. Ask; people often do not mind. If they say no, find another spot!

PRELIMINARY NOTES TO THE RAMBLES

- Each ramble description gives directions starting from Ottawa, the common "hub."
- "Trailhead" means the start of a trail.
- Abbreviations: NCC = National Capital Commission; NCR =National Capital Region; P-7, P-11, etc. represent parking lot numbers in and around Gatineau Park and Mer Bleue ... but not all lots are numbered.
- **Important:** If you see something amiss on Gatineau Park trails, such as a fallen tree or a flooded spot, report it to appropriate authorities such as the NCC Visitor's Centre for Gatineau Park and Mer Bleue.
- **Final note:** Because of the amalgamation of the City of Ottawa with the surrounding towns in Ontario and City of Hull with the surrounding towns to become the City of Gatineau in Québec, some street names are going to change.

EXAMPLES OF NATURAL ENVIRONMENTS FOUND IN THE RAMBLES

I chose each ramble because of its unique offerings. As you explore, you will discover several different ecological habitats, from upland forest to wetland, from river to bog.

Here's a short review of these habitats, particularly wetland areas whose definitions can be confusing. There are three basic types of wetlands:

- **Marshes** are usually flooded; plants live in shallow water or saturated ground. Typical marshes are seen along the North Service road approaching Petrie Island, where water circulation is fairly constant. (Rambles that include marshes are Rideau Canal, Petrie Island, and Mer Bleue.)
- **Swamps** feature plants that live in standing water, but these areas may dry out at certain times. Water tends to be more stagnant.
- **Peat lands** contain decomposing material, which over time forms beds of rich organic soil called peat. Fens are peat lands fed by groundwater, while bogs are replenished by rain and snow, have a high acid content. (Mer Bleue is a peat land bog; Gatineau Park contains another peat bog at Ramsay Lake on the Eardley-Masham Road in the Pontiac.)[9]

Rideau Canal

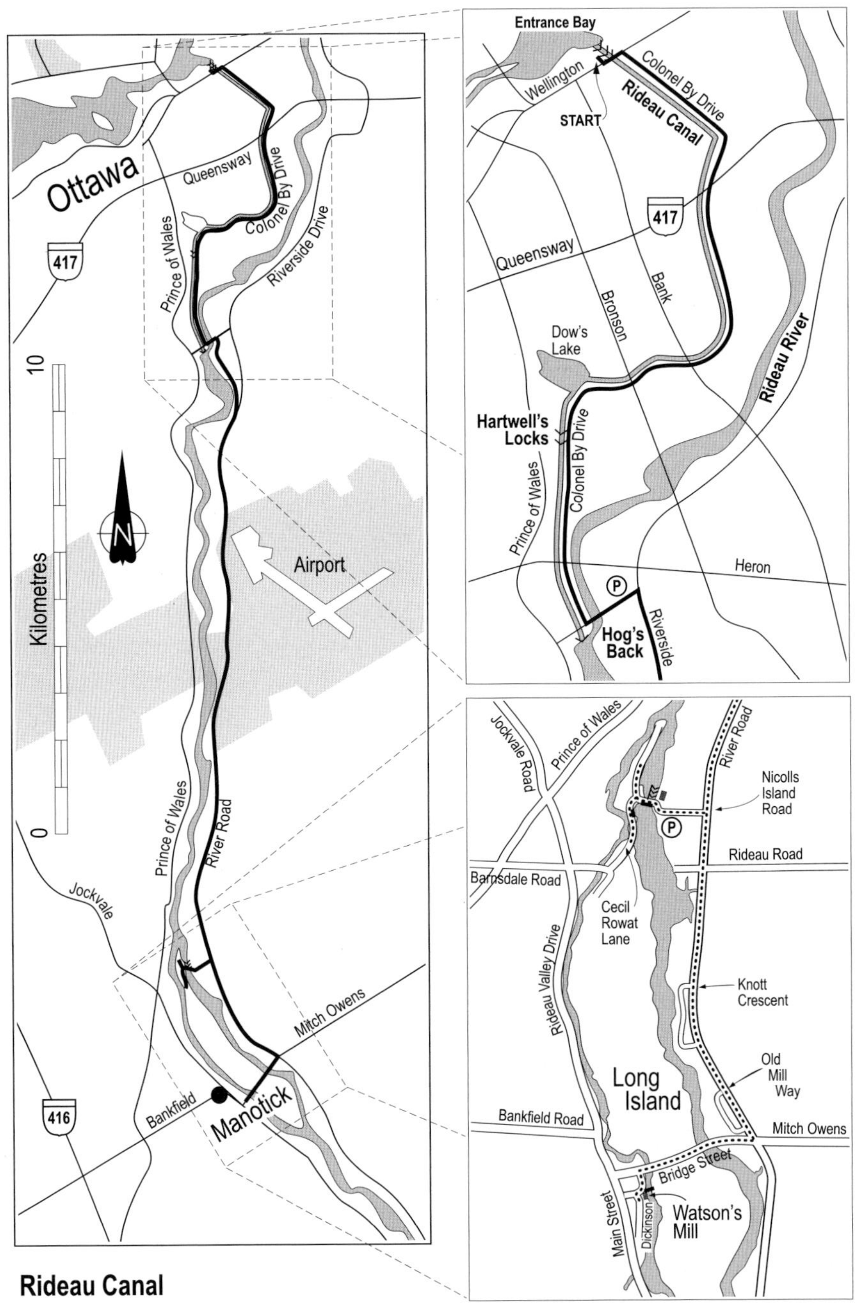

Rideau Canal

Spooning for Christmas: John MacTaggart's Tale of the Rideau Canal

While surveying the Rideau Canal in 1826, Colonel John By's team of men experienced some profoundly miserable moments. John MacTaggart was By's Clerk of the Works and fortunately for us, he wrote a descriptive account of his experiences.

MacTaggart spent part of November 1826 staggering through dense, dark, wet cedar swamps extending from the Entrance Bay Locks (below the Château Laurier) to what was then called "Dow's Great Swamp," after settler Abraham Dow. In his personal account of his labours, MacTaggart wrote how he and his men crawled on their hands and knees through dense brush, often through freezing cold water, en route to their goal. In fact, the men had to cease their efforts, as the going was too tough.

The job had to be done so eleven of them returned after the frost, which came on December 20 that year, along with a snowstorm that deposited over a foot of snow. Progress was tediously slow and the woods so dark and impenetrable that the man in the lead blew on a horn so those who followed knew where he was. The leader waited until the rest caught up, then the process started again. MacTaggart openly envied the Algonquin and other native peoples who had no need of compass to guide them.

It is one thing to stay warm while moving about during daytime, but banishing the cold and wet after nightfall is considerably more challenging. What were they to do? The men slept together, clustering around a fire behind which they had placed a large tree trunk that served dual purpose as a heat reflector and windbreak. This exercise in swamp camping was hardly comfy, as MacTaggart eloquently relates:

> *... after having lain an hour or so on one side, some one would cry Spoon! — the order to turn to the other, which was often an agreeable order, if a spike of tree-root or such substance stuck up beneath the ribs. Reclining thus, like a parcel of spoons, our feet to the fire, we have found the hair of our heads often frozen to the place where we lay. ... In Dow's Great Swamp, one of the most dismal places in the wilderness, did five Irishmen, two Englishmen, two Americans, one French Canadian, and one Scotchman, hold their merry Christmas of 1826 — or rather, forgot to hold it at all.*[10]

The Winter of Six-Metre Drifts

At 11:00 in the morning on 11 February 1869, Patrick Whelan was hanged after being found guilty for the murder of popular orator and Father of Confederation, Thomas D'Arcy McGee. An appreciative crowd jeered while they watched him die. (The curious among you will be interested to hear that these same gallows can be visited at the supposedly haunted International Hostel on Ottawa's Nicholas Street.) Proclaiming his innocence to the end, Whelan's guilt is still hotly debated and it's widely felt he was a convenient scapegoat because of his (equally debated) association with the Irish Fenian movement.

As often happens in fictional stories, that very February day, Nature seemed to sympathize with Whelan's anguished spirit.

That very morning, a fierce snowstorm blew into the capital. The blizzard shut roads, rendered bridges impassable, and stranded thousands of bystanders in the city. From that day until after St. Patrick's Day, March 17, the snow continued to fall. Six-metre drifts accumulated, forcing people to remain indoors. We can only imagine how tavern keepers' initial delight descended into dismay: how could they feed the good folks stranded for days on end at their pub? City and country dwellers alike panicked because known landmarks disappeared amid the drifting snow, making venturing any distance at all unthinkable.

In fact, those living on farms could barely move from house to barn. In *100 Years Ottawa and the Valley: A Backward Glance from Centennial Year*, Harry Walker quotes from a diary written by William Upton, who owned a farm where the Macdonald-Cartier Airport is today. Upton and his wife Ellen did not travel into Ottawa to watch Whelan hang. Instead, busy with his chore of cutting meat, he absent-mindedly jotted down in his diary that the temperature had fallen and that a blizzard was blowing. After a day or two of such weather, it was difficult to get around the farm to feed the livestock. Anxiously, the Uptons fretted over their daughter Mary who was trapped on Long Island where she was visiting friends. In his diary, Upton wrote that the government "ordered out the garrison troops at Ottawa to dig out trains of the Ottawa and Prescott Railway in the cuts where the drifts were over 20 feet high."

The situation grew desperate: hay and grain was so scarce that farm animals perished because they could not forage through the accumulated snow. People travelled by sleigh, and snowshoes were the only way to get chores done. Upton's entries reveal how complicated everyday activities were:

> *Friday, February 16. Went with Ellen to water the cows in Wood's bush. On the way back all but one lay down as the path was so narrow and the snow so deep that the cows could not keep their balance on the elevated ridge. We got them all home except one which having fallen several times, when about half way home could get no farther so had to be left in a deep hole sheltered by the snow all round. We protected her with boards and a horse blanket and gave her hay for the night and water to drink. Went to E. Reynolds for a little hay for the horses. It snowed heavily all day.*

On April 19 rains fell, but not as a gentle drizzle. Instead, nature conspired treachery again, swelling the banks of the Rideau River which "went on a rampage that flooded the countryside. The river road was four feet under water.[11]

HUMAN HISTORY

The 202-km Rideau Canal is a National Historic Site of Canada. Although the canal extends from Ottawa to Kingston on Lake Ontario, for the purposes of *Capital Rambles* our exploration only covers the length from Ottawa to Manotick because this section lies within the National Capital Region (NCR). The entire watercourse is well worth exploring, however, particularly the stone-arched dam at Jones Falls, a personal favourite.

The history of the Rideau Canal is fraught with intrigue, fears of war, and the British government's urgent need to fill its colony with loyal settlers to deter American attacks. As the international border, the St. Lawrence might have seemed the logical choice for a supply route, the river left the British vulnerable to attack along its full course. It was important that an alternate network be found (or constructed) to allow the transport of military supplies quickly, dependably, and defensibly.

Sites for such a supply route had been proposed as early as 1783 when Lieutenant-Colonel George McDonnell suggested using the

Cataraqui and Rideau river watersheds. Time passed and plans were set aside for a variety of reasons, one of which was cost: Britain pondered how to justify to a sceptical public, the spending of some £25,000 (McDonnell's estimate) on the remote colonies. Nothing was done.

American progress proved the catalyst particularly after the War of 1812. In early spring 1817, Americans commenced work on the Erie Canal. Upper and Lower Canada awoke to the potential threat of trade slipping away from their control, and both governments began to lobby Britain for support. In 1818 work began on the Grenville Canal, which ran almost 10 km and by-passed the extensive Long Sault Rapids between Ottawa and Montréal. A year later work commenced on the citadel at Québec City, and in 1821 workers began to build the Lachine Canal at Montréal.

Finally the timing was right for the Rideau Canal. The Duke of Wellington, Britain's Master of the Ordinance during these canal-building years, sent Samuel Clowes to survey the Rideau route in 1824. In his book *Building the Rideau Canal: A Pictorial History*, author Robert W. Passfield wrote that Clowes reported "it would require extensive canal cuts and more than 53 locks to overcome a total difference of

First Eight locks, Bytown, Rideau Canal, watercolour by P.J. Bainbrigge, 1838. Foreground depicts rafts of square timber with sails floating down the Ottawa River. NAC C-11864.

elevation of 422 feet, and it would be a costly undertaking."[12] But despite the cost, the project was sanctioned, and in 1826 Lieutenant-Colonel John By arrived to commence work.

On 26 September 1826, the first sod was turned at the current site of the eight locks at Entrance Bay, located in the dramatic cut through the cliffs between today's Parliament Hill and Château Laurier. Lord Dalhousie, Governor-in-Chief of the Canadas, joined By and a celebratory group of onlookers at the ceremony. Work commenced in earnest.

By was a visionary who saw not just the military but also the commercial opportunity offered by the Rideau Canal, and he was well aware of American progress on the Erie Canal. Boat technology was changing rapidly. Shallow (6-m) draught bateaux had more-or-less been replaced by the larger Durham boats because of their far greater carrying capacity. By 1826, another class of conveyance was gaining prominence upon the waterways: lake and river steamboats. By realized these vessels could convey not only commercial trade goods, but also thousands of troops, satisfying two goals at once.

By's efforts were hampered by a British government which still balked at the projected budget. Samuel Clowes' 1824 assessment of the scope and cost of the waterway was incomplete: Clowes had greatly underestimated the costs and this mistake had serious consequences for By for the duration of the construction of the Rideau Canal. Ordinance orders from By's superiors in England often took a month and a half or more to arrive, so By often was following one direction while another updated order was held up in the mail.

What confused matters even further was By's vision of a canal that would accommodate steamers. This meant the canal had to be wider and deeper. Britain balked, hemmed, and hawed, and time passed. Contractors threatened to sue the Crown, By continued as best he could. Finally, in 1828, members of the Kempt Committee arrived in Kingston on June 15 to assess By's progress and to consider the steamboat angle once and for all. They commended By, and although interested in his scheme, which would include navigation by the larger lake steamers, they asked him to scale down his plans so that, the canal would accommodate the smaller river steamers.

By was delighted. Author Passfield notes that the river steamers were side-wheelers, "108 feet long by 30 feet wide across their paddleboxes, with four-foot draughts and it was calculated that their 32-horsepower engines could easily tow two fully laden Durham boats at a speed of four to five miles per hour in quiet water."[13]

Even more interesting to By and the committee, perhaps, was that Durham boats could venture up the Ottawa, down the Rideau and Cataraqui to Lake Ontario, and from there through the Erie Canal without being unloaded and reloaded. This meant there would be no trans-shipment of goods, which always entailed an additional investment of labour and time. The Kempt Committee's report, completed on June 28 the same year, gave By the go-ahead he required.

As work proceeded on the Rideau Canal, workers, merchants, and lumbermen continued to settle the little community on the Ottawa opposite Wrightsville (renamed Hull in 1875 and incorporated into the mega-city of Gatineau in January 2002). In 1826, more than 800 residents lived in Bytown, (today's Ottawa); this was merely a handful compared to populations of 2,849 in York (Toronto) and 1,677 in Kingston. The gap demonstrates how urgent it was to populate the Ottawa and St. Lawrence with loyal British subjects who could be called upon to defend the Canadas from the Americans, if needed.

The canal had an immediate effect upon settlement, because after canal workers completed their jobs at particular locations, some stayed, homesteading where they had toiled. This is what happened to Long Island and Manotick, where this capital ramble terminates. The first settler on Long Island was Andrew Gamble, from Balleymena, Ireland, in 1828. Possibly he or his family members worked on By's canal project at Hog's Back Falls, where Gamble first settled prior to moving to Long Island. Did Gamble work on that first set of locks, then move southwards, realizing he could obtain a larger chunk of property before other homesteaders raised the price of land and before the next wave of canal work was completed? There must have been many who speculated on land as Colonel By's project gained credibility, progressing steadily southwards well within its six-year mandate.

Robert Bell's survey map of 1849 shows the "Village of Long Island," although the on-island settlement did not evolve as everyone expected. Two factors influenced the village's growth: the building of a dam on the east branch of the Rideau River, and the building of a mill by Moss Kent Dickinson and Joseph Merrill Currier in 1850. Both millers were Americans: Dickinson was from Massachusetts, Currier from Vermont. After forming a partnership, they became the first to ship sawn lumber — the new industry of the 1850s that rapidly overtook the square timber trade — to Boston.

By 1859, the two businessmen had acquired the rights to the water power at the dam site. They hired Scottish stonemasons to build the

Settlement on Long Island on the Ottawa River, 1830. Watercolour by James Pattison Cockburn. NAC C-040048.

stone gristmill — which still stands beside the dam. Instead of building an exterior water wheel common to the times, Dickinson and Currier powered the mill with six interior turbines — the brand new technology for the times. The original Cornish tin roof remains intact. The imported grinding stones from France ground more than one hundred barrels of flour daily, and in its heyday and during the height of the season, the mill employed twenty men.

Legend tells us this mill is home to a ghost. In 1861, a year after the mill officially opened, Dickinson's partner Joseph Currier was showing off the interior of the building to his wife. Ann Crosby's inspection proved all too brief: tragically, a revolving wheel snatched at the corner of her dress and in a dreadful moment, she was hurled against a supporting beam before its motion could be stopped. She died instantly, a bride of just two months. Her distraught husband abandoned his partnership with Dickinson three years later. Currier moved to New Edinburgh, and started a lumber mill and sash factory at Rideau Falls. In 1867–68, he had 24 Sussex Drive built in the Gothic villa style. This famous address has been home to all Canadian prime ministers since 1950, when Louis St. Laurent reluctantly moved from the Roxborough Apartments to this now much-altered grand home overlooking the Ottawa River.

Dickinson left more of a legacy than a single stone gristmill. This industrious fellow built a sawmill opposite the gristmill (also in 1860) and three years later, a carding mill, which was razed by fire in 1869. The sawmill employed twelve men and produced two million feet of lumber. It was replaced in 1870 with a different mill whose purpose was to prepare wood required for carriages and wagons. After that mill was destroyed by fire, Dickinson rebuilt: his new mill was partially powered by a cable connected to one of the gristmill's wheels, an ingenious, shared use of power for its time. Dickinson shipped product from this mill to Glasgow, to a distillery owned by John Moncur.

By 1862, Dickinson had the town surveyed and land prices soared from $8 to $40 an acre. In 1864, the population was one hundred persons. Dickinson personally owned 200 acres and in 1870 he, his wife (Elizabeth Mary Twigge of Toronto), and four children moved from Ottawa to reside on Long Island.

There exists a solid connection between Dickinson and Ottawa, for he was mayor of the capital between 1864 and 1866 — the tumultuous

Manotick, Ontario showing steamer Olive on Rideau River at bridge, c. 1880. Photo: William James Topley. NAC PA-8808.

years leading to Confederation. Moreover, Dickinson understood the promise of the Rideau Canal: he started the Dickinson Line of river steamers, including the *Olive*, *Britannia*, and *City of Ottawa*.

Today, visitors who paddle canoes and motor in houseboats on the waterway, or drive or cycle alongside it, can continue to marvel at By's project, which constituted one of the greatest engineering feats of its day.

NATURAL HISTORY

From its start at Entrance Bay to its completion in Kingston, the waterway offers a fascinating glimpse into one of Eastern Ontario's major watersheds. Travelling southward along the Rideau Canal provides plenty of opportunity to explore geology and landforms, as well as the varied wildlife found in woods, open pasture, and wetlands.

The cliffs at Entrance Bay in downtown Ottawa are Ordovician limestone. They are much younger than the Gatineau Hills, which are Precambrian. The Entrance Bay cliffs are faulted and uplifted (just like at the Chaudière). Cedar trees are visible around the eastern side of the cliff face (best seen, east of the National Gallery), recalling the cedar-filled bog By and his workers contended with almost 200 years ago.

Faulting is prominently visible again at Hog's Back Falls. Close examination of the rock configurations shows some folding, but the faulted uplift is most evident. (If you want to read more about this, check the bibliography for the work of geologists Dr. Alice E. Wilson and Dr. Donald Hogarth. Wilson wrote, "The whole region around Hogsback is criss-crossed by faults as though the surface had been struck by a mighty hammer in the long ago."[14])

There is more than geology to notice along the Rideau from the Ottawa to Manotick. Watch out for wetland denizens: mammals such as muskrat (which have a pointed, furry tail) and beaver (which have a flat, hairless tail) are often swimming about. Blue heron can be seen hunting for frogs and small fish by the shore, and watch for the osprey, or fish hawk, swooping down, plunging into the water to catch a fish. In early spring, the call of those returning migrants, red-winged blackbirds, might prompt a welcoming smile from you as you realize winter is on its way out. Watch for eastern bluebirds along the fences as you drive through the countryside: their slim, hunched silhouettes are easily identified on overhead wires.

The waterway route presents a wide variety of vegetation from water lilies to bull rushes and cattails, along with stands of sugar, silver, and other maples. Look for primitive species such as horsetails, which grow where "their feet are wet." This watershed is protected by the Rideau Valley Conservation Authority, a non-profit environmental and watchdog group whose mandate is the preservation of this precious, ancient watercourse.

BEFORE YOU GO ON THE RAMBLE

Why go? The Rideau Canal is North America's oldest-operating nineteenth-century canal. Parks Canada staff operate the entirely navigable waterway during late spring (usually the Victoria Day long weekend) to mid-October. Although the canal continues to Kingston, I invite you to explore 20 km of its length to Manotick, a town still within the NCR.

Distance: 50 km round trip on paved roads.

Modes of exploration: The ramble includes walking. You can drive or bike on roads that skirt the canal, rent a boat, bring your own motorized boat, or canoe/kayak part or all of the route.

The Ramble: Start at **Entrance Bay Locks** located between Parliament Hill and the Château Laurier, and continue to Hartwell's Locks, Hog's Back Falls, Black Rapids, Long Island, Manotick, and the Manotick Mill.

Parking: At the beginning of the ramble find street parking or else park your car at city lots (there is one behind the Château Laurier). Throughout the ramble there is (so far free) parking at the locks.

Facilities: There are washroom (outhouses) and picnic facilities at all locks.

Of special note: Entrance Bay locks features the Bytown Museum. (Because it was threatened with closure thanks to the City of Ottawa's spring 2004 budget, the museum might have closed — or the Commissariat building that houses it might have morphed into a different function.) The roadways along the eastern side of the canal, south of Hogs Back Falls comprise part of Ontario's "Eastern Bluebird Trail."

THE RAMBLE

Start at **Entrance Bay Locks**. Parliament Hill is on your west (left), the Château Laurier to your east (right). Below the East Block of Parliament, find the stone staircase descending to the Ottawa River.

Walking down the steps, you first pass the **Blacksmith Shop** (built 1826–29), then the **Lockmaster's Office**, the 1884 limestone building standing at the head of the locks, beneath the Sapper's Bridge. The other building on the west side of the canal is the 1826 **Commissariat**, once the storehouse for the canal builders' tools and supplies and a military warehouse, now the **Bytown Museum** and home to the **Historical Society of Ottawa**. The museum has an excellent permanent display of paraphernalia associated with the canal-building period, plus various seasonal temporary exhibits focusing on a different aspect of life in the capital in days gone. On the far side of the locks, you'll spy the foundations of a fourth building which was the Royal Engineers' Office, a contemporary structure to the Commissariat, which was demolished in 1911. Look north to the **Interprovincial (Lady Alexandra) Bridge** built in 1900 for the railroad from Ottawa to Maniwaki: the trains shook the old building so much that it was demolished.

If you're here during summer's navigation season, you'll want to join the onlookers who enjoy picnicking here while watching boats of all sizes navigate the locks. Well-informed Parks Canada staff answer your questions, and are fascinating to watch while they open and close the locks by turning cog-like hand-turned mechanisms.

While here, gaze about you at the limestone cliffs. When By and Lord Dalhousie joined in the little ceremony of sod-turning here on 26 September 1826, this immense cut in the rock was merely a goal in their minds. This cut was laboriously dug by scores of French and Irish labourers under the supervision of the Royal Engineers. The navvies worked with pickaxes, shovels, and gunpowder, all too frequently blowing themselves to bits or maiming themselves in the process.

The eight Entrance Bay Locks raise boats from the level of the Ottawa River to the basin behind the National Arts Centre where there used to be a turnaround called the Canal Basin (located south of the Sapper's Bridge). The locks enable an elevation of over 24 m (almost 80 ft).

The Rideau Canal, Ottawa, Ont., c. 1912. At left, Union Station is under construction plus the railway is there; to the west (right) are warehouses where the NAC is today. NAC PA-45644.

Many famous Ottawa names were contractors on the canal: Thomas MacKay (who built Rideau Hall and planned New Edinburgh), won the contract for the masonry work on these eight locks. John Redpath (who along with MacKay had also negotiated contracts for the Lachine Canal at Montréal) worked here too.

Depart Entrance Bay Locks and drive south on Colonel By Drive, which you will find on the east side of the canal. Your next destination is the two locks at **Hartwell's Locks**, which raise the water level another 6.5 m. They are located between Carleton University and the Central Experimental Farm's Arboretum and Fletcher Wildlife Garden. As you drive from Entrance Bay Locks, you travel alongside the canal, which courses to Dow's Lake, then passes through Hartwell's, towards the next system at Hog's Back Falls. This is the exact route through the cedar swamp that John MacTaggart and the other surveyors slogged through during the Christmas of 1826! Once cleared of its trees, Dow's Lake used to flood every spring. The canal builders erected the St. Louis Dam to prevent the annual flooding of Preston Street.

Hartwell's Locks comprise the southernmost extension of the skating rink formed by the Rideau Canal come wintertime, when students and bureaucrats alike can be seen skating to work. Maintained at taxpayer's expense by the National Capital Commission, at 7.9 km the Rideau Canal forms the longest skating "rink" in the world.

In 1912, Aletha Davidson's father, Arthur Dale, moved his family to Ottawa from Shawville, Québec, a village just west of the NCR. Dale served as lockman, living with his family in the original blockhouse on the west side of the locks here. Built of cut stone, the house was sturdily designed for the military defence of the locks. Today, however, it has lost its heritage look due to a façade of wooden clapboard.

Mrs. Davidson recalls her life at Hartwell's as published in *Memories of the Lockstations:*

> A story has been told down through the years that there is money buried near this building. It is supposed to have been the wages for the men working on the canal at the time. There has been a number of persons down through the years using scanners, shovels, etc., to locate this money, but to date it has never been revealed whether it has been found.

Another of her recollections speaks of the freight boats plying the canal.

> Captain Jim Yelland was in charge of the *Rideau* dredge and Captain D. Pritchard was in charge of the *Agnes*, later called the *Agnes P.* Every year in the spring the channels were cleaned out by the dredge. The *Ottawan* was a freight boat. It did not carry passengers. The *Wanikewan* was a pleasure boat and carried passengers as far as Smiths Falls. It also took cruises as far as Kars where there was a large cheese factory. We would leave the boat and go into the factory to watch the cheese being made. We looked forward to this trip several times each year.
>
> Captain Ned Fleming was in charge of the *Loretta*, which was a service boat that checked the canal and waterways for damages and defects to the gates and locks. The government carpenters kept the gates in repair and built new gates as they were needed. All of the work on the stations was done by hand, such as mixing the paint that was used for the upkeep of the buildings, cutting grass, etc.

Mrs. Davidson also described how the locks were opened by hand, as they still are today, although now Parks Canada summer staff does the job. Mrs. Davidson called the hand-operated wheels "crabs," and others who are familiar with the terminology use "locking" to describe the action of boats going through the locks.

> The crabs were operated by hand … turned to open the gates and operate the sluices which let the water flow from one basin to another while boats were being locked through. The locks were kept open 24 hours a day but seldom would there be a lockage after dark. I do remember just one as I helped to carry the lantern from one basin to the other.[15]

In 1924, Arthur Dale was promoted to the position of lockmaster, and transferred from Hartwell's to the next lock we'll visit: **Hog's Back**. To get there, continue south on Colonel By Drive, to Hog's Back Road. Turn right (east), and almost immediately left into the parking lot. Walk to the Falls. (**Note:** there is a network of paths here along the east shore of the canal leading north through Hogs Back Falls Park to Vincent Massey Park. Both are extremely popular summertime destinations for families, and in the height of summer parking may be difficult.)

Hog's Back Falls got its name from the craggy rocks — supposedly resembling a hog's spine —jutting out of the falls here. One of the best spots to view the foaming rush of water is from **Hog's Back Park** where footpaths descend alongside the impressive falls. Good lookouts are also located on the **Hog's Back Bridge** immediately overlooking the chasm created by the dam and corresponding chutes. To the west is a walkway that is particularly interesting during spring's melt-water rush because you feel as if you are virtually "in" the falls — especially when the wind blows the spray over you! Note that in winter ice formations make an inspiring subject for photography.

Hog's Back Falls is dramatic, and we can only imagine how it must have appeared in 1827 prior to any containment:

> the river was 170 feet wide … with a discharge of about 170,000 cubic feet per minute, and in flood the boiling water rose 16 feet up its banks. By decided to take advantage of the lofty riverbanks at the spot by building a 45-foot-high dam across

> the channel to flood the Three Island Rapids further upstream and provide a navigable depth of water all the way to Black Rapids, four miles away.[16]

New Yorker Walter Fenelon was the first contractor to attempt to tame the falls' wild fury, and in July 1827 he began to build a 15-metre-high stone dam. In February 1828, earth and stone fill that Fenelon had dumped into the partially completed structure was washed away. By decided to rebuild immediately, but although his Royal Sappers and Miners set a timber crib and rocks to span and fill the gap left between the end of Fenelon's dam and the embankment, the rushing waters once again ripped open the gap on 29 March 1828. The indefatigable By encouraged his men once again, and a year later, the gap was closed. Or so they thought, until the mighty current ripped By's handiwork asunder in the spring floodwaters of 1829. This third breach prompted By to rethink his strategy. In July 1829, 160 men started work on a permanent weir, and two years later the dam at Hog's Back Falls was completed.

According to Mrs. Davidson, by the 1920s, Hog's Back was a summer resort relatively remote from the city limits. "There were numerous cottages along the east side of the Rideau River in Gloucester as far as Vincent Massey Park. On the west side below the locks was a large campsite called the Valley of Dreams."

Mrs. Davidson mentions Teskey's Tea Room and another popular spot:

> In 1930 a very attractive take-out food service was built on the canal road. It was called the 'Old Dutch Mill.' Customers were served food in their cars by attractive girls in Dutch costumes. It operated for several years and then was taken down for the widening of the road which was renamed Colonel By Drive in 1953.
>
> The McCallum's poultry farm, Brûlé's quarry and several houses on the Hog's Back Road in Gloucester were expropriated for development of road widening and park land. On the southeast side of Mooney's Bay where the Marina now is built was a large ice house. There was also St. Patrick's Summer home for girls and boys.[17]

These days, Mooney's Bay is a favourite picnic grounds with a swirl of beach as well as boat rentals.

The next lock and dam is at **Black Rapids**, approximately 2.5 km south of Hog's Back. To get there, connect to Riverside Drive South (go east on Hog's Back Road, then turn right, south). Proceed through the Mooney's Bay area, along what has become River Road, passing the Black Rapids locks here. (**Note:** You can only access Black Rapids from the west side of the Rideau, whereas you are able to explore Long Island from both approaches.) By completed **Black Rapids** locks in 1830. The lockmaster's house was removed in 1914, and a concrete dam built between 1949 and 1954 replaced By's stone dam.

Continue southwards, passing Cedardale, Gloucester Glen, and Honey Gables communities before arriving at our next Rideau Canal destination: **Long Island**. You are now three kilometres south of Black Rapids. Turn west towards the river on **Nicolls Island Road**, at Rideau Park, to locate the **Long Island Locks, lock numbers 14, 15, and 16**. A cluster of buildings ahead on your right includes the lockmaster's home and service buildings. Proceed across the bridge but look immediately to your right (north) to view the locks.

Dam at Nicolls Island. Photo: E. Fletcher September 2002.

At the far side of the bridge you are on **Nicolls Island** (although the locks, rather confusingly, are known as the Long Island Locks). The road forks. Walking north via the right-hand fork on Nicolls Island Road lets you explore a little community nestled together amid the shelter of a mixed woods.

According to author Mel Rowat, another contributor to *Memories of the Lockstations*, this was land first leased by Edward McGrath, who invited many of his friends to summer here near his own cottage. "In the summer," Rowat recalls, "it was usual to hear the musical sounds of the piano from the McGrath cottage while the young people danced on the long surrounding veranda."[18]

Return to the fork and walk south on **Cecil Rowat Lane** to cross the newer dam and look back towards By's **slackwater system dam**. Stand upon the bridge (actually the top of the new dam) and look for blue heron below. Perhaps you'd like to do as I did, and scramble down the side of the embankment here, to stand beside the west branch of the Rideau River to gaze up at the dam's impressive size.

By's vision of what he would build at Long Island was unprecedented in its scope. He devised a slackwater system "in which high dams raised the water level to flood the rapids and back up the water to a navigable depth. Each stillwater so created would stretch upriver to the base of the dam at the next set of rapids."[19] Author Robert Passfield makes the point that land values were so low that By could afford to use the "waste land" for this construction, whereas in Britain the government could not possibly have purchased or expropriated this amount of land at anywhere near market value.

The Irish and French labourers in By's employ had a dreadful time of it. "The life of a labourer on the Rideau Project was extremely arduous. Not only did he work 14- to 16-hour days, six days a week, as was customary in the early 19th Century, but he did so under the most primitive and taxing of conditions.... Once the line of canal was selected, axemen cut the trees and oxen dragged the logs and boulders off the site. Then excavation began with pick, shovel and wheelbarrow."[20]

According to Passfield, the Irish didn't prepare for winter, often refusing to purchase blankets or otherwise get ready for the bitter months of snow, ice, and frigid temperatures. Already ravaged by famine and poverty — not to mention the arduous Atlantic crossing — they suffered tremendously. Passfield notes that French labourers knew Canada and its harsh winter, so they would stop the canal work, and retreat to their homes or find work in the logging shanties, while the

Irish, "lived in rude huts or caves in the riverbank on the outskirts of Bytown (Ottawa) and Kingston."[21]

Now retrace your steps to your car at the parking lot. The Rideau Canal proceeds southwards through **Burritt's Rapids**, culminating at Kingston. However, to continue our exploration of the Rideau system within the National Capital Region, we now travel westwards towards the village of Manotick, a name derived from an Ojibwa word meaning "island in the river."

First continue south on River Road, passing **Walter Upton-Collins Park** on your right, then both Knott Crescent and Old Mill Way. Directly after it, turn right into **Manotick** via Bridge Street (this is County Road 8, rather confusingly also called Mitch Owens Road when it heads east of the traffic lights). Proceed to the **Manotick Mill** (known also as **Watson's Mill**) by turning right on Dickinson Street. Park at the mill. Operated by volunteers, Dickinson Square is the sight of a lively farmer's market in season (generally speaking, late May through October).

This gristmill was built by merchant Moss Kent Dickinson and his partner, Joseph Currier, from limestone they quarried on the west side of the river in 1859. The mill has had four names: Long Island Flouring Mills Enterprise, Long Island Mills, Manotick Mills, and, since 1946, Watson's Mill. This last appellation has supposedly stuck, though the structure is still known colloquially as "the old Manotick Mill." Aleck Spratt purchased it in 1929; he lived in the adjacent Dickinson home. Ownership of the mill subsequently fell to Harry Watson when he purchased it from the Spratts in 1946. Watson knew the business well. He moved to Manotick from England in 1924 and worked for the Spratts as manager of milling operations. Possibly, to avoid confusion with names, Watson immediately established his presence by putting up a sign over the doorway: Watson's Mills.

Manotick offers many historical buildings for your inspection. Guided tours are available in season, so you can linger here and make a day's exploration of this still-vibrant milling town. Moss Kent Dickinson — known as "the King of the Rideau" thanks to his industriousness and specifically, his "Dickinson Line" of river steamers — would surely be delighted.

Return to Ottawa. You can backtrack the way you came, else connect to Old Highway 16 via Main Street, or else return via the new Highway 416. Alternatively, consider heading south to the Baxter Conservation Centre. There you can wander boardwalks and woodland trails to explore the wetland area and its denizens. Perhaps you can imagine yourself back in time, working on the canal route alongside By as he oversaw the labourers working on his world-class project.

OTHER PLACES OF INTEREST

The Rideau Canal by boat: You can boat the entire 202 km to Kingston. There are fourteen sets of locks from Kingston to Newboro, which raise the water a total of 50 m (Newboro is the highest point in Upper Rideau Lake). From here, boats are lowered 83 m through a series of thirty-one locks to the Ottawa River. An offshoot, called the Tay Canal, transports boats through two locks, raising them 7.6 metres. Boats 27.4 m (90 ft) long and 7.9 m (26 ft) wide maximum can fit through the locks and canal cuts; it takes roughly 15–20 minutes to negotiate the locks but during the height of summer, the journey can take longer due to line-ups. Navigation charts are available (and essential) for safe boating.

Entrance Bay boat tours: At Entrance Bay Locks on the Ottawa River, there are summer boat tours, which travel from the Portage Bridge to Pointe Gatineau. This is a fun way to view historic Ottawa "from the river."

Shared cycle/walking paths: The central section of this ramble is easy to bike because of the path network from Entrance Bay to Hog's Back. At **Hartwell's Locks**, for instance, you can also connect to other beautiful cycle and walking paths beyond the canal, which lead to the **Central Experimental Farm** and **Arboretum**. Walkers can clamber up trails on the rise of land immediately beyond the lockmaster's house to arrive in the **Fletcher Wildlife Garden**. Bicycles are not permitted along this sanctuary's trails. The garden is an oasis for wildlife: many species of birds can be seen here, and gardeners are able to see which type of flower or flowering shrub attracts what kind of bird. As well, there is a native species garden, which is a super teaching aid for those of us learning to identify indigenous plants we can find during our rambles. **Vincent Massey Park** is located adjacent to Hog's Back Falls and contains a large picnic area as well as walking trails.

Baxter Conservation Centre: an important component of the Rideau Valley Conservation Authority, this centre is located near **Kars**. It is a 68-hectare park on the banks of the Rideau River, approximately a half-hour drive from Ottawa, just outside of the southern boundary of the NCR. To get there directly, take Highway 416 South and pass the turnoffs to North Gower. Turn onto the Dilworth Road exit and head east to the Rideau River, following signs to the Baxter Conservation Area and park here. There are super trails here. (I enjoy the 2.2 km **Fiddlehead Trail**.) Often there are guided tours, but a free self-guiding pamphlet explains flora and fauna, like fiddlehead ferns (the edible type you see in grocery shops). It is always useful having an informed naturalist guide; when I visited last time, my guide showed me a cavity in a tree that housed a nest of wild bees. I would never have noticed this nest if she hadn't been there. Baxter is also home to the **Filmore Park Nut Grove** where you can learn about thirty types of nut- or bean-bearing trees, including the Kentucky coffee tree, a rare species here in the NCR. All trees have identification tags.

Mer Bleue

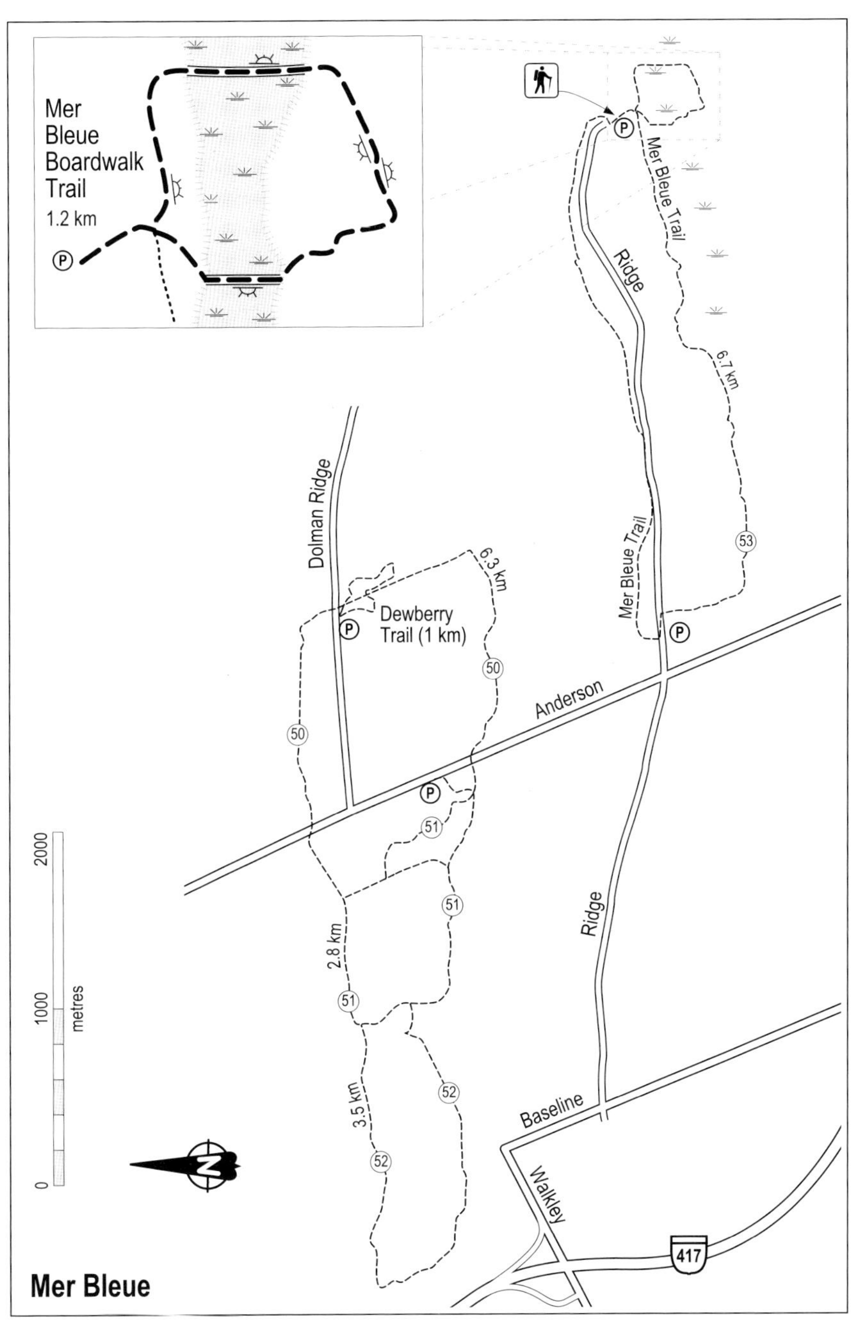

Mer
Bleue
Boardwalk
Trail
1.2 km
P
Mer Bleue Trail
Ridge
6.7 km
53
Mer Bleue Trail
P
Dolman Ridge
6.3 km
Dewberry
Trail (1 km)
P
50
50
Anderson
P
51
51
2.8 km
51
3.5 km
52
52
Ridge
Baseline
Walkley
417
0
1000
2000
metres
Mer Bleue

East of Ottawa lies almost 5,000 acres of peat bog with the mysterious name of "Mer Bleue" which, in English, means "Blue Sea." How did this fascinating spot get its name?

During the early days of homesteading east of Ottawa, when weather conditions were right, swirling mist obscured the vast wetlands. Local residents called the area "Mer Bleue," and the name stuck. Today Mer Bleue is a wildlife sanctuary and conservation area managed by the National Capital Commission (NCC).

One of the first buildings erected near Mer Bleue was an 1845 square timber homestead. George Gray, formerly of New Edinburgh (the village built in Bytown by Thomas MacKay for his millworkers), built his residence on Borthwick Ridge, where he owned and operated a 200-acre farm with his two sons, John and Allan. The Grays were by no means alone on the ridge, which recalls the name of another early settler, Thomas Borthwick. The Borthwicks were quite prominent here and recognized the value of the natural spring water that was so abundant here. They founded the Borthwick Mineral Spring, and began to bottle the natural product, which they sold in Ottawa.

As mentioned, water defines the NCR — and it's not just potable water or rivers that I'm thinking about. Just as much as we enjoy spas these days, in the late 1800s in Canada, sulphur baths and "taking the waters" was considered healthful and trendy. After all, on 25 November 1895, Banff National Park was created as Canada's first national park, largely because of the Cave and Basin, a natural sulphur spring. In Europe, spas had been associated with natural healing for years and their touristic value was well known in places such as Germany and Hungary. Here in the capital area, we are blessed with many potable springs, and yet the legacy of the saline Champlain Sea has also left us with valuable "sulphur waters," too. Carlsbad Springs is one such former site, located southeast of Mer Bleue. In days gone by, it was a popular spa where Ottawans and others came to "take the baths." Lesser-known Victoria Sulphur Springs was located further north, near Green's Creek. Just like its neighbour, it was known for its hotel, which was owned by the Lafleur family, where in 1887 guests paid $5.00 for a dozen tickets to enjoy the baths.

It is not surprising that water was such a desirable, and hence valuable, economic commodity in the area. Cholera and typhoid were all-too-common diseases well into the early 1900s. Ottawans suffered significant typhoid epidemics in 1911 and 1912. No wonder then, back in the late 1800s, that clear and pure spring water provided full employment for the Borthwick family.

Descendents of yet another pioneering family who homesteaded on this ridge — the McCartneys — are still there. Their white trucks decorated with a cartoon chicken can be seen throughout the city, delivering poultry meat to various locations. Here on the ridge, you pass their farm when you near the Mer Bleue boardwalk trail. Some 3 km north of Borthwick Ridge lies a parallel ridge that takes its name from John Dolman, a Justice of the Peace and health inspector who settled here between 1880 and 1890.

So far, I've talked about human history "around" the bog. But who is associated with Mer Bleue bog itself? In 1919, a high school teacher named James Collins, who lived in the nearby village of Russell, penned an unpublished manuscript entitled *The Chronicle of Carlsbad Springs*. Author and late NCC historian Courtney J. Bond excerpted several paragraphs of it in his now out-of-print classic guide and history, *The Ottawa Country*. Collins evocatively describes the Mer Bleue area while on a canoe trip along Bear Creek to Ottawa:

> The sun was setting behind the forest of spruce and tamarack in the Mer Bleue. On the edge of the clearing was the large potash-kettle supported by huge boulders from which the grey smoke of the smouldering elm and ash logs rose slowly skyward. A smudge burned before the door of MacDonald's shanty to chase the mosquitoes, painfully troublesome about the Forks at that time. The voice of the cuckoo sounded far above the trees towards the meadows. The oriole piped sweetly in the neighbouring woods...
>
> The next morning was perfect. The mist hung over the bank and the clearing. A few of the whip-poor-wills were still singing. The smoke from the potash fire smelled crisp and invigorating as it rose from the still smouldering embers. ... The cock flew up on the fence near the old stable and gave one last crow before he started his day's roaming with his flock. The breakfast being over, Angus MacDonald is seen down by the brook putting the last finishing touches on the cargo of potash and adding anything else he may have had of marketable value. His wife is now seated in the canoe in the place prepared for

> her. MacDonald goes back to the shack and brings something out laying it carefully near where he shall sit and row. It is his old trusty musket which perhaps saw service in the Glengarry Light Infantry.[22]

This last military note calls to mind another human "use" of Mer Bleue. Ten years after Collins wrote his memoirs, the Great Depression was in full swing. Just as in what is now Gatineau Park, where at least one trail (Skyline) was built by unemployed men as a make-work project, a similar scheme happened here. Workers dug ditches at the east end of the bog but fortunately, they did not succeed in draining it. Sometime later, during WW II, the Royal Canadian Air Force used the "worthless" bog as a practice bombing range.

Today, Mer Bleue is a treasured gem of the NCC's Greenbelt system of parklands — itself a legacy of Jacques Gréber's 1950 master plan of the capital. Thankfully, wetland systems are recognized as precious ecological habitats that need protection from human intervention and development. Enter the international body responsible for their preservation, the Ramsar List of Wetlands of International Importance. As part of our unfolding human history, Mer Bleue is now a preserved wetland under the 1971 Convention on Wetlands signed in Ramsar, Iran. This intergovernmental treaty identified wetlands and their resources and today there are 136 contracting parties to the convention, with 1,267 protected wetland sites throughout the world totalling 107.5 million hectares.

NATURAL HISTORY

Mer Bleue's almost 3,300-hectare wetland represents a throwback to the eras of the Laurentide Ice Sheet and the Champlain Sea. Over 9,000 years ago a southern branch of the Ottawa River coursed through here. If the Parliament Buildings had existed during that great sea, they would have been submerged in saline water where whales and seals swam. Dolman and Borthwick ridges were islands, large sand and gravel "bars" created as ice withdrew. Approximately 8,000 years ago, the southern branch of the estuary disappeared, replaced by a wetland created by underlying clay that prevented water from escaping. Cattails grew in the algae-rich waters. Meanwhile, just north of the Mer Bleue wetland, the channel of the Ottawa River watershed was narrowing as the land rebounded from the weight of the ice sheet.

Today's Mer Bleue bog lies north of Bear Brook and Carlsbad Springs, two other vestiges from the ice age. Vegetation in the bog includes deposits of sphagnum peat moss forming a dense mat up to 6 m deep. Although the sphagnum moss on Mer Bleue's surface looks dense, as if it would hold your weight, it won't, and this is why bogs are particularly treacherous. The moss mats fulfill a significant ecological function, helping the wetland serve as "lungs" of the earth, much in the same way as mangrove trees do in the tropics. Mer Bleue bog is critical to the health of its surrounding landscape because it filters contaminants from the watershed region. It also serves as natural reservoir by replenishing the water table. More than 75 percent of Ontario's wetlands have been drained, so it is particularly important that the NCC remains committed to maintaining Mer Bleue as an internationally significant conservation area.

Nevertheless, there is more to life at Mer Bleue than sphagnum moss. Dramatic dark green spires of black spruce trees grow here, as well. Come autumn, the green needle-like leaves of the deciduous conifer, the tamarack (or larch), turn brilliant gold before dropping to the mossy mat. Carnivorous plants are also visible; look for the pitcher plant and sundew. Other plants typical of northern boreal forest ecological zones exist here, including leatherleaf, bog cranberry, and bog laurel. Another feature of Mer Bleue is a series of islands inside the bog, where birch and aspen grow.

Mer Bleue also features a "lagg," a term referring to the moat of water surrounding the bog. The lagg was created by beavers that, doing what comes naturally, dammed all the outflows of the bog. Mer Bleue's lagg is becoming increasingly choked by cattails. Here you will surely hear that harbinger of spring, the red-winged blackbird. Also listen for the comical-sounding, "gurgling water" call of the well-camouflaged American bittern.

While strolling along the Mer Bleue boardwalk, you will see evidence of beavers and their rodent relatives, muskrats, whose "swimming channels" cut narrow swathes through the cattails encroaching the bog. Look also for muddy "preening tufts" where black, mallard, and other ducks stand to clean themselves. Tell-tale feathers floating on the water's surface reveal these areas to you, even if their former owners have flown off at your approach.

Beaver activity along path at Mer Bleue.
Photo: E. Fletcher, September 2002.

Mer Bleue is home to many unusual birds. The boardwalk offers birdwatchers a rich variety of species, as does an amble along the ridge. Nashville warblers; northern shrike; black-backed woodpecker; northern mockingbirds; several unusual sparrows: Lincoln, clay-coloured, and Henslow's; sedge wren; olive-sided flycatcher; and orchard oriole have all been reliably identified in Mer Bleue, according to area birders Larry Neily and Tony Beck.

Amateur zoologists among you will delight to realize that Mer Bleue is also home to some creatures that are extremely rare throughout North America, if not the world. One such critter is the spotted turtle. With its black carapace and bright yellow or orange spots, this small amphibian (127 mm shell length) is easily recognized — if you are so fortunate as to spot it. If you have ever tried to approach wild turtles, however, you already know that even your softest footsteps (or paddle strokes) warn them of your presence from many metres away. Frustratingly, these truly wild creatures tend to slip into the water well before you can get close enough to observe them. (That's another good reason to bring binoculars along on your ramble.)

Hopefully Mer Bleue will survive for many more thousands of years despite inevitable urban sprawl. Other factors threaten the bog. For example, while we attempt to prevent destructive wild fires we have to recognize that we are impeding the natural evolution of landscape. Without such checks and balances, and with the ever-constant unchecked activity of beavers, the vegetation of Mer Bleue is becoming less diverse.

BEFORE YOU GO ON THE RAMBLE

Why go? Mer Bleue is a rare example of a sphagnum bog wetland system. Boardwalk and other trails permit you to get "up close and personal" to an otherwise impenetrable, rare ecosystem.

Distances: Mer Bleue is roughly a 20 km drive from Parliament Hill. The Boardwalk Trail is a gentle 1.2 km walk.

Modes of exploration: You can cycle to the bog but note that bikes are not permitted on the boardwalk itself. In winter there are cross-country ski trails here but again, stay on trails to conserve the bog habitat and biodiversity.

The Ramble: Highway 417 east to Walkley Road, Baseline Road, Ridge Road and Mer Bleue Boardwalk Trail.

Parking: Parking lot on-site.

Facilities: There are washrooms (outhouses) at the trailhead. The path and boardwalk are wheelchair friendly, but remember: in inclement weather you are totally exposed. If you are in a wheelchair you must be very well prepared as there is no shelter from wind, sun, or rain. As you might expect, insects like black flies and mosquitoes are fierce here in season (mid-May through July, minimum). Pack bug repellent and wear wide-brimmed sunhats for both bugs and sun.

To get to Mer Bleue Boardwalk Trail take highway 417 east of Ottawa. Exit at Walkley Road, turn left (east) to cross over the 417. Walkley Road ends almost immediately at Baseline where you turn right and then left onto Ridge Road (named after the Borthwick Ridge). Continue east atop the ridge, crossing Anderson Road. Stay on Ridge Road, driving slowly along the spine of the gravel ridge where there is a mixed forest of hardwoods, conifers, and shrubs. To the north, enjoy the superb views of the farmland below, as well as the Ottawa River in the distance. Scan the sky for turkey vultures, scavengers easily identified while soaring on updrafts of air, scanning the ground for carrion. When you look up at them, you notice the telltale broad bands of white underneath their wings.

At the end of the Borthwick Ridge Road, park your car in the Mer Bleue Boardwalk Trail lot. Bring your binoculars, because almost as soon as you get out of the parking lot there are shrubs and trees to identify, and it is rewarding to scan for birds. There are remnants of

Snapping turtle along path at Mer Bleue, September 2002.
Photo: E. Fletcher.

an apple orchard to your right, as well as large shrubs such as buckthorn, nannyberry, and honeysuckle. Be on the lookout for critters; particularly from mid-May to September you might see turtles as you approach the boardwalk.

Continue down the path to the trailhead marked by excellent interpretation signs followed by the short descent to the boardwalk. The sign tells us about the creation of the acidic sphagnum bog. One describes how the current topography of the bog was created 9,500 years ago thanks to the Laurentide Ice Sheet and Champlain Sea.

Start walking the boardwalk now, keeping a lookout for interpretive signs. First, you cross a wide channel in the bog: can you find the large beaver lodge here? The next sign describes the water, stating it is 1,000 times more acidic than milk. As you stroll the boardwalk, you will particularly note the different types of vegetation. Soon the cattails disappear, replaced by deep sphagnum moss. The more you look around, the more types of plants you'll see.

White (silver) birch, black spruce, and tamarack are the main tree species here. Low-lying plants include the fascinating "carnivorous"

Beaver lodge in channel of Mer Bleue bog.
Photo: E. Fletcher, 2002.

round-leafed sundews, as well as leatherleaf and bog laurel. The latter two have similarly shaped leaves, but completely different flowers: the leatherleaf has a white bell-shaped flower whereas the laurel blossom opens to the sky. Bog cranberry and blueberry grow here, too. Remember, picking these in the conservation area is forbidden: look, but don't sample berries here!

Look about you into the distance while you walk and note how the forest verge contains the bog. You can see the island formations, with their aspen (poplar trees) and birch.

Pause and take a moment to squat down on the boardwalk to peer over its edge. Stop for a while, if you can, to *really* listen to and identify the sounds made by bog denizens. In spring particularly, listen to the frog chorus and to the twitters of returning songbirds, calling for mates and generally bustling about, building their nests. Search for leopard, green, and bullfrogs; watch for blue-winged teal, black and mallard ducks; search for pied-billed grebe diving birds or the great blue heron. Do the smaller birds suddenly fly away? If so, look around you for the northern harrier or marsh hawk, which dines on smaller fry.

The boardwalk at Mer Bleue. Photo: E. Fletcher, 2002.

Towards the end of the boardwalk, you cross through another expanse of cattails that ring the peat bog. This is the lagg. Crossing through it, check for the channels in the cattails made by beaver and muskrat and look for the little peaks of mud protruding from the water where ducks and Canada geese preen their feathers. If you are extremely fortunate, you might see another mammal — the river otter — though they are very shy of human contact. Instead of actually seeing the creatures, particularly on a day where there are many visitors, search for tell-tale paw prints in the muck.

As the lagg peters out, the boardwalk ends and you walk through a mixed hardwood forest. The gradual elevation here is perhaps 6 m on a broad well-maintained path. Look and listen for woodpeckers: can you find the big oval-shaped holes left by the largest woodpecker in North America, the pileated woodpecker? These birds are not particularly shy, and are relatively common. Other species here are nuthatches (they make a nasal-sounding *tzeet! tzeet!* sound), brown creepers, chickadees, blue jays, and both downy and hairy woodpeckers.

After you emerge from the woods, the trail continues its gradual rise, eventually levelling out as it rejoins the original fork and set of information panels that marked the beginning of the trail. Ahead of you is the parking lot. Now, with the panels on your left, turn right at the fork, back to your car (or bike). As you walk, look left to see the old orchard, shrubs, and trees such as buckthorn.

OTHER PLACES OF INTEREST

Mer Bleue's other trails: There are several trails in the Mer Bleue area. Trail numbers 50, 51, and 52 represent a 12.4 km loop; trail numbers 53 and 53A represent a 6.7 km loop; Dewberry Trail is a 1 km circuit. At the time of writing, dogs are not permitted on the boardwalk trail, but are allowed on a leash on these three very lovely circuits. Get an NCC Greenbelt trail map in order to explore these and other trails.

Carlsbad Springs: This was once a prominent resort. People flocked here to drink, bathe in, and otherwise enjoy the waters here. The springs originally were called "Cathartic," due to the renowned healing effects of the water's medicinal qualities, which were purported to cure rheumatism and other ailments such as skin diseases. By 1846, the name was altered to Eastman's Springs, after Daniel Eastman, who had by this time purchased 200 acres from Charles Billings. Six years later, Eastman had built a stopping place used by the lumbermen who travelled the valley. By 1870, however, a canny group of Ottawa businessmen bought him out, erecting the Dominion Springs Company Hotel, which thrived here, accommodating visitors to the mineral springs. Fire swept through the hotel later that year. Its manager, James Boyd, rebuilt a brick hotel here, using a clever design whose interior housed several mineral baths; the popular Dominion House spa was in operation in 1878. Twelve years later the Boyd family renamed it the Carlsbad Springs Hotel, after the famous spa in Austria named Karlsbad. They ran it until its closure in 1968. Other families — the Tenenbaums and Epsteins — also opened hotels and spas here, particularly catering to the Jewish community who enjoyed their kosher menus. All the hotels had closed by 1968.

Petrie Island

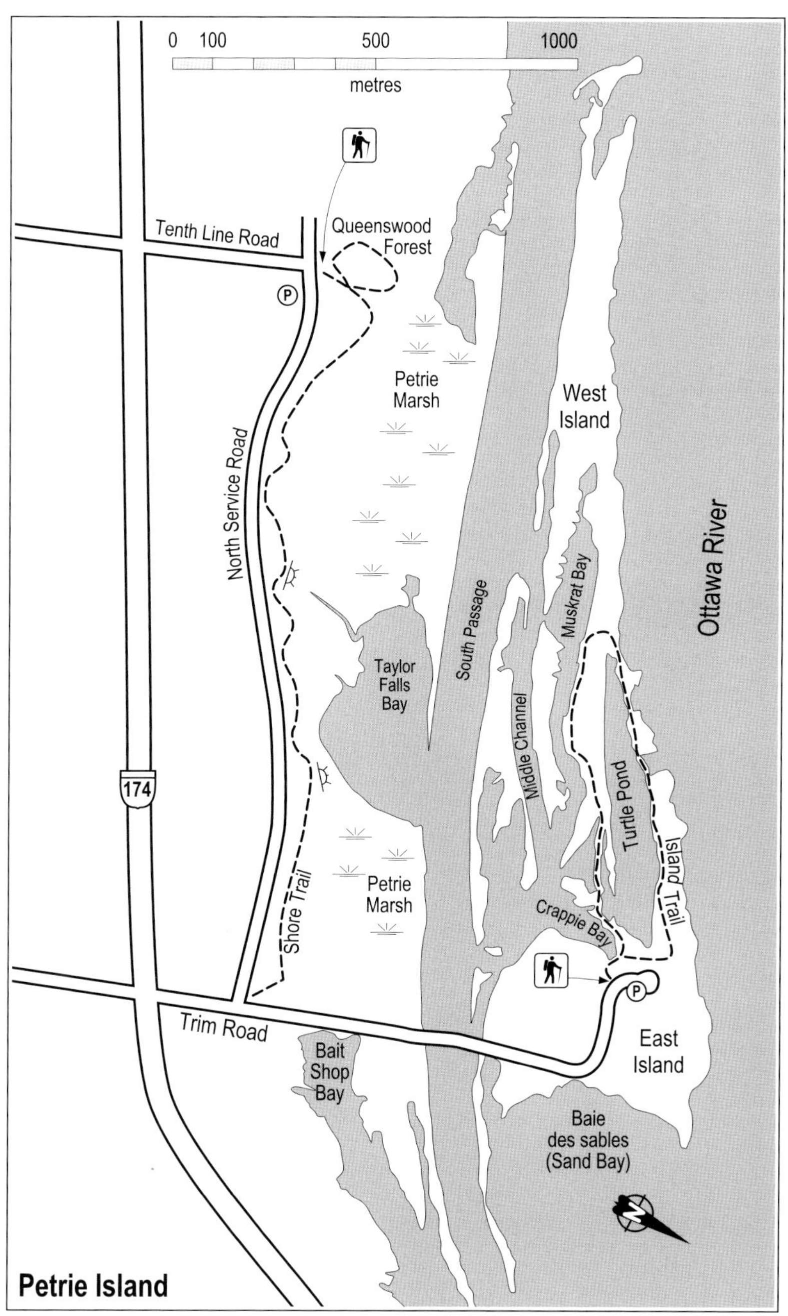

East of the confluence of the Ottawa and Gatineau rivers, and north of Mer Bleue, there is a little group of islands in the Ottawa River. The gravel and sand islands known collectively as "Petrie Island" are a glacial remnant. Not a single island, Petrie is actually a cluster of several small islands that form their own "unit" in the Ottawa River east of neighbours Duck and Kettle islands.

Thousands of years ago, in the Archaic-Indian Period, these islands were home to Native summer encampments. The fishing and hunting were probably excellent, as the group of little islands created their own natural shelter for ducks, geese, and mammals such as squirrel and deer.

Captain Archibald Petrie arrived here in the early 1800s. Born in Scotland in 1773, he became a purser in the Royal Navy, and saw action on Lake Ontario in the War of 1812, serving on *HMS Princess Charlotte*. After his retirement, the British government granted him land both as a reward for his years of military service and as a way of settling the area with loyal colonists with a military background. Petrie settled east of Bytown (now Ottawa), west of Cumberland, on land overlooking the islands that bear his name, which he leased from the Crown in 1834. Three years later he fought as Captain of the First Regiment in the 1837 Rebellion. This experience apparently fostered in him the notion of developing a land route on the south shore of the Ottawa River leading from Bytown to Montréal.

Petrie built his home along what was known as the King's Road, or Old Montréal Road, which extended from Lachine outside of Montréal to what was then Bytown. (The road was constructed in the late 1820s so that supplies could be brought to By's canal project from Montréal.) In Petrie's day, this was a toll road. Petrie evidently believed in community involvement at every level: between 1844 and 1847 he was a member of the Legislative Assembly of the Province of Canada; from 1852 to 1864 he served as a councillor for Cumberland; and between 1852 and 1856 he served as reeve. He died in 1864.

The next notable date for the islands was 1900, the year of the Ottawa-Hull Great Fire. The three islands, Kettle, Duck, and Petrie, became a campground for over 8,000 homeless people whose homes had been razed.

Later, the islands evolved into a popular recreational destination. Locals knew it to be a pretty picnic spot with sheltered bays and inlets that provided safe swimming, boating, and fishing, protected as they

House built alongside Ottawa River for log drivers. COA CA-1214.

were from the strong current and winds along the main channel of the Ottawa. But the islands weren't purely used for recreational pursuits; people hunted and trapped there, and bought parcels of land to serve as woodlots. Always in need of ice to keep ice boxes cold in summertime, the islets also provided a logical and easy access to the Ottawa River in wintertime, where ice was cut for early refrigeration. Teams of horses stood hitched to stone boats (think of a wheel-less wagon) while men with long saws cut blocks of ice up to one metre thick from the river. These were heaved onto the stone boats; then the horses hauled them to storage areas where they were usually packed in sawdust. When warmer weather arrived, the ice was delivered to households and businesses.

In 1939, the island was officially given its current name (hitherto it had been variously called Snake, Leonard, Petrie, and O'Connor Island). Despite being a little group of small islands sheltered by a larger, long "sandbar," it generally takes the singular, not pluralized name.

The next known date of significance, 1943, saw two enterprising individuals — John James Farmer and Gerard Bouthillier — procure fishing and trapping rights to the exclusion of anyone else on-island.

In addition to fishing and trapping, this sandy leftover from the Laurentide Ice Sheet was also an industrial site. By the early 1920s the Rivington family had built and operated four concrete wharves on-island, the foundations of which still exist. The easternmost island of the Petrie Island group was the site of a sand and gravel operation in the 1950s. Mr. Donat Grandmaître purchased the east side of the main island and developed it as a sand pit, selling that commodity for concrete and other uses until 2003. The Grandmaîtres industrial interests meant that a bridge to the south banks of the Ottawa River finally made sense, and soon a road connected Petrie Island to the Old Montréal Road.

Once these connecting links were built, cottage lots were developed but although fifty lots were created, only four were built upon. You can still view these cabins on the north shore of the main island.

Back in the 1950s Petrie and its associated islands were larger than they are today. When the Carillon Dam located downstream was built in 1964 it raised the Ottawa River's water level some four centimetres. This was enough to permanently drown most of the approximately 8-m wide beach on the north side of the main island, to create deeper channels and marshy areas in the backwater parts of the islands, and to completely submerge a few smaller islands in the group.

The Carillon Dam directly affected the Grandmaître family who hitherto had "mined" the sand using a dragline. The permanent rise in water level caused them to rethink their methodology, and they started mining sand using a process of suction from the river.

Twenty years passed and in 1983 the Grandmaîtres sold the island to the Regional Municipality of Ottawa–Carleton. With the city's amalgamation in 2001, the island became part of the City of Ottawa, and as of 2003 the City approved a budget of $2.4 million to develop the northeastern sector of the island. At time of publication in early spring 2004, the actual "improvements" were not completed. The Grandmaître's sand operation is closed, replaced by a sandy beach complete with beach house, along with additional parking plus some environmental work such as erosion control. As well, the Friends of Petrie Island are planning to have an interpretive centre on-island, and erect signage to identify trails more clearly.

Other developments threaten this island. This stretch of the Ottawa is the possible site of a bridge to connect the provinces of Ontario and Québec, whereby trucks could avoid having to pass through Ottawa's downtown core via King Edward Avenue. From the mid-1970s to the present, seemingly innumerable studies have been conducted regarding bridges on the Ottawa, and the fact of the matter is that no one who is environmentally sensitive really wants to see another one. Some people have suggested a bridge might be palatable at Britannia Bay, others point to Petrie Island. Both sites are important migratory bird nesting grounds, so neither possibility is looked upon favourably by naturalists. Nonetheless, traffic congestion appears to demand another bridge. Accordingly, yet another plan, this one prepared by Cumberland in 1994, proposed a bridge to be supported on pilings, to preserve the Petrie Islands wetlands as much as possible.

What is certain is that this pretty 250 ha island complex, with its quiet backwater eddies and stretch of shoreline will continue to attract recreationalists who want to get away from the city to kayak, canoe, stroll, sit and read, snowshoe, fish, and ice fish. Today, the island's biodiversity is protected as much as possible by the Friends of Petrie Island, a conservation-minded group who organized themselves in 1998. These days, hunting and trapping is no longer permitted: fortunately, critters are only "shot" by keen photographers!

NATURAL HISTORY

This is a wetland woods area, meaning that every spring much of the vegetation on these islands is flooded. Of course, trees are not entirely submerged, but you will be able to detect water marks and ice marks on tree trunks if you examine them closely. The constant flooding/drying fluctuation means indigenous species have developed special adaptive capabilities to survive spring's flooding and summer's heat, followed by winter's deep freeze. Winter's conditions are harsh not only because of plunging temperatures, but also because of ice build-up (which causes scouring and gouging of tree trunks) and desiccation, due to the air being so dry.

Because the mainland along both the north and south shore of the Ottawa River has been stabilized for farming, housing, or other developments, these islands are rare examples of fluctuating shoreline. This is one of the reasons why Petrie Island constitutes a separate ramble apart from its neighbour, the equally fascinating Mer Bleue. Indeed, Petrie Island is a designated Class 1 wetland system, being an easily accessed island environment that remains surprisingly intact, notwithstanding years of development on the main island's easternmost tip.

What species can you see here? Because the island was subdivided into woodlots, old growth has been logged. Consequently, many trees such as butternut, bitternut hickory, hackberry, basswood, and both red and black ash are less than eighty years old. Two grasses were identified by naturalist Dan Brunton in 1998: one is Gattinger's Panic Grass, which is unique to the NCR here on Petrie Island. The second is the rare — and romantic-sounding — Mossy Love Grass.

Well-known NCR birder Tony Beck and others compiled a list of 109 species here between 1994 and 1998.[23] Species listed include water-based birds such as American bittern and pied-billed grebe, along with woodland thicket species such as vireos and house wrens, various flycatchers, rose-breasted grosbeaks, and the melodious catbird and brown thrasher, members of the *Mimidae* family renowned for their lovely songs. The rarely seen great gray owl has been sighted here in winter, along with its more commonly seen cousin, the great horned owl.

The islands are also home to several turtles. The painted turtle is very common, but both map and spotted turtles are uncommonly sighted and rare. Best time to find turtles is in May through September, but if you drive here, please watch for and avoid them if you see them slowly crossing the road!

BEFORE YOU GO ON THE RAMBLE

Why go? Petrie Island is actually a group of islands that are remnants of an old sandbar in the Ottawa River left by the Champlain Sea. The cluster of islands is a haven for birds and wetland wood species such as the rare spotted turtle and wood duck.

Distance: Petrie Island is 24 km east of the Parliament Buildings; all trails are just a few kilometres in length.

Modes of exploration: Drive/cycle there, then you can choose from many activities. Take your kayak or canoe so you can safely paddle on the protected inner (south) side of the islands, stroll footpaths (footpaths are not for bikes), else explore by ski come winter.

Getting there: Only 24 km east of downtown Ottawa, Petrie Island is readily accessible via Highway 417 (Queensway) then Highway 174 east. Exit at Trim Road. Turn left (north) at the traffic lights where you'll cross over the causeway to Petrie Island. (Good signs help to direct you to the island.) After you are on-island, the road curves west; simply follow this road and park at the sandy lot. (Note: during the summer of 2004, a new parking lot may be installed straight ahead of you so that you will no longer veer left at this curve.)

Facilities: The island's trail network, beaches, information kiosks, picnic area, and benches are looked after by volunteers. Ice fishing huts may be rented. Kiosks post the latest bird or other information from the Friends of Petrie Island.

Of special note: In spring 2004 signs on-island stipulate that unauthorized access between 9:00 p.m. and 6:00 a.m. will result in a fine for trespassing. This is because this is an ecologically fragile area.

Take care on the north side of the main island: there is a very strong current in the river. Swimming is not encouraged, and canoeists and kayakers also need to respect the current. Poison ivy grows here abundantly. In bug season this sheltered ramble is challenging and the worst time for bugs is the very best time to view nesting songbirds such as warblers, so come prepared. Bug jackets and hats are worth their weight in gold! Wheelchair access is possible along the old roadbed, now the main stone-dust Island Trail.

Finally, because the island may be developed more, trails and access points outlined here might not be absolutely precise. Despite potential changes, I decided to include this island in *Capital Rambles*, as it is — and will continue to be — an intriguing, precious destination for canoeists, kayakers, hikers, and skiers. **Note:** in winter this is a popular place to ice fish, and there is good cross-country skiing and snowshoeing (trails are ungroomed).

THE RAMBLE

Petrie Island is a complex of several islands: East, North, and West being the main three. When crossing the Trim Road causeway to the eastern sector of Petrie Island's East Island, you cross the body of water known as the South Passage. Just beyond view, further west of the bridge, is Taylor Falls Bay, which you could explore by canoe or kayak if you wish. In the foreground is the Petrie Marsh. There are several trails associated with Petrie Island and I've described three super pathways I've thoroughly enjoyed.

🚶 ... SHORE TRAIL

Shore Trail is a 2.3 km walk along the south shore of the Ottawa River; in other words, it overlooks the South Passage, or Petrie Channel, and is not actually located on Petrie Island proper. The trailhead is on the North Service Road, which heads west from Trim Road just south of the causeway to Petrie Island. Drive west along the North Service Road and park in the lot at the junction of Tenth Line Road. As you drive, look north to the Ottawa River: the trail skirts the most ecologically sensitive area of this wetland region, known as the Petrie Marsh. It is so designated because it is particularly vulnerable to the variations in water level during spring flooding.

There are two sections to this trail: the walk heading east to Trim Road crosses creeks, wet areas, and culverts to give you good views of the marsh and, beyond it, the islands which you can explore later on. Find the second part of this shore trail opposite the parking lot at the junction of the North Service and Trim roads. A small sign marks the start to this Cumberland Township trail, known as the Queenswood Forest Trail. This 0.4-km trail traverses a significant woods dominated by hemlock and sugar maple trees.

🚶 ... CANOE TRAIL

Note: To date a *formal* trail by this name has not yet been developed. Designed as a self-guided canoe "trail," the concept is that markers placed on trees or signs will guide paddlers around a logical circuit.

Paddlers among you will thoroughly enjoy exploring the backwaters of Petrie Island by kayak or canoe. As a general orientation, here's a basic introduction to the named bodies of water at Petrie Islands. The first "backwater bay" on your left (west) after the Causeway is Crappie Bay. To the north of it on the main island is the Turtle Pond, a practically enclosed body of water (shielded from the Ottawa River by dense mats of cattails). Canoeing is discouraged on Turtle Pond because it is a sensitive breeding area for a variety of wetland species. Muskrat Bay is another channel cut into the main island, connected to Crappie Bay.

It is entirely possible for you to spend a happy day paddling about in these backwaters. Have a close look at a map (in fact, take one with you), then head off for a canoe or kayak exploration of these remarkable wetlands. If you want to picnic, do so in your canoe or kayak so you don't degrade the embankments as you clamber in and out of your boat.

While paddling, look for muskrat and beaver lodges. Muskrat lodges are made primarily of cattails and reeds, and are held together by muck. Beaver typically use branches of trees they have felled and subsequently trimmed down. Both types of lodges are conical in shape, and although they have underwater entrances their peaked tops stick out of the water. Although more adventurous in early morning or dusk, both types of rodents can be observed during the day. Can't tell the difference between them? Beavers have oblong, flat, and hairless tails (which they slap on the water's surface when alarmed), whereas muskrats have thin, furry tails.

As you paddle, watch for turtles sunning themselves on logs or look out for their snouts sticking out of the water, perhaps observing you as you pass by. The main season for turtles is mid- to end of May until September. If you're lucky you might see a female laying her eggs in the sand. Always be on the lookout for turtle nests: look for scraped sandy soil where the turtle's claw marks can be seen. Sometimes you'll see evidence of a predator like a raccoon or a skunk having dined on the delectable eggs; check for paw prints in the sandy soil and see whether you can tell which critter made them. If you are extremely fortunate, you could even witness a hatching or see the tiny turtles making their way down to the water. Timing for this is species dependent: snapping turtle hatchings were seen and documented by the Friends of Petrie Island in September 2002, for instance.

... ISLAND TRAIL

This path's trailhead heads west from the main parking lot and picnic area. It is roughly 1.8 km in length. At first it wends along the inside backwater channels, lending superb views of the wetland landscape. Pause at the riverbank to look for paw prints, listen for birdsong, and scan the water for turtles.

Painted turtles can often be viewed basking on logs in the water: your binoculars will assist you in identifying them. Map turtles are also seen here. How can you tell them apart? First, maps are so-called because the narrow yellow marks on their otherwise black carapaces (shells) resemble lines on a topographical map. Painted turtles don't have these. Map turtles also do not have the red line defining the rim of their shells. Maps are quite large: they can be 15 cm long and as is usual for turtles (and many other species, actually) females are larger than males. The plastron (bottom of the shell) is completely yellow.

Proceed along the path that wends its way through the woods to the paved stone-dust trail leading westward. There is an old roadbed that leads to the four cottages on the north shore of the island complex overlooking the Ottawa River, which is quite broad here. On a windy day, whitecaps form quickly: beware of these and of the current if you are considering canoeing or kayaking into the open water here. Several footpaths lead to the Ottawa River's edge, although most such trails are deeply eroded into the sandy soil. Vetch and other plants crowd you until you emerge onto the windy top of a small rise overlooking the river. The view northwest reveals a spectacular open sweep of river.

Return the way you came. Note that beyond the parking lot you can continue walking east towards the south of the old sand extraction site. This path may have been extended and developed by the time you explore it. The basic route, however, will probably remain the same. Enjoy!

OTHER PLACES OF INTEREST

(See nearby Mer Bleue and Cumberland Village rambles.)

Cumberland Village

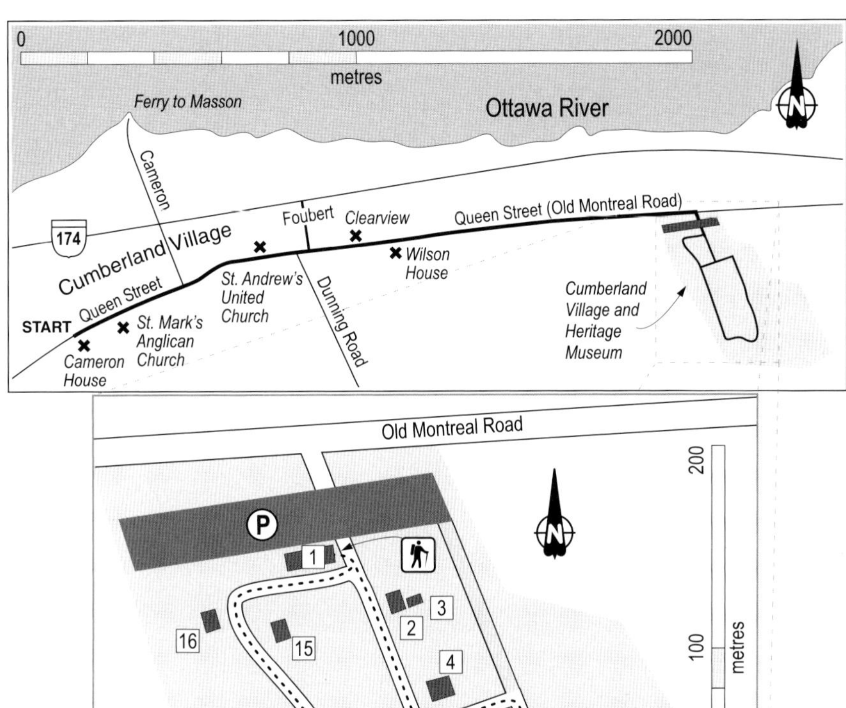

Cumberland Village

Cumberland Municipality represents Ontario's most northeasterly sector of the National Capital Region. Cumberland Village lies immediately inland from the southern shore of the Ottawa River, straddling the Old Montréal Road. Originally known as the King's Road, it was built during the late 1820s from Lachine near Montréal to Bytown (early Ottawa) to transport goods during By's canal-building years (1826–32). But communities existed prior to the construction of the "King's Road." What was this region's story?

Although Cumberland was first surveyed in 1789, only the northern section bordering the river was laid out then, not the entire municipality. Ten years later it became a township in Russell County. In 1801 — one year after Philemon Wright founded Wrightsville — the first settler, Abijah Dunning, and his four sons settled the property where the Cumberland Village now stands.

Six years later in 1807, Amable Foubert bought part of the Dunnings' land, and built and started operating a fur-trading post that was destroyed by fire in 1900. Foubert built a homestead near the corner of Foubert and Queen streets (the latter here being the Old Montréal Road). His original homestead was demolished, probably in 1915, and replaced with a simple gable-roofed, two-storey L-shaped home originally featuring a wooden shingled façade.

Another important first occurred in 1819, when the *Union* became the first steamboat to ply the Ottawa River. This heralded a new era of transportation, which saw steamers navigate the waters from Hawkesbury and Bytown beginning in the early 1820s. This traffic was key to the development of Cumberland, and in the 1840s the village was a bustling forwarding centre. This meant that at its two wharves (Cameron and McLeod) goods were loaded onto steamers heading either up- or down-stream to markets such as Bytown or east to Montréal. A third, Wilson Wharf, was built in the 1860s and subsequently rebuilt in the 1880s, proving that steamers and their forwarding as well as passenger and tourism businesses enjoyed a long life.

During the early years of the steamship forwarding business, settlement took shape, slowly attracting homesteaders. By 1822 Russell Township was joined to Prescott, becoming known as the "United Counties of Prescott-Russell." According to a chronology given to me at the Cumberland Historical Village Museum,[24] only six settlers occupied the riverfront here at Cumberland in 1822; ten years later there were fifteen. By this time, the community of Bear Brook, to the south, had started, and in 1841 a road connected it to Cumberland.

Relative prosperity seemed to be a sure thing, as growth continued to advance, and so Cumberland Township became incorporated on 5 January 1850. The next decade witnessed a large influx of French Canadians and Irish settlers. The French populated nearby Cyrville and St. Joseph (now Orléans) located in Gloucester Municipality immediately west of Cumberland. In his 1879 *Atlas of Carleton County*, author Belden wrote,

> Cyrville is another Village settled exclusively by French. The land was first taken up by Joseph and Michael Cyr, about 1850, and being cut up into small lots was leased at nominal rentals and very long terms to habitants. The place is a nearer approach to the old Seigniorial Tenure communities of Lower Canada than any other, probably, west of the Ottawa River. There is a population in the Village of several hundred, though there is scarce a place of business of any kind in its limits. The official name of the Post-office is Delorme.[25]

Cyrville became a popular stopping place where teamsters (the men who drove teams of horses hauling commodities by wagon) could stable their horses — or procure a fresh team — and stay overnight if they wished before heading into Bytown. It's hard to believe that hectares and hectares of cabbages used to grow here, but they did, on land owned by market gardeners such the Seguin family.

The township of Cumberland borders Gloucester on its east side and French settlement continued to populate this county here; Sarsfield and Leonard villages were both predominantly settled by French Canadians or French-speaking European emigrants.

Although other roads were developed, communities remained fairly isolated until the 1890s when the Canadian Atlantic, Grand Trunk, and Canadian Pacific railroads penetrated the township, connecting the little communities to each other and to markets hitherto accessible primarily by seasonal steamer traffic.

The year 1883 saw the Grand Trunk come through Vars; in 1897 the CPR reached Leonard (a largely French community south of Cumberland and Sarsfield), which had been established in 1867. The railway stations were catalysts for growth, constructed at logical intervals along the railway lines. As stations and town sites developed, merchants came to start businesses; cheese factories sprang up (thanks to many nearby dairy farms); wool mills, gristmills, and sawmills prospered. All such industries served to buy and then transform raw materials that were processed then packaged for rail shipment to a variety of destinations.

Technologies have their impacts and their heyday. Rail proved the death knell for steamers because the latter could not operate year-round. Nonetheless, steamers plied the Ottawa River until 1925. And although rail reigned supreme for years, it eventually succumbed to vehicular transportation as paved roads were laid down and as the internal combustion engine was perfected. By the 1890s a network of toll roads connected the township. Dunning Road was completed in this period while Old Montréal Road was the first in the area to be paved between Cumberland and Orléans in 1900.

Relative prosperity declined to unemployment in the Great Depression years of the Dirty Thirties. Here in Township of Cumberland several government-sponsored initiatives gave people gainful employment to the tune of approximately a dollar a day. Projects included the leveling of French Hill, replanting of the Larose Forest, and a farm relief system whereby farmers who couldn't pay their mortgages were offered assistance.

As you will note when visiting Cumberland Village, two stone homes of prominence flank either side of Queen Street (as the Old Montréal Road is named in "downtown" Cumberland village). The stately cut limestone mansion on the south side of the road is the Wilson residence, still owned by that family. Norman Frank Wilson was the MP for Russell County and his wife, Cairine Wilson, was the first female Canadian Senator, appointed to that position in 1930.

Nowadays, Cumberland is a very pretty albeit small village community, home to the Cumberland Historical Village Museum — and the ferry that crosses the Ottawa to Masson just south of Buckingham, at the confluence of the Lièvre River (see Lièvre River ramble). Closely associated with the river, Cumberland grew up in what was to be a largely French-speaking settlement. When you visit, you'll notice the prevalence of French for it remains the mother tongue of many of the residents, most of whom are fluently bilingual.

Today, Cumberland and the surrounding villages are experiencing a resurgence in prosperity, with many enjoying a revival as bedroom communities serving the capital. Land is again becoming valuable because workers from the city want good views and the peaceable kingdom that, in theory at least, a country community offers. As well, residents are taking pride in their surroundings: the Cumberland Local Architectural Conservation Advisory Committee started up in the 1990s and began to research and compile an inventory of notable buildings.

NATURAL HISTORY

The surrounding countryside is comprised of rolling hills of sandy outwash, sedimentary deposition left by the Champlain Sea.

As you drive towards Cumberland Village and the museum, you travel along the riverfront, glimpsing excellent views of the Ottawa River. Watch carefully after you pass the Petrie Island turnoff: once past it, and still on Highway 174 (old Highway 17), you may note a limestone quarry cut into the ridge that parallels the Ottawa River. The hillside quarry, on your right, is fenced off, but remains as testament to the forces of nature that created the landscape of the National Capital Region.

While walking around the Village Museum, watch for migratory song birds in the thickets.

BEFORE YOU GO ON THE RAMBLE

Why go? The Cumberland ramble comprises an exploration of two heritage sites: the living village itself and the Cumberland Village Heritage Museum. Because it showcases how ordinary people lived and worked in the early days before the creation of the NCR, the museum is of invaluable heritage significance — and a great way to increase you and your family's understanding of how settlement evolved here in the Ottawa Valley.

Distance: Cumberland Village is 32 km from Ottawa's downtown core.

Modes of exploration: Drive to Cumberland. You could bike to Cumberland, too, but you'll need to walk when you explore the museum itself.

Getting there: To get there, drive east along the Queensway (Highway 417) to "the split" where you continue east on Highway 174 (old Route 17) along the river. You will see signs for the ferry as you approach Cumberland Village. (This ferry crosses the Ottawa River to Masson; see Lièvre River ramble.) At the traffic lights at the corner of Cameron Street, turn right (south). At the stop sign (Queen Street) turn right onto this road, the Old Montréal Road, to start this ramble.

The Cumberland Village Heritage Museum is located further east at 2940 Queen Street. You cannot miss it, for the parking lot is well signed and you will see the old Vars (not Cumberland) railway station at the rear of the lot. **Special Note**: In spring 2004, the City of Ottawa proposed closing Cumberland Village Museum for budgetary reasons. Since no decision was made at time of publication, and because the museum grounds are home to many interesting heritage buildings, I decided to leave this component of the ramble as it is. My thinking is that the valuable property may find another sponsor — let's hope so. When you go on this ramble, if the museum has been closed, see whether you can get permission to enter the grounds: it's well worthwhile as it's the only museum of its kind in Ottawa east. Traditionally it is open seasonally and charges a modest admission.

Facilities: The museum has a generous parking lot, washroom facilities, a gift shop, and simple snacks (chips, soft drinks and juices) can be purchased.

Of special note: At the museum there are plenty of spots to enjoy a picnic. Get yourself a map of the extensive museum property. The area is flat, so walking shouldn't pose a problem, though wheelchair access to the interiors of some buildings could be challenging and stairs are the only access to the second floor of old houses. The site is exposed: take along a sunhat and the regular gear so you can enjoy yourself, and an umbrella if it's rainy. The living village is also fun to explore: there is a restaurant, antique shop, old-fashioned corner store, and churches.

🚶 ... CUMBERLAND VILLAGE

Start this ramble by turning right from Highway 174 onto Cameron Street, then right again onto Queen Street. Briefly drive west to Cameron House, along the old toll road partially financed by Captain Archibald Petrie, who gathered £4,000 after the Rebellion of 1837 to upgrade the road.

Cameron House is a cut limestone central-gabled Regency style farmhouse, an architectural style common to Ontario between 1810 and 1840. Located on the south side of the Old Montréal Road (here named Queen Street), the house was built for John Cameron from 1851 to 1861. The front façade is sheltered from the north wind by a porch, whose decorative columns lighten what would otherwise be an austere entryway. The overall effect is symmetrical: windows, chimneys, and doorways are well balanced and functional.

Turn around here, carefully, and return eastward towards the village. The third building to your right is **St. Mark's Anglican Church**, which has a surprising story. It was moved to this location in 1893 from the nearby community of Martin Corners where it had been in use for twenty-three years. (Martin's Corners was at the junction of Queen Street and Frank Kenny Road, west of Cumberland and east of Petrie Island, in the community known now as Bella Vista). The booklet *Cumberland Heritage* informs us the church was purchased by the Crown "for five French shillings" and moved here because Cumberland had more Anglicans.[26]

Proceed past Cameron Street east of the stop sign. Next is the brick **St. Andrew's United Church**, located on the north side of Queen Street. It was erected in 1879, as the Presbyterian church. It makes a nice contrast to the clapboard and aluminium-sided St. Marks; both are examples of rural Gothic Revival architecture, though each uses completely different materials. In his book *The Ottawa Country*, former NCC historian Courtney C. J. Bond claims the white marl brick probably was transported here from the Clarke brickyard located at MacKay Lake, in the former village of Rockcliffe Park (now part of the mega-city of Ottawa).[27]

This church stands on the site of the so-called "Auld Kirk," dated 1828, which was destroyed by fire in 1878. The cornerstone of St. Andrew's is dated 6 October 1879. Next door to the church is a corner store that's fun to go into, where you can stock up on snacks for your adventure and picnic at the Village Museum.

Proceed east on Queen to **Clearview**, the Ferguson house, now the Heritage Inn Restaurant. This remarkable heritage structure sports an extremely decorative, two-storied wraparound porch that adds a southern air of luxurious distinction to this former home. The third storey of the former mansion is sheltered by a deep mansard roof. Dormer windows pierce the top of its roofline, a detail that further lightens the look of the home by carrying the eye upwards.

Clearview was built in 1883 for Dr. James Ferguson who had a medical practice in Cumberland from 1861 to 1921. His first home, Spratt house, is now one of the houses you'll see in the Cumberland Village Heritage Museum. It was after he wed Susanna Rice MacLaurin that he purchased the land on which this mansion still stands. If it is open, do go inside to view the highly detailed woodwork on the interior. The ceiling is particularly decorative.

The Ferguson house, Clearview, now the Heritage Inn Restaurant.
Photo K. Fletcher, 2002.

The home was probably named Clearview for the clear view of the Ottawa River it once enjoyed. In its early days, the gardens would possibly have cascaded down to the riverbank, but today, no such luck: the land has been severed and built upon. "There goes the neighbourhood!"

Just down the way, on the opposite side of Queen Street you will find the circa 1861 **Wilson House** along with its accompanying farm buildings which make this a particularly delightful complex to view. Find a spot to park just on the side of the road and get out so you can have a very close look at an all-too-rare example of a mid-nineteenth century farmhouse, barn, chicken coop, and associated structures.

William Wilson was born in Edinburgh, Scotland. He worked in Montréal, and then in Buckingham as a Crown Timber Agent. In 1848 he moved to Cumberland and this present stone house is shown in the 1861 census. Cairine Wilson was appointed the first woman Senator to the Canadian Senate on 15 February 1930, ending her career there in 1962. Wilson family members still own the fine 2-1/2-storey residence. Take a look at its symmetrical lines by standing in front of it on the opposite side of the road. Basically a Georgian style home, a neo-classical portico was added on later. Its sturdy Doric columns (arguably a bit of overkill for the structure itself) support a pediment over the doorway, whose door features sidelights as well as an Adamesque fanlight transom. These sidelights must surely permit light to flood the interior central hallway that is typical to such houses.

Stroll east of the house itself to enjoy a view of the manicured lawns, old barn, and other outbuildings. Then continue east to the Cumberland Village Heritage Museum on the right (south) side of Queen Street. The Wilsons are inextricably linked to the museum, for the family donated the land for it.

… CUMBERLAND VILLAGE HERITAGE MUSEUM

Drive into the village and park in the lot, then proceed to the Vars railway station where you can pay the entry fee. You will want to wander freely or possibly procure a guide. Get a copy of the booklet *Cumberland Heritage*, which is sold at the gift shop inside the station.

Vars Grand Trunk Railway Station is a completely wooden structure. Its well-worn floor evokes memories of all the people who must have bustled around inside, purchasing tickets, sheltering from inclement weather, and anxiously awaiting the return of a loved one "on the rails." The first station at Vars was built in 1881 for the Canada Atlantic Railway. This one replaced it in 1908. The station building was donated to the museum by the Canadian National Railway in 1975.

The Station is kept "alive" through the efforts of the Telegrapher's Society, a group of volunteers dedicated to keeping the concept of telegraphy alive in the minds of visitors. Here you can see examples of wooden poles with loops at the end, which were used by telegraphers to deliver printed messages to the train drivers so they did not need to stop and disembark.

Once outside, find the marker commemorating the creation of the township and village. To the east is the **Knox United Church**, built in 1904. There's a delightful quality to the interior, which is ornamented with an unusual stencil decoration above a wainscoting of tongue-in-groove stained pine, which is continued around the windows. The church was originally located across from the Catholic Church, so the congregation asked their minister if they could decorate their church. The stencils fit the bill. There is a delightful Christmas carolling service here during the festive season, and couples can rent the church for their wedding ceremonies.

The Knox United Church. Photo K. Fletcher, 2002.

The stained glass is original, albeit very plain — in keeping with its origin as a Presbyterian church. (The United Church came about after Presbyterians and Methodists formed a "union" with one another.)

Behind Knox Church find a **hearse shed**. The original was not attached to the church. If you can, look inside to see the 1890 pall bearer's wagon and also a funeral coach, circa the same date. Both were made by Mitchell & Co. of Ingersoll, Ontario.

Return to the main walkway and continue south. The next board-and-batten exterior building is the **Firehall**, home to a 1938 International fire engine. Kids can try on a fire fighter's uniform and hat.

Once outside again, find the pumpkin-coloured **Community Hall** with its milk-chocolate brown trim. In times past you would have seen it at the start of this ramble, at the crossroads of Cameron and Queen in the heart of Cumberland Village. A typical community hall, it was used by just about everyone for just about everything. It served as the Orange Hall (is this why it is painted pumpkin?), Girl Guides, and Boy Scouts meeting hall. These organizations and others used the building before it was moved to its present location in 1983.

Next to the Community Hall is **Foubert House**, constructed for Napoleon Foubert, and built at the corner of Foubert and Queen streets. This was probably the family's second house; the Fouberts were the second family to settle in Cumberland Village, but their first dwelling would probably have been a more humble log structure, built circa 1807.

This house is shingled, which makes the façade rather unusual. The L-shape allows for the generously proportioned yet compact porch. Step inside: the original ceilings are intact, and are made of pressed tin whose rather gaudy pattern is different in every room.

Continue west down the shaded lane. The sugar maples are a glorious gold in October. At the corner is **Spratt,** or **Grier house**, the circa 1857 log house where Dr. Ferguson lived prior to his marriage and the subsequent construction of imposing Clearview, which you just visited. This far more modest squared log building contains the overflow collection of the museum, and is a beautifully preserved and tidy reminder of how settlers' early homes would have appeared.

Cross the road to step inside **French Hill School**, which served children in grades one through eight south of Cumberland until it closed in 1936. In 1976 it was moved here. Examine the interior walls and ceiling: all are composed of tin, but do you notice something rather odd? The fleur-de-lis design is upside down, consistently. Why is this? The answer is lost to time.

The circa 1857 Spratt house. Photo K. Fletcher, 2002.

Other interesting items of note include the "Favourite Box" brand of wood stove. Children had to bring sticks of wood from home so that the teacher wouldn't have to cut and haul wood herself. The interior of the school is extremely well lit by virtue of the sash windows' generous dimensions; however, the schoolchildren may have wished for similarly spacious desks. Instead, each desk seated two students. On your left as you enter, read the page of the open Ontario Reader dated 1932, and note the slogan "One Flag, One Fleet, One Throne."

Now walk south (keeping Queen Street and the train station behind you). You first pass **Watson's Garage**, a gasoline station — the oldest surviving Imperial dealer in the world, according to the museum guide.

The next farmhouse on your left was new to the museum in 2001 and was undeveloped when I visited. It was moved here from Canaan Road, almost at Rockland.

Beyond it, beginning at the southwest corner and running along the south side of the walking path lie several **farm outbuildings** where old farm machinery such as ploughs is displayed. Also here are the museum's few animals: perhaps a team of horses, a pair of pigs, goats, and poultry. All crave your attention and enjoy a friendly pat.

The French Hill schoolhouse. Photo K. Fletcher, 2002.

At the southeast corner find the **sawmill**. It is not a completely original entity: the sawmill's mechanical parts came from Poltimore, Québec (see Lièvre River ramble); the wood for the mill structure came from the Chrysler Farm on the St. Lawrence (immediately adjacent to Upper Canada Village); and the Fairbanks-Morse diesel engine came from Shawville, Québec. The composite structure is nonetheless fascinating and operational.

Before turning the corner to proceed north back towards the main village, look due south. You'll see a pretty ravine and hill opposite, which are part of the museum property — and an ideal place for bird watching.

While proceeding north, look for a path leading to your right (east), through a **pine plantation**. The fragrance of pine in summertime is deliciously spicy. On your right, a once-cleared area is succumbing to "natural infill" by virtue of the presence of vegetation such as hawthorn trees. Look for northern shrike here; nicknamed butcher birds, these fascinating birds impale their prey on such thorns as these on the hawthorn tree so they can return and eat them later.

After passing the pine plantation a big surprise awaits you: a **model train track**, a permanent installation. If you're fortunate, you might happen upon an enthusiastic group of men and women, members of the Ottawa Valley Live Steamers and Model Engineers Club, perched in a rather ungainly fashion on a miniature train that circles a perfectly graded and maintained track! Although most of the volunteers who maintain both track and engines are men, some females are beginning to make inroads on this once predominantly male territory.

While returning to the gardens located behind the Community Hall you will stroll past **Dale Cemetery** where you can find the final resting places of many early Cumberland residents. Looking for gravestones of French settlers and community members? Drive south to Sarsfield, which was predominantly French.

Turn left to stroll west along the short driveway in front of the Community Hall. At the schoolhouse, turn right this time to veer north. Find the **Duford House** on your left, built circa 1825 by a family who originally came here from Montréal. The property remained in the family until 1976, at which time house and land were expropriated to create Place d'Orléans.

Can you believe that fourteen children lived here with their parents Elphege and Exilia Duford? Because of the home's small size, it seems impossible ... but it's true. Step inside and just imagine how tightly packed they would have been. Then look at the tiny kitchen: how could Exilia possibly have managed to cook for sixteen people here? Note the hand-operated water pump mounted inside: this was a luxury item in the early years.

Perhaps it's Exilia who is sometimes spotted in the window located beneath the central peak of the home. Her ghostly form may be seen looking out wistfully, and sometimes she rearranges toys and other items inside the house. Don't believe me? Sceptics among you ought to chat with museum staff, who know a thing or two ...

Further along the road on the right, find the **Mainville/Wilkes home**, built circa 1880 and donated to the museum by the Wilkes family. Its "six over six" paned sash windows are larger than the "two over two" of the Dupuis home you'll see next. The exterior is finished with board and batten, proving that by this time homes were being constructed of sawn timber, undoubtedly produced at a local sawmill. Note too how the roof sports an ever-so-slight curve at its eaves, being reminiscent of the "bell-cast" French Canadian roofs built this way so that when snow would slip off, it would land away from a person who might be standing below. The house contains an extensive collection of radios, the prized former possessions of Ottawa resident Bill Beaton, who at the time of writing still comes to clean and operate them. If you're lucky, you'll find him here busily at work. He enjoys questions.

As you approach the final curve in the road, the 1820 **Dupuis house** on the left rather resembles some crazed architect's concept of a mushroom, to my mind. Its tall doorway is out of proportion to the tiny building, and the gambrel-style "barn-like" roof seems oddly out of place. The half-squared timbers are fascinating: take a close look and you'll notice that the interior side of the logs still have their bark, while the exterior of the logs have been squared so that the bark has been removed. Miss Eva Dupuis called this dwelling home. She lived a frugal life: the house had no plumbing or electricity until after her death in 1983.

How did Miss Dupuis cope? The *Cumberland Heritage* booklet tells us, "She heated the house with a wood-burning stove and lighted it with lanterns. Water was pumped from a well and food stored in an ice-box." When you go inside, note the dimensions. It's perhaps

The Dupuis house. Photo K. Fletcher, 2002.

fortunate that Miss Dupuis lived on her own, because there is truly not much space.

This completes our ramble: return to your car by exiting through the gift shop inside the Vars railway station.

OTHER PLACES OF INTEREST

Beckett Creek National Bird Sanctuary: Further east of Cumberland Historical Village is another tributary of the Ottawa River: Beckett's Creek, which crosses beneath the Old Montréal Road immediately west of the road sharing the Creek's name. There are walking trails here, as well as at the **Beckett Creek National Bird Sanctuary**, located beyond the creek and road. At the junction of the Old Montréal Road and Highway 174 is a campground bordering the Ottawa.

St. Albert Cheese Factory: Want to explore other quaint villages in the region? At Sarsfield find the **St. Albert Cheese Factory**, a solitary reminder of earlier years when there were many in this region. At Navan, nearby, is the fairground where, in season, the **Navan Fair** takes place. (Its fiftieth anniversary was celebrated mid-August of 1995.)

Still another spot of interest that harkens back to olden times is the **Navan and Cleroux Greenhouses**, reminders of the early market gardens of the Cyr brothers.

Lièvre River Loop

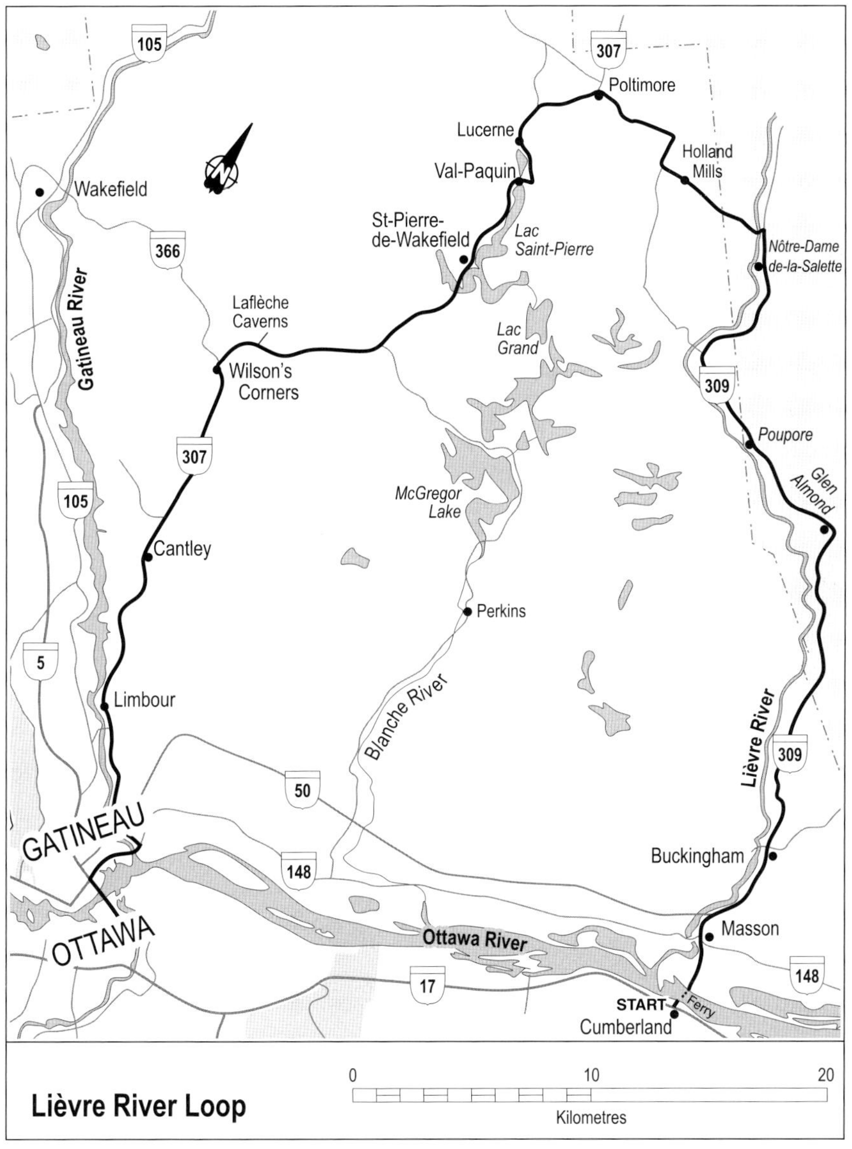

Terror before dawn: Landslide at Nôtre-Dame-de-la-Salette

Imagine you are fast asleep in the pre-dawn of Sunday, 26 April 1908. Your home on the hillside overlooking the quiet village of Nôtre-Dame-de-la-Salette on the Lièvre River is cozy enough. Perhaps there's still a nip to the early morning air that makes you glad to be in your toasty warm bed. After all, there is still ice on the river. Soon you and everyone else in the village will rise, begin your chores, and head to Mass.

All of a sudden, all Hell breaks loose and you are in the midst of it: your bed is propelled — headlong and with a dreadful groaning — into the icy waters of the Lièvre River. Horrified, you realize you're on top of a hay bale floating downstream. Bewildered, you see your mother floating past you clutching a makeshift raft of broken boards. Everywhere there is mud, jagged splits of ice thrusting upward from the river, and shattered timber. Meanwhile, the dead and dying lie buried beneath a deluge of mud and ice. Groans, cries, and the river's incessant flow are your new world.

What happened?

Twenty-two year-old Camille Lapointe survived the landslide at Nôtre-Dame-de-la-Salette, although thirty-three townspeople lost their lives. Camille's six brothers and grandmother were among the dead. Many people probably never knew what happened: asleep one minute and, literally, buried alive or drowned the next.

Almost fifty years later, Mr. Lapointe recalled his experience: "I was lying asleep in my room on the second story of our home." Heroically, although stranded on a bale of hay in the Lièvre, he refused to be rescued until his mother had been safely removed from the "raft." The paper noted that horsemen galloped to the village of Buckingham to ask for help. One home had the second storey completely shorn off: amazingly enough the entire family walked out of it, unaided. Others were not so fortunate.

So what did happen? The land slipped into the river, forcing "knives of ice" up onto its east embankment, which destroyed parts of the village here. A permanent remnant of the hillside remains in the midst of the Lièvre, as an island. *The Ottawa Journal* noted: "A small island in the river is all that is left of the land that for a short time completely blocked the river and sent floodwaters rushing up into the wrecked village to add to the toll of death, damage, and injury."

Today the western embankment of the Lièvre River is an open field and the island can still be viewed, just downstream of the bridge at Nôtre-Dame-de-la-Salette.

Bear reveals underground cavern to hunter

One wintry day in 1865, Joseph Dubois was minding his own business, intent on tracking his prey, a black bear. When the creature disappeared into a crevice in the rocks, Dubois ever so cautiously followed it.

Suddenly, Dubois forgot all about his furry quarry.

He had entered a place where possibly no one had ever been before: the underground caverns of the Laflèche Cave, the largest known cave in the Canadian Shield. Incredulous, Dubois returned later with a light. Its illumination revealed a magical world of stalactites and stalagmites. The cave was formed over millennia by fissures in the rock through which, over time, water flowed. Ever so gradually, the soluble marble dissolved as a result of the carbonic gas formed while the water flowed through the fissures, making it more acidic and hence more able to dissolve the marble.

Stalactites and stalagmites twinkled and shone in Dubois' lantern. (Stalactites hang like icicles from the ceiling, whereas stalagmites rise from the ground. Confused? Remember the "c" in stalactites represents "ceiling"; the "g" in stalagmite reminds you of "ground.")

Interminable numbers of drips create these types of formations because minute particles of calcite are suspended in the water. While drips extend to reach the cavern's floor, a stalactite forms, and, as the tiny spray of mineral-rich water splashes to the ground, a bump forms. Over time, a stalagmite develops. Who knows how many drips there are in a day, in a week, in a year? Apparently, it takes a thousand years for one centimetre of stalactite to grow. Over many thousands of years, when the two formations join, a third geological formation is created: a column.

Despite Dubois marvelling at this natural phenomenon, somehow it took years for the site to develop into a tourist destination. The Hull Attraction Company opened the cave to visitors in 1923, but problems arose as soon as the cavern's entryway was enlarged to enable more people to enter more easily.

The intake of fresh air altered the micro-climate of the ancient grotto. Then vandals broke so many of the marvellous stalactites, stalagmites, and columns that not one of the magnificent large specimens Dubois saw now survives in the main caverns.

How did the caves get their name? In the 1930s, Zephyr Laflèche bought the 315 acres of land surrounding the cavern. Much damage occurred during the 1950s and 1960s, specifically after another entryway was blasted. A decade later the cave was closed. Kids knew it was there, however, and vandalism continued. The Municipality of Val des Monts purchased the property in the 1980s, determined to restore the cave as a tourism and educational site. Fifteen years passed before the Laflèche Cave reopened. The site is well worthwhile visiting, although I've never seen a bear there ... yet!

Canoe landing at the foot of the portage, Lièvre River, Québec, 1877.
Photo: William James Topley. NAC PA-26485.

The Lièvre (Hare) River is important watershed that tumbles down some 320 km from Kempt Lake in the north to join the Ottawa River east of the Gatineau River. There are five hydroelectric plants along its course; two of the most important are at Masson and High Falls (the latter one lies north of the National Capital Region).

In the 1800s, while Philemon Wright and many others were developing the lumber industry in this region and its hinterland, the watercourses of the Ottawa River watershed provided the means of getting logs to market. Yet, the same rushing waters that enabled lumbermen to bring their commodity downstream also presented serious difficulties at every cascade and rapid.

Here amid the jagged rocks, timbers would shatter or, perhaps worse, pile up, creating spectacular but dangerous log jams. Rivermen would then do their "dance" across the floating "sticks," as the trimmed logs were called, to find and free the key logs creating the pileup. Then, with pike-poles, peaveys, and cant-hooks, these dexterous athletes would pry the jam loose. This was challenging, dangerous work: many men were crushed, drowned, or blown apart by the gunpowder used to free particularly pernicious logjams.

J.R. Booth, the "Chaudière Carnegie," as he was sometimes known, with square timbers loaded on railway cars, c. 1924. NAC-PA-120161.

During the latter half of the nineteenth century, Ezra Butler Eddy, John Rudolphus Booth, and the Maclaren brothers were among the significant players in the Outaouais region's timber industry. Eddy and the Maclarens owned timber rights extending up the Lièvre River and its watershed.

Just as the lumber industry had shifted from squared timber in the early 1800s to sawn timber by the mid-1800s, so it was to change again in the latter half of the century. As easily obtained red and white pine was logged out, other softwoods such as spruce became more available. Concurrently, the lumber industry in the United States needed product; eager eyes turned northward to Canada's remaining stands of pine and spruce. Not only was lumber needed for American cities, but newsprint and paper made from wood were also in hot demand. (The old technology of manufacturing paper from linen and other rags was replaced by the emerging pulp and paper industry.)

People like E.B. Eddy were already aware of the power inherent in the region's waterfalls. After all, he had built his empire at the Chaudière Falls where the Ottawa River provided a source of both power and transportation. The latter was crucial: Eddy was well situated at the falls to procure sticks of timber for processing at his water-powered factories, then use the river and the Rideau Canal to send finished materials south to market in Southern Ontario and the United States. By the 1870s he and the Maclarens owned timber rights along the Lièvre. They eyed the rapids, pondering the way to harness the energy of the falls.

At the turn of the last century, trade with the United States grew into a contentious issue — much as it still is today. They needed pulp and paper, lumber, and many other commodities. Canada was doing "its thing": far too often shipping raw materials out of the country for manufacture off-shore. In 1900, Ontario became the first province to ban the export of pulp and ten years later Québec followed suit, ordering that "all timber felled on Crown lands … be processed into pulp within the province."[28] Three years subsequent to this, the American Congress passed the Underwood Act such that no duty was imposed upon imported paper. West Québec was well placed to capitalize on this expanding market. The Maclarens, Booth, and Eddy developed their technologies to take advantage of the hydroelectric power provided by the rivers. With a ready labour force of men, women, and children (child labour was significant at the time) living in Lowertown (Ottawa), Hull, and Pointe Gatineau, the NCR offered a good supply of workers to these industrialists.

Maclaren's Mills, Buckingham, Québec, 1890. NAC C-15307.

But although Eddy owned timber rights up the Lièvre, the main players here were the brothers Maclaren along with patriarch James Maclaren. This family owned the timber rights to the Lower Lièvre valley. By 1900 the five brothers owned the water rights to High Falls and "both banks of the Lièvre from Buckingham down to the Ottawa River."[29] Two years later they had built a pulp and paper mill "with a projected output of fifty-four metric tonnes."[30] By 1911 they dammed the Lièvre at High Falls; by 1929 they built the Masson Mill; and by 1930 the power plant they built just above Buckingham became a significant regional supplier of hydroelectric power.

All this development of mills, processing plants, and hydroelectric power stations was increasingly dependent on one crucial factor: a reliable source of power. Sawmills, gristmills, and other industrial sites built alongside rivers were hampered by irregular water flow. Water levels fluctuated not just with annual precipitation levels, but also seasonally due to winter's freeze-up. What could be done to provide a steady source of power? The answer was twofold: the construction of dams and reservoirs. Companies who had purchased land rights surrounding watersheds could now erect hydro dams that flooded land they actually owned outright. Accordingly, up the Lièvre and other rivers such as the Gatineau (see Gatineau River ramble) land was flooded, and homes and businesses expropriated or abandoned to create the reservoirs required to power mills and plants and to provide water for residential, commercial, and industrial needs.

So the story of the Lièvre goes hand in hand with the industrialization of the Outaouais and Ottawa region, the obliteration of topographical features after the damming of the river, and settlements that pre-dated the reservoirs. In the first quarter of the last century Canadian International Paper (CIP) arrived in West Québec. At the same time, its major competitor International Paper and Power Company (IPP) also arrived. Both were based in America; both not only invested in paper plants but also in hydroelectricity. By 1929 IPP was the world's largest producer of paper and electricity. But CIP was no slouch, acquiring 3,600 square kilometres of Crown woodland in the upper valleys of the Ottawa and Gatineau rivers between 1925 and 1928, all to supply its new plant in Gatineau.[31]

What was the effect of such industrial competition upon the Ottawa region? First of all, CIP alone employed between 1,000 and 1,500 workers in its pulp and paper mill. In his book *The History of the Outaouais*, author Chad Gaffield comments that "during logging season the company employed teams that could vary between 2,400 and 4,000 men at Maniwaki, the centre of its logging activities."[32]

Although both companies jostled for territory and power, the Maclaren brothers maintained their control of the Lièvre and their Buckingham and Masson interests. The Maclaren operations remain a mainstay of the Lièvre today, continuing the family's long association with the prosperity of this easternmost sector of the National Capital Region.

But we cannot speak of the Lièvre, or of Buckingham and the Maclarens without mentioning the labour unrest that sparked a demonstration in the village park known as "The Landing." On 8 October 1906, four hundred striking workers demanded to be paid a minimum wage; however, the Maclarens refused to negotiate and locked them out. This prompted the workers to march to The Landing (so-named because the river steamers used to dock here to unload minerals and other goods from the Lièvre's rich hinterland) to make speeches and lobby for better working conditions. Impatience grew as workers milled about. Tempers flared, people jostled, and a grand melée ensued. Suddenly, the command, "Shoot them!" rang out. Shots were fired, many workers were injured and labour leaders Thomas Bélanger and François Thériault were killed. The Maclarens couldn't contain the crowd and two days later called in the Royal Canadian Dragoons. One hundred and seventeen soldiers restored calm to Buckingham.[33]

(**Note:** When on this ramble, you will pass by the cemetery south of Buckingham where you can visit the graves of Bélanger and Thériault.)

Of course, there is more to the Lièvre than just power, pulp, and paper. This ramble takes you through some of the prettiest countryside showcased in this book. That is, if you like undulating countryside dotted with remote farms and rugged outcrops of island-like rocky hillocks where mixed hardwood and softwood forests grow. This is a spectacular drive in autumn, when the hills are cloaked in the magical colours of gold, scarlet, and purple.

At Gatineau Mills, logs are guided towards the ramp, Gatineau, Québec. Photo: Bud Glunz. n.d. NAC PA-121658.

NATURAL HISTORY

Today's enthusiasts of challenging whitewater kayaking and canoeing — or those of us who simply enjoy spectacular natural scenery — can thank the forces of physical geography for the opportunities the Lièvre offers. Rapids and waterfalls are created by two significant geological factors: faulting and terraces. Over millennia, faulting along fractures in the Canadian Shield rock underlying this region created the series of rapids along the Lièvre, Gatineau, Mississippi, Rideau, and Ottawa rivers. While the land rebounded after the weight of the glacier receded, the Champlain Sea receded and elevations rose. Natural terraces formed marking "beaches" or old shorelines of the sea.

Most of the lakes here drain to the east into the Lièvre via their own mini-watersheds. After traversing the bridge located at Nôtre-Dame-de-la-Salette you cross the stream called Ruisseau du Prêtre (Priest's Creek), the most significant waterway other than the Lièvre itself. It is here, west of the Lièvre, that you start noticing all the lakes: McLeod, Saint-Pierre (on which the hamlets of Val Paquin and St-Pierre-de-Wakefield are located), Grand, McGregor, McGlashan, Girard — these and many others are either on our route or signposted on the highway.

When the ice from the Laurentide Ice Sheet melted, salty waters of the Champlain Sea flooded the landscape here to a height of 150 metres or thereabouts; many of the craggy hillocks you see on this ramble would have been islands in that sea! As the land rebounded after the weight of the ice was removed, more deposition occurred. This is why productive farms can exist today amid this rugged-looking landscape.

In addition, the land became pocked with basins, crinkled with valleys, and dotted with plateaus, which you can look for while you explore. Water was trapped here, so the landscape you travel through today takes you past many lakes of various sizes. Lac St.-Pierre-de-Wakefield is large, filling a valley and hence being called a "valley lake." Smaller lakes are usually of the basin type, often being quite dramatically circular in shape, and formed where ice gouged out a bowl shape in the rock. Another clue to the type of lake you are viewing is the presence — or absence — of a beach, which would have been formed by deposition of sand and gravel. Valley lakes typically have beaches while basin lakes may not. Remember, however, that before the days of environmental rules and regulations, many people brought in sand or dredged lakes to create unnatural shorelines and beaches.

Watery destinations on this ramble include the fascinating Laflèche Cavern, created some 20,000 years ago. Water penetrated faults in the rock and over thousands of years dissolved and eroded these fissures into large spaces, variously called galleries, chambers (or rooms), and dome pits (or chimneys). Here you can see other natural phenomena inside the cave such as stalagmites and stalactites, and on the exterior you can view sinkholes and furrows, other signposts of glacial activity. The cave is one of the largest and oldest in Québec, with some 400 m of connecting spaces operated as a tourist destination throughout the year.

Natural history in the region does not usually incorporate underground denizens, but here in the Laflèche Cavern you can learn about creatures with antennae called troglobites who live their lives in complete darkness. (The prefix "troglo-" is from the Greek word meaning "cave.") In addition, there are trogloxenes, animals that sometimes venture inside the caves. These include porcupines. As you can imagine, the cave is also the haunt of the flying mammal, the little brown bat. These can be seen hanging upside down in crevices in the gallery ceilings. (Don't fret: bats are far more concerned about you than vice-versa. Typically they remain hanging upside down, possibly hoping you'll quickly go away and leave them be.) The cave is also home to species called troglophiles, animals that reproduce inside the protection of a cavern. The *Meta menardi* spider births its young here in Laflèche Cavern. (Don't be disturbed if you find spiders and bats unsavoury or even scary. The cave is spacious and although I've visited a few times, I have never seen one of these spiders. I did see bats, but they never took flight.)

The caves allow us to glimpse and wonder about not just the rocks but also the minerals that abound in the region. Around 1865, minerals such as graphite and apatite began to be mined near the villages of Glen Almond and Nôtre-Dame-de-la-Salette.

The Lièvre valley was once a prosperous mining region. Geologist Dr. Donald Hogarth's book on the geology of the Gatineau-Lièvre area describes many mines: the Back, Daisy, Derry, Aetna, and Emerald mines, along with Pednaud and Cadieux quarries.[34] There were two "heydays" of mining for the Lower Lièvre. Mining graphite and apatite were major industries between 1865 and 1895. Apatite is used to make fertilizer, and so Buckingham developed this industry, too. Also during this period Buckingham produced over 90 percent of Canada's feldspar — in fact, in 1878 a sample of Buckingham feldspar was exhibited at the World Exposition in Paris. Later, between 1920 and 1970, mica, graphite, and feldspar were mined near here. During this fifty-year span, feldspar was processed into powder by the company Flint and Spar of Buckingham and shipped all over the world.[35]

The number of lakes, rivers, and streams make this sector of the NCR ideal cottage country. This region of lakes, rugged outcrops of Precambrian rock (the Canadian Shield), undulating cleared land with picturesque farms, and dense mixed hardwood forest is not well travelled. Consequently, this ramble is one of the most picturesque that appears in this book.

Why go? This is a little-known but delightful backroads ramble introducing you to some extremely picturesque countryside of wooded hills, farms, and valleys. The views are delightful, the watershed history intriguing.

Distance: Approximately 144 km round trip from downtown Ottawa, includes some good gravel roads.

Modes of exploration: You probably will drive this route, at least at first. Consider cycling, consider taking your canoe after you've checked out some of the lakes and rivers.

Getting there: Drive 30 km east on Highway 417, then take Highway 174 (old Highway 17), colloquially known as "the split" to Cumberland Village. Cross to **Masson** in Québec, by ferry. Your route now continues through Buckingham, Glen Almond, Poupore, Nôtre-Dame-de-la-Salette, Ruisseau du Prêtre, Holland Mills, Lucerne, Lac St-Pierre, Val Paquin, St-Pierre-de-Wakefield, (turnoff to Laflèche Caverns), Wakefield, Cantley, Limbour, Gatineau, and Ottawa.

Facilities: The towns variously offer restaurants, washrooms, inns; parks offer washrooms (outhouses) and picnic areas.

Left to right: George Cross, Maria Cross, unidentified man, and Kenneth Cross at the Pelissier Caverns in Wilson's Corners, c. 1930. HSG 01757.

Of special note: This is a full day's ramble for you to enjoy at your leisure and there are such lovely views that I particularly recommend you take not just binoculars but also your camera. Good picnic potential here, too!

THE RAMBLE

Prelude: before setting off, we ramblers of the twenty-first century should realize we are not the first to appreciate the Lièvre's outstanding beauty. Canada's famous Confederation poets Archibald Lampman and Duncan Campbell Scott, among others, also loved the Gatineau Hills. In 1889 Lampman penned "A Dawn on the Lièvre," one of his most famous poems, in which he praises the river's outstanding beauty after paddling his canoe along it:

Up the dark-valleyed river stroke by stroke
We drove the water from the rustling blade;
And when the height was almost gone we made
The Oxbow bend; and there the dawn awoke;
Full on the shrouded night-charged river broke
The sun, down the long mountain valley rolled
A sudden, swinging avalanche of gold,
Through mists that sprang and reeled aside like smoke.

With Lampman's words firmly in our minds eye, it's time to explore this river ramble. First, drive east to **Cumberland**, approximately 30 km east of Ottawa's downtown core. Take the Queensway (Highway 417) to "the split" where you continue east on Highway 174 (old Highway 17) along the Ottawa River. Your destination is the **ferry crossing** from Cumberland to Masson: watch for ferry signs as you approach Cumberland. At the traffic lights at the corner of Cameron Street, turn left (north) to the ferry docks. The ferry operates twenty-four hours daily, year-round.

Crossing a river on a ferry is always rather fun, and it is a grand introduction to this particular ramble that courses alongside the Lièvre and many other watersheds. While crossing, note the sign on board listing prices: the cost breakdown (as of 2004) included the highest charge of $30 for a prefabricated house, then descended through charges for a ten-wheel loaded truck, a recreational vehicle, a car, and finally culminated with the lowest charge of $1.00 for a walk-on (pedestrian). Rather surprisingly, houses cross the river here frequently, according to the ferryman. While crossing, look for tugs and float planes amid the more ubiquitous cottages crowding the north shore.

Once on the Québec side, proceed north on **chemin du Quai**. You probably won't be able to miss the sight (or smell) of the pulp and paper mill here in Masson. I can never understand how anyone could become so used to its sulphurous odour to enable them to live here! People are adaptable, however, and homes here are of a plain, sturdy architectural style typical of mill towns in North America. At the junction of Quai and chemin de Montréal (Highway 148), look right before proceeding north on what becomes **Route 309** (rue Nôtre Dame). The old, two-storey clapboard building of heritage note here was recently renovated into a pub.

Proceed north on Highway 309 after the junction with 148 East. North of the industrial park of **Masson-Angers** you come to the outskirts of **Buckingham**, named after a county and city in England.

Continue slowly in Buckingham: just beyond the **Rhéaume Dam** (on your left) you soon come to a cemetery. Pause here if you wish, to search for the graves of Bélanger and Thériault, the two labour leaders who were shot during the strike of 1906. Opposite **St. Andrew's United Church** (1890) and rue Lamennais find a small park, **Parc Maclaren**, just before the bridge heading left (west) over the river. This is **Pont Brady**. Later on we'll walk over this bridge to look at **Barrage Dufferin Dam** below. While noting St. Andrew's, look opposite it to find Maison Kenny House, built in 1850, which has always been the residence of a Maclaren.

The next road on your right is rue Joseph which is Highway 315 heading northeast to Mayo County and the next river system: the watershed of the eastern Blanche River (confusingly, there is a second Blanche River lying to the west between the Lièvre and Gatineau). At the corner of Highway 315 and rue Principale, facing the jog in the road and bridge, is a late 1800s flat-topped heritage building that boasts an angled front entryway with a large clock inset. This is the **McCallum-Lahaie** building, now a Sears store.

On the left-hand side of the road are some typical late-eighteenth century flat-topped brick commercial buildings full of shops. A few metres further north, on the east side of the road find number 408 rue Principale, a square-timbered log home with dormer windows punctuating its sweep of roof. Continue north on Principale until you reach a split in the road where you'll veer left (at rue Fall). Park in the small lot here. Behind you is a small building at 379 rue Principale, home to the **Buckingham Historical Society** which always has a small exhibit on display as well as information on the region. In the 1800s a lively agricultural market was located here. The eastern extension of rue Fall becomes rue Market here, so you cannot miss where farmers used to bring their produce to sell.

If you want to explore the Lièvre closely now, leave your car here at the lot and find the 1994 **riverside pathway and cycling park** by immediately heading toward the river and walk or bike along it. The entire circuit walk can take you as little as thirty minutes, but you can stretch it out for as long as you like. Within a few metres of the start of the circuit there is a lookout over the Lièvre and the old ERCO plant (see below). For now, continue north on the east embankment, passing the entryway to the boardwalk built on the old log sluice. Continue along this paved path, passing some installation art along the way. Signs along the path offer some fascinating factoids. For instance, in 1871 Buckingham council adopted a bylaw prohibiting dog and cock fights; in the 1880s the mica industry replaced phosphate manufacturing as the town's primary industry; and women were gainfully employed in the mica manufacturing industry because they were so adept at splitting its finely layered sheets with their thumbs and a knife.

You soon find yourself at a second parking lot and **Parc R.W. Scullion** where Pont du Progress, the railway bridge, spans the river. Beyond is a third park: **Parc Landing**. The latter derives its name from some nineteen river barges, such as the *George Bothwell* (apparently parts of it can still be seen when river levels are low, although I've not witnessed this), that used to land here. This barge not only transported goods along the Lièvre, it also took tourists who came to view the falls. Other boats included the *Eva*, *Nelson*, and *Worthington*. The last was a sidewheeler — a steamship. The *Nelson* was the last passenger boat to work the Lièvre: it cost $1.25 for a round-trip from Buckingham to view High Falls (north of the National Capital Region).

Electric Reduction Company plant and log chute, Buckingham, Québec, on the Lièvre River, c. 1916. NAC PA-110883.

Electric Reduction Company, Buckingham, Québec, on the Lièvre River, c. 1916. NAC PA-110882.

Return to the log chute boardwalk. You are walking alongside a man-made embankment. On the far side of the river is the **Electric Reduction Company of Canada**, incorporated in 1897. André Joyce of the Buckingham Historical Society wrote to me, explaining how the company operated, and what working conditions were like. In 1898, "the company employed 50 men, who worked 10 hours a day, 60 hours a week at the rate of 10 cents an hour." ERC has produced a wide range of products in its lifetime: in 1918 it produced "495,000 pounds of phosphorus to the American War Department." In 1941, 528 workers were employed here, and a year later, in 1942, ERC began "production of red amorphous. 'Project 29' is constructed in order to supply the armed forces with phosphorus filled smoke bombs." In 1952 the head office, previously here in Buckingham, moved to Toronto and five years later, the town's last phosphorous furnaces closed. In 1972 the company was purchased by a firm in Texas, but in 1987 they sold; now it is the **Albright & Wilson Amèrique** plant. As of 1995 this plant produced "food phosphates." Quite a transformation from chemicals and bombs, isn't it?

Before reaching the boardwalk you pass the 1893 brick building that once served as the Buckingham Water Works. Pause and look to

Walking trail crossing the Lièvre at Buckingham on the old log chute. Photo: E. Fletcher 2002.

its immediate south (to the left when facing it) so you won't miss examining a segment of original log chute. Unlike the metal chute supporting today's boardwalk, this remnant is constructed of wood.

Now turn right to start walking over the Lièvre on the boardwalk. The walkway is an excellent example of how to put heritage structures to good use in today's world. The old **log chute,** or sluice, was built in 1959 by the James Maclaren Company. It transported timbers for processing at their pulp and paper mills in Masson and, apart from this little section, the main stretch was disassembled in 1993.

In summertime look for white swans swimming about on the basin created by the dams. You cannot miss the poison ivy covering the hillsides on either side of the river: if you don't know what this noxious plant looks like, identify it now and avoid it.

All too soon the boardwalk ends and you emerge onto a grassy embankment, part of **Parc des Ancients Combatants** where there is a section of a warship, the *HMSC Buckingham,* mounted here in memory of area residents who lost their lives in WW II.

Turn left at **Pont Brady**, named for Father John Brady, priest of St.-Grégoire-de-Nazianze church (built in 1855, demolished in 1974). Carefully cross to the bridge's south side. From here you get a good view of the **Dufferin Dam** below. Continue to rue Principale, and turn left to return to your car. Once in it, return to Highway 309 north (the main street) and turn left (north). After you pass rue Market, watch for another old residence, **Château Kelly,** once home to Buckingham's mayor William H. Kelly (1907–1908).

Drive north on Highway 309 towards **Glen Almond**. Once a mining centre, there is only a small community here today. While driving, note the hummocky hills protruding from the old river valley floor, now knolls upon which a mixed hardwood and softwood forest grows. After a few kilometres of countryside, the road suddenly brings us back to the Lièvre; we'll be flirting with views of the river from now on. While driving, watch for crosses on the hillsides commemorating those who have lost their lives on the road and in the surrounding bush.

After passing Glen Almond, watch for **Poupore**, a community that sprung up because locks were built here to permit riverboats like scows and barges to navigate the waters that hitherto had only been navigable by canoes. Boats such as the *Eva* transported goods destined for the mines upriver, such as those near Nôtre-Dame-de-la-Salette; indeed, there was a healthy forwarding industry here on the Lièvre during the mid- to late 1800s. Goods were portaged around all the falls and rapids, while the riverboats transported supplies to the next navigable point. They were not empty on their return route: they were full of phosphate mined at High Rock and Centre Lake mines.[36] These bigger industrial boats disappeared on the Lièvre after the erection of the Maclaren Dam at High Falls.

The village of **Nôtre-Dame-de-la-Salette** is next, 11 km north of Buckingham. When approaching it the highway swings down and up, veering westwards, with an old farmhouse on the west side. The hillside directly in front has a protected southwest aspect; can you see the small vineyard here?

As you enter Nôtre-Dame-de-la-Salette watch for the small park on the left and park your car. While standing near the interpretive sign, look to the west embankment. There is a small island in the river, and a field across from you. A small sign in French describes the fateful day when tragedy struck here. Suddenly, without any warning, at 3:30 a.m. on 26 April 1908, a landslide swept many who lived here to their deaths. The ice that still covered the river sliced upwards onto this eastern bank along with a sudden influx of water. The combined actions of slumping, ice, and flooding wreaked havoc on the village: twelve homes were destroyed and thirty-three people died. The island remains, a remnant of soil, mud, and vegetation left behind after the landslide.

Church at Nôtre-Dame-de-la-Salette. Photo: E. Fletcher 2003.

Resume driving. Check out the village and its church if you wish, then turn left on **rue Pont** to cross the bridge to the west side of the Lièvre (continuing north brings you to Mont Laurier area). This bridge represented the death knell of the river boats, as roads and bridges permitted cars to take over from the seasonal boat transportation network, year-round. Prior to the bridge, a scow transported people from one embankment to another near here. According to writer Fred E. Robinson, the original covered bridge collapsed during its construction in 1923. Workers such as Herdus H. Last, Adelard Brassard, and Charlie Gowan used teams of horses and sleighs in winter to haul the rocks for the bridge's piers. When the wind blew the rafters off the structure that day, Brassard and Last tumbled down; fortunately neither was harmed.[37]

Now we say goodbye to the Lièvre. We will skirt the **Ruisseau du Prêtre** (Priest's Creek) and head west to Poltimore via Holland Mills.

On the west bank of the Lièvre, pass Domaine la Maison Blanche on your left and proceed up the hill. On your right, note the farmhouse with a tin façade and an old barn. A few kilometres beyond, find the next community of **Holland Mills**, so-called for the mills that once lined Ruisseau du Prêtre. On the right-hand side of the road here you'll find True North Ferme des Cerfs (deer farm), where you can admire many of these creatures, which are raised for meat, breeding stock, and for their antlers, which are a popular component of much Asian medicine.

In the 1870s there was a school here, where the road forks to Harper's Lake. In 1904 the schoolmistress was a Miss Zelda Draper, from Shawville. By the 1930s, writer Rupert Last notes teacher's salaries were $50 a month. This was not much even in those days, particularly as they had pay for room and board at a farmhouse nearby. Sometimes these were two or so miles away — all considered well within walking distance.

Last reminds us that the pupils helped the teacher look after the school premises. "The first boys to get to school split kindling, lit fire, and split wood for the day. At the first break, two pupils walked half a mile to Ned Woodstock's for water with a pail slung on the broom handle between them."[38] They fetched water because the school's well water was so muddy. The "janitorial services" were also supplied by the girls whose duty it was to sweep the floor with a corn broom which, Last writes, "only served to displace the dust."

In the 1940s the Holland Mills and Poltimore schools merged and this hamlet's school closed. There were many associations between these two villages and Nôtre-Dame-de-la-Salette: after all, they were not far apart even in the days of horse and wagon. Cheese factories such as the one at Poltimore, mills, and other enterprises spurred entrepreneurial local residents into starting a farmer's cooperative in "la-Salette" — as well as a fall fair in Poltimore's agricultural grounds.

After crossing Ruisseau du Prêtre turn right at the fork in the road to **Poltimore**. (Note that there is a seasonal ferry crossing the Lièvre River that you can reach via the left-hand, southerly fork on chemin des rapides.) You soon get to another fork: here turn left (to stay on the paved road) instead of going north.

Postcard of Poltimore, n.d. HSG 01890–001.

Now you enter a broad valley and **Poltimore**. Although the name is derived from a town in England north of Exeter, this village — and the area itself — was settled by many German-speaking peoples. Families such as Brunkes (who came from Germany's Sleighzinger region close to the Polish border) and Tscheschlocks (changed to Cheslock) settled here. Many immigrants to Canada also settled the adjacent townships of Mulgrave–Derry and Mayo, just east of the NCR along the Blanche River watershed.

Although there were many German-speaking homesteaders here at Poltimore, as well as Polish and Norwegian settlers who arrived in the 1930s, there were many English and French-speaking people here, too.

Several Irish settlers came, among whom were John Littleton, hired by Mike Cooligan, a cheese maker in Poltimore. Scots settlers such as the McMillans and James Greer homesteaded here; Greer died at 35, leaving a young family. His wife numbered among the French-speaking community: Philenese Pelletier hailed from Québec City. She was a midwife who was kept occupied administering not only to help with deliveries, but to be of medical assistance in any way she could. The Bonsall family came to Poltimore from Manchester, England, and it was Mrs. Elizabeth [Pegg] Bonsall who gave the village its name — her birthplace was Poltimore, England.

Postcard of Anglican church in Poltimore, n.d. HSG 01890–005.

Travel slowly through the village, noting the architecture of churches, residences, and commercial buildings as you go. Find **St. Louis de France** Roman Catholic Church with its two statues out front. After passing rue St. Louis de France, the plain **Anglican Parish of Christ Church** appears, with **J.B. McClelland's** shop on the left. You also pass chemin Pinkos, named for a family who left Krakow, Poland, to come to the region circa 1866. Martin Pinkos first worked at the mine at Ironside (on the Gatineau River) before moving across to the Lièvre region. Here he worked at High Rock Mine prior to moving again, this time to Poltimore. Descendents of the family still live here.

On your right you pass a clapboard house with a pretty turned wood porch, before coming to the **Dépanneur Renaud**, a combination corner store and snack bar on the corner of rue Pont. In the 1920s the Poltimore Cheese Factory stood opposite Renaud's, operated by Mike Cooligan.

This was the Bonsall/McCallium House, Poltimore, at 39 chemin du Pont, 1891. HSG 01889–002.

At Renaud's Dépanneur you might want to turn right, briefly, to venture north to the agricultural grounds and school. You pass by the **United Church** here, too.

Otherwise, stay on the main Poltimore road to join Highway 307 beyond George E. Last's Polled Hereford farm (a right-hand turn here on chemin Voyageur leads to Denholm and then to the Gatineau River village of Low). The farm was built by Fred Sharp, and is where the aforementioned Herdus Last lived. Author Rupert Last, who wrote the book on Poltimore's history, was born here.

Take Highway 307 south towards **Lucerne, Val-Paquin, St-Pierre-de-Wakefield:** you pass alongside the large valley lake, Lac Saint-Pierre, where there are many pretty views, lovely cottages, and accommodations including Hotel sur le Lac. A signpost announces you are 12 km from Cantley. Very soon on your right (west) note a large sign pointing to Laflèche Cavern; shortly after it you come to the junction with Highway

366 Nord. Stay right (south) on Highway 307 here. Note that turning north takes you to Edelweiss Valley ski area and also Wakefield (see Gatineau River ramble). Keep a watch for **La Ferme de Deux Mondes** soon appearing on your left, which offers intriguing glimpses into how farms were operated in the mid-1800s.

Now you are in **Cantley**, named in honour of a Colonel who worked with Colonel By on the Rideau Canal, and fought in the War of 1812. He obtained a grant of land here that By supposedly arranged. Cantley, however, was not the first European to settle here. That was Andrew Blackburn, in 1829, closely followed by Irishmen James Brown and Dominic Fleming.

On your left, don't miss the **Milks family farm** (number 694), an original homestead farmhouse and outbuildings dating from between 1867 and 1869. The beautifully preserved white clapboard farmhouse with ornate wraparound porch and red roof is a heritage landmark, particularly because its yard outbuildings and rear summer kitchen are complete. The unique mailbox is a replica of the house.

Anthony Milks, son of pioneers John and Mary Milks, was born in Cantley on 17 May 1859. When I interviewed the late Nellie Milks (wife of Anthony's son Hector), she told me that during the November freeze-up, Anthony would go north to work on the lumber camps where he soon became foreman. In 1884, however, he joined the Canadian Nile Voyageurs, that famous and special contingent of 350 volunteers who sailed to Egypt to rescue General Gordon at Khartoum. (There is a plaque at the Kitchissippi Lookout, on the Ottawa River Parkway, which commemorates this historic event.) The Milks' family history describes Anthony's many talents and his keen energy level:

> After returning to Canada, he worked with his father. ... He was capable in many trades: as a carpenter, cabinet maker, millwright, blacksmith, plasterer riverman, etc. He bought a sawmill, set it up at his home, and during the winter months he sawed logs for the surrounding farmers. He built his own blacksmith shop and worked for the neighbours when requested to do so. During the construction season, he contracted all around the country and, to this day, many a fine church stands as evidence of his ability.[39]

Collège Saint Alexandre at Limbour. Photo: K. Fletcher 2003.

Beyond the farm, watch on the left hand side for the **Farmer's Rapids Generating Station**: call ahead if you want a tour. The road is now rue Principale, and hugs the Gatineau River.

At the traffic lights (corner of des Érables) you cannot miss the grand sweep of playing fields and imposing buildings on a rise of land: this is the **Collège Saint Alexandre**. Turn left beyond the lights to drive onto the grounds. You can drive in front of the building and look at the immense gold-coloured statue of Jesus. Drive around the half-loop paved driveway and at the northwest end (towards des Érables) pull over to park for a moment. Walk west (towards rue Principale) and slip inside the little grove of trees at the corner of the streets, still on-property. Here you'll discover a tiny bridge over a little watercourse, and a stone grotto; unfortunately the statue has been removed. Return to your car, turn left on des Érables and left again on rue Principale.

Shortly afterwards you arrive at the Alonzo-Wright Bridge spanning the Gatineau River: turn right (west), cross the river and immediately turn left on Highway 105, (south), where you pass through the city of Gatineau and cross the Ottawa River, returning to the capital.

Logs at Cascades on Gatineau River, Ottawa vicinity, August 1900.
Photo: William James Topley. NAC PA-8969.

OTHER PLACES OF INTEREST

Laflèche Cave: This is a must-see, and can be a destination unto itself. Because it is an official tourist site, you cannot explore on your own. Guided tours are approximately one hour and fifteen minutes. You are provided with a hard hat and headlight. Cave temperature is constant at approximately 7°C, so dress accordingly. There are interior ladders so you can descend into the nether regions of the cave. Wear sturdy hiking shoes with ankle supports. And when you telephone the site to book your tour, please confirm these facts as details can alter from time to time. (**Note:** If you are a spelunker, enquire whether there are more in-depth tours still available whereby you can crawl into narrow spaces that the average visitor never sees.)

La Ferme de Deux Mondes (Farm of Two Worlds) is approximately 10 km north of Gatineau. It illustrates how the pioneers cleared the land and farmed, offering an interesting comparison to rural life today.

Farmer's Rapids Generating Station offers tours of the plant.

Edelweiss Valley and **Val des Monts**: these two ski hills are yet another way of appreciating the physical landscape!

Wakefield Women's Institute Picnic at Laflèche Caverns. In front row are President Mrs. R. H. Kirby (2nd from right) and Vice President Mrs. H. Cuthbertson (end, at right), n.d. HSG 01357.

Dam under construction. International Pulp & Paper Co., Chelsea and Farmers Rapids, c. 1936. Collection: Department of the Interior. NAC PA-44394.

Gatineau River Loop

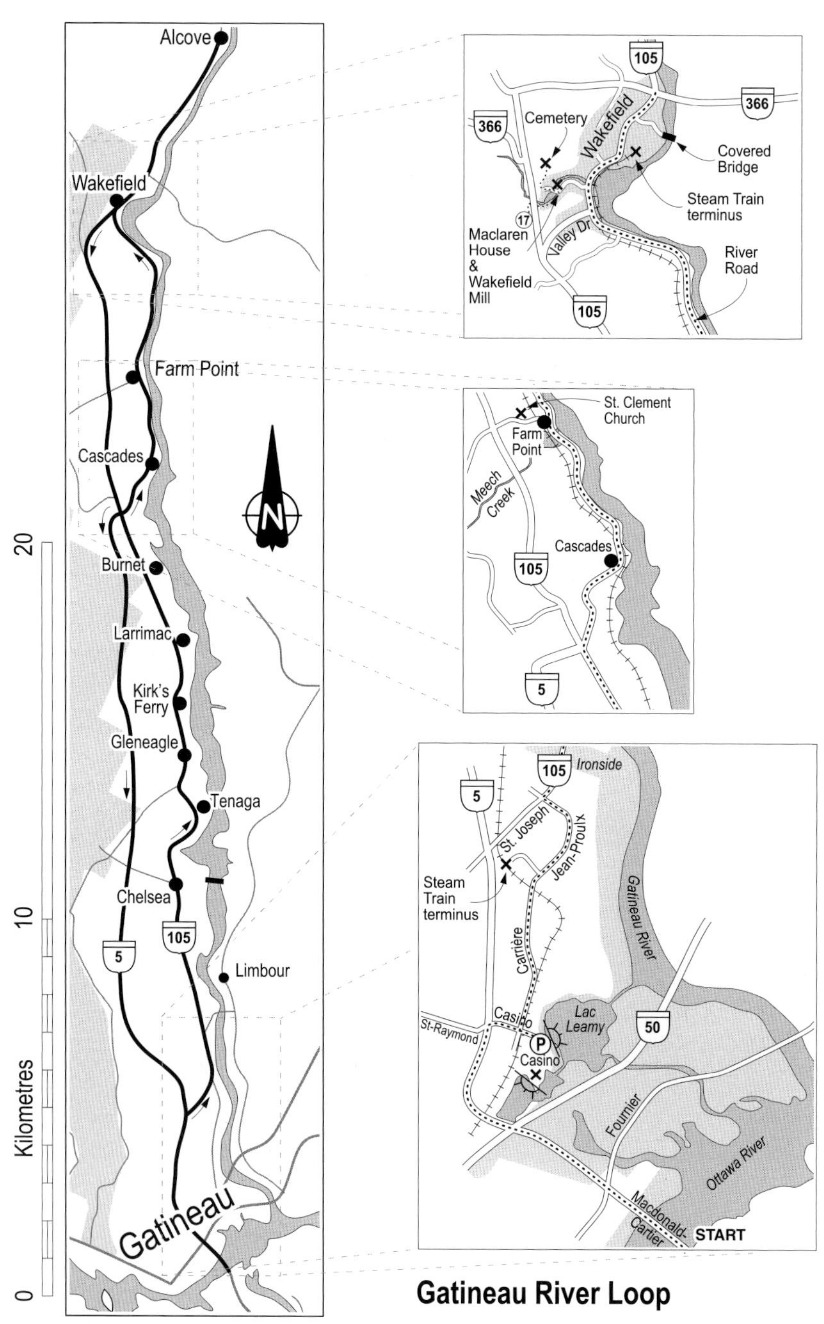

Gatineau River Loop

The Legend of Fairy Lake

I "discovered" Anson A. Gard in 1985. This American raconteur and travel writer explored Ottawa at the turn of the last century, romantically recounting the wonders of the valley to an American audience he hoped would come to marvel at the scenery and Canada's capital. Although his conversational style sounds affected today, Gard has his merits. In *The Hub and the Spokes*, he documents drives, walks, museums, and attractions, as well as listing famous persons in Ottawa and the surrounding villages in the early 1900s. He also walked the entire Mountain Road at the foot of the Eardley Escarpment, meeting, chatting with, and sometimes even staying overnight with every resident who lived along that road. Published as *Genealogy of the Valley*, this chronology gives a fascinating snapshot of life in North Hull during that brief window of time. As well, it is Gard who first revealed the legend of Fairy Lake to me in his book *Humours of the Valley*, published in 1906. Fairy Lake — *en français*, Lac des Fées — is nestled in the hills at the foot of Gatineau Park, and gives its name to a Parkway, too. Some people call it Haunted Lake, according to Anson Gard. Why? Who was the fairy of this pretty lake? Gard spun the tale.

Once upon a time, a beautiful Indian maiden lived amid the Gatineau Hills. One summer, she fell in love — but as fate insists on complicating matters sometimes, not with one young man, but two. How could she choose? Both suitors were attentive. They competed for her hand, bringing her gifts, showing off their prowess in hunting, fishing, and in the mastery of battle. She dithered, undecided, loving them both dearly. Then her lovers were called to battle, a skirmish in which both brave souls lost their lives. Grief-stricken and overcome with guilt, the young maiden drowned herself in the pretty lake in the fold of the hill. The spirits of the three doomed lovers swirl around the lake in their quest for peace.

And so it is, on a clear moonlit night, you might sit by Lac des Fées and feel the presence of regret and longing.

Although Samuel de Champlain's journal contains many fascinating observations of his 1613 journey up the Ottawa, his entries are often all-too elusive and short. Nonetheless, his impressions of the Gatineau River are fascinating to read, penned on the fourth day of his trip west of present-day Montréal:

> On the fourth day we passed near another river which comes from the north, where some tribes named Algoumekin lived. It is not wide, but filled with a vast number of rapids which are very difficult to pass. Sometimes these people go down this river to avoid meeting their enemies, knowing they will not look for them in places so difficult of access.[40]

However sparse this entry is, we can glean much from Champlain's three sentences. The "Algoumekin" were the nomadic Eastern woodland peoples whose name we more commonly spell as "Algonquin" or "Algonkin." Champlain tells us they dwelled here, along the Gatineau River, which he says was not wide, but full of rapids. Although these were an obstacle to easy navigation, rapids also provided welcome protection from warring bands of Iroquois who challenged the Algonquins for supremacy of the old trade route along the Ottawa.

Such notations inspire far more questions than they answer. How did the Algonquin peoples live? Were there well-worn portages alongside the tumultuous waters of the rapids, or were there some "secret" bypasses of calmer waters, known only to the Algonquin? What was life like, back then, just prior to and subsequent to European contact?

As the Champlain Sea receded, over time, the delta of the Gatineau River at the confluence of the Ottawa River formed a broad estuary. It was a region rich in wildlife, a flat area where the native traders plying the Ottawa could rest, hunt, fish, replenish their food stores, and continue on their journey. Did other peoples decide to encamp here and grow their food, as was happening in other parts of Québec and Ontario? Research is not conclusive on this point. Still, some things we do know include:

> At present, all the evidence suggests that the delta of the Gatineau River was used by more than one group during Late Woodland times. Groups of various origins followed one another and might even have shared camps as well as the resources of

> the delta, at certain times. It appears that groups from the west, carrying with them earthen pots decorated with motifs called Laurel and Blackduck, frequented the delta of the Gatineau River regularly at the end of the Middle Woodland Period and at the beginning of the Late Woodland Period, between A.D. 900 and A.D. 1200. From the eleventh century and until the arrival of Europeans, the resources of the delta seem to have attracted people who were related or at least had strong ties with representatives of the emerging Iroquoian culture in the southern parts of Québec and Ontario.[41]

But how did these people live and what were their daily domestic lives like? Recent archaeological digs around Leamy Lake Park revealed much, particularly about what life was like around the time of contact with Europeans.

Writer Claire Saint-Germain explains that a hearth was unearthed during excavation at the Gatineau River delta. We can imagine a group of people clustered around it, perhaps enjoying the heat cast from the fire, waiting for food to finish cooking, and speaking of the day's activities and chores. Saint-Germain notes that the hearth contained a "large quantity of food residue," and a little distance away from it, "stone tools were manufactured and bones fractured. Here and there, on the living floor, appear chipping debris and bones which had been inadvertently moved there by the occupants or perhaps by roots and burroughing [sic] animals." The writer also mentions that "we also found small glass beads and the rusted blade of a knife acquired, without doubt, through commercial exchanges with Europeans. We also noted the presence of earthenware pots which bear a strong resemblance to those made by sedentary populations in south-eastern Ontario, namely the Huron."[42]

Much more is known after the arrival of Europeans. Wildlife became a trade commodity and the Hudson's Bay and North West Company made a fortune from beaver pelts. As land was taken from the native tribes while European's settled their former hunting grounds, the Algonquin peoples were given reserves of land upon which they still live. All of these lie just beyond the limits of the National Capital Region: For instance, one group called the Kitigan Zibi Anishinabeg live near Maniwaki, north of Wakefield and the NCR, while another lives west of its boundary, near Golden Lake on the Bonnechere River waterway near Algonquin Park.

Native remains are a sensitive issue. European archaeologists such as Clyde Kennedy, who researched, excavated, and carefully documented many archaeological sites in the Ottawa Valley was among several seminal leaders who furthered our knowledge of aboriginal life pre- and post-contact. Although such scientists as he made valuable contributions, the bones they dug up, catalogued, and researched are the subject of much debate. The Kitigan Zibi Algonquin group of Algonquins based in Maniwaki, for instance, have been negotiating with the director and archaeologists at the Canadian Museum of Civilization (CMC) for years. They want to have all human remains returned to them, so they can be given a proper ceremony and perhaps be re-interred, so that the ancestral spirits can rest in peace.

In an *Ottawa Citizen* article, reporter Randy Boswell quotes the director of the CMC's archaeology department: "it is our opinion that human remains which are several thousand years old are too old to be affiliated with any modern community without other substantiating evidence."[43] What will happen to the bones of these ancient people who dwelt in the Ottawa Valley? Whatever is decided, the debate reveals much about how two cultures view spirituality and science.

The CMC was erected west of the Gatineau River delta (see Brewery Creek ramble). Ironically, the museum was built on top of an excavated ossuary — a communal cemetery — that held some twenty or so aboriginal skeletons.

But the Gatineau River's human history does not begin and end with bones of contention. Its story is inextricably tied to the resource industries of logging and mining.

Philemon Wright started the timber industry so as to increase his family's fortunes. Due to his efforts, a document called the Gatineau Privilege was created, in which the rights to vast amounts of timber alongside the river and its watershed were reserved, largely for the Wrights. In their seminal work, *Hurling Down the Pine*, authors John Hughson and Courtenay Bond wrote:

> In 1832 the so-called Gatineau Privilege was granted by the Crown Timber Office, permitting Ruggles, Tiberius and Christopher Columbus Wright each to take out 2,000 pieces of red pine timber yearly on the Gatineau. This wild river had been left untouched until then by lumbermen. In addition, Peter Aylen and Thomas McGoey were permitted to take out 2,000 sticks each.[44]

Three years later, the document was re-written and the territory expanded. Effectively, it locked up rights to the best and most accessible timberlands for a privileged few.

As for that other resource, minerals, in 1801 the deflection of a compass indicated the presence of iron ore in the hillsides along present-day Mine Road in Gatineau. Iron ore soon started to be mined at the Forsyth Mine whose adits (entrances) are now almost totally obscured by saplings. The hamlet of Ironsides got its name and *raison d'être* from this mine, and after the Rideau Canal was completed, millions of tons of iron ore were shipped to the United States via an efficient water route network. By the 1850s and 1860s, barges plied the Gatineau and Ottawa rivers, then proceeded south along the Rideau Canal to Kingston and beyond into the Great Lakes system to Cleveland, Ohio (see Rideau Canal ramble). Iron and other goods were also conveyed east to Montréal and Québec City, and from there to Europe. The Paris World Exposition of 1855 displayed a one-ton sample of iron ore mined at the Forsyth Mine in Gatineau.

Iron is not the only mineral in the Gatineau Hills. Along River Road there has been extensive quarrying of magnesium ore, as well as marble, and talc. Mica mines were also dotted about the region, and the peculiar layers or sheets of this mineral were used on the front of many an early wood stove. In some cases, mica sheets were used for windows, too.

As industry and settlement sprang up, the development of the railway became crucial to the opening up of the region. At the end of the 1800s, the railway pushed north from Ottawa and Hull to Wakefield and Maniwaki along the Gatineau's western embankment. Today's Wakefield Steam Train continues the tradition that allowed people to commute and ship goods up and down the waterway in all seasons. The train you can ride today is Swedish-built and never saw service in Canada until brought here for this tourism venture. Transportation trends again shifted with the construction of Highways 105 and 5; the advent of truck transport combined with cars and buses on paved, all-season, and well-maintained roadways sounded the death knell the era of railway transportation.

Concurrent with the development of the roadways came the harnessing of the Gatineau's rapids. Hydroelectric dams were constructed in the 1920s and 1930s. Farmer's Rapids, the community that sprang up on the site of pioneer William Farmer's property, also proved to be an excellent location for a power dam on the lower Gatineau. The

Farmer's Rapids Hydroelectric Dam can be toured (see Lièvre River ramble).

The designation of Ottawa as the capital of Canada greatly influenced the development of the land alongside the Gatineau River. The city's population rapidly expanded due to the number of civil servants plus the influx of merchants, businesspeople, and others who correctly anticipated opportunity while the young capital grew. The "suburbs" of Sandy Hill, then Rockcliffe Village, and eventually the Glebe developed after Confederation.

During summertime's torpid heat, people who could afford it looked longingly to the Gatineau Hills for respite amid its mountains, lakes, and rivers. By the 1870s summer residences were being built alongside Jeffs Lake — now called Kingsmere Lake in today's Gatineau Park. Well into the turn of the century, inns, bed and breakfasts, and cottages sprang up along the Gatineau River.

Portrait of William Farmer and his wife, n.d. HSG 00582.

Automobile and two women and dog, possibly near Larrimac, Gatineau River outing. Car may be a 1923 or 1924 Franklin, c. 1920. HSG 01020.

Winter had its attractions too. In the 1920s, the Ottawa Ski Club started to develop trails at Camp Fortune, along with other lodges up the Gatineau River, at communities like East Templeton. Skiers would catch the Ottawa Electric Company streetcars in Ottawa and cross the river to Hull, then they boarded the train to Ironsides or Kirk's Ferry, where they disembarked and skied to various lodges in what is now

Gatineau River at Kirk's Ferry, depicting the horse and wagon era along with rail, before river was dammed, c. 1898. NAC PA-85907.

Gatineau Park. When the cars came on the scene, people quickly forsook the rail in preference of the independence of choosing their own times of departure and return.

Despite being altered by dams, and no longer being used for picturesque log booms, the Gatineau River still flows downstream to join the Ottawa, opposite to the confluence of the Rideau River and its pretty falls as it has done for thousands of years. Today's recreationalists paddle the Gatineau's eddies in canoe and kayak, stroll along its pathways, or cycle along its embankments on paved bike paths that form part of the Trans-Canada Trail.

This mighty river was named in memory of Nicolas Gatineau, Sieur du Plessis, who was a notary at Trois-Rivières and Montréal. Perhaps he got bored of his desk job: whatever the case, in the mid-1600s he paddled up the Gatineau, in search of more land where furs could be harvested for export to France. Legend has it he drowned in the river that bears his name.

It is both a fitting and sobering tale upon which to end this section, for Nicolas Gatineau's drowning death reminds us of the water's powerful forces. Today, when we explore the river by canoe, kayak, on skis in the winter, or plunge into its depths and swim in its dark waters, we must respect the currents of this still-mighty watershed.

What's in a name? Romance, often! The river's Algonquin name is Tenagatin, meaning "the never ending river." As we watch the waters of the Gatineau descending to the Ottawa, it's this more whimsical name that I think of — see what you think when you sit beside it on a summer's day!

NATURAL HISTORY

Most estuaries are rich feeding grounds for all sorts of wildlife, whether they are amphibians, reptiles, mammals, fish, or birds. In spring the estuaries become both temporary staging grounds as well as summer homes for returning waterfowl such as Canada geese, great blue heron, American bittern, as well as common mergansers, mallard, black, and wood ducks. Redwing blackbirds chortle as they grasp cattails bending before spring's early breezes, and songbirds such as warblers, sparrows, and wrens bring their welcome songs back to the red and silver maple woods along the river's shallow mouth.

Further upstream, along the River Road just south of Wakefield, marshes throng the west embankment. I found a night heron here once, perched in a tree alongside the road. Also look for painted turtles basking on logs that still bob up from the river bottom, recalling the time when giant log booms floated downriver.

Geology did not just create the opportunity for mining. Just as with the Lièvre, the Gatineau River's many rapids were created by fault lines and shifting plates, as well as from terraces or old beach heads marking water levels. At the Paugan Falls Dam at Low, just north of the NCR and Wakefield, there is an outcrop of white marble visible below the falls. Marble is dissolved relatively easily by water, a fact that has given us both the Laflèche and Lusk Caves, which allow us to explore below the surface of the NCR (see the Lièvre and Gatineau Park rambles). Tours of the caves offer us an all-too-rare opportunity to examine the erosive powers of water over geological spans time.

BEFORE YOU GO ON THE RAMBLE

Why go? The Gatineau River loop offers spectacular views of a river once famous for its tumultuous rapids. After being tamed by hydro dams, the river was used for transporting logs to the sawmills, and pulp and paper mills. Today it's a historic, recreational river that is the beloved "home" to many a resident living along its shores.

Distance: Approximately 72 km round trip from downtown Ottawa.

Modes of exploration: Described as a drive, the loop makes a super bike route. You can also take your canoe or kayak to explore the river, particularly around Wakefield.

Getting there: Cross to Gatineau at the Macdonald-Cartier Bridge and drive north on Highway 105, exit at the Casino to Lac Leamy and the Parc écologique du lac Leamy, rejoin Highway 105 Nord to Ironside, Chelsea, Tenaga, Gleneagle, Kirks Ferry, Larrimac, Burnet; take River Road to drive along Chemin-des-Pins to Cascades, Farm Point, and Wakefield, then explore North Wakefield, otherwise known as Alcove before returning to Ottawa.

Facilities: Wakefield is home to a thriving artists' community, excellent lodgings, and pretty hikes.

Of special note: Highway 105 and River Road routes are paved, but are winding, old roads. Take care driving since many driveways abruptly open onto them, many with practically hidden access points.

Winter at Jim Hammond's home on Chelsea Road, Highway 105, near Ironsides, now a part of Hull. Home now demolished, n.d. HSG 00090.

Wakefield Bay looking south, 1900. COA CA-1435.

Horse and buggy pass through original Gendron covered bridge, constructed in 1915, n.d. HSG 00278.

THE RAMBLE

Head to Gatineau by crossing the **Macdonald-Cartier Bridge** named in honour of Canada's first prime minister, Sir John A. Macdonald, and Sir Georges Étienne Cartier, one of the Fathers of Confederation. Take Highway 5 north to Boulevard St-Raymond and exit right (east) on rue Casino. Cross the tracks into the parking lot for the Casino and the Lac Leamy Hilton. Park here and walk to the former quarry now "transformed" into a picturesque lake with a truly amazing **fountain**. Its steep sides show off the sedimentary layers of Ordovician limestone to great effect. Behind the Casino — a dramatic example of "showcase" architecture if there ever was one — find a narrow channel leading to **Lac Leamy**.

A footpath wends its way around the lake to **Parc écologique du lac Leamy** and more pathways — including a section of **Trans-Canada Trail** that links northwest to Gatineau Park and south to Ottawa. In summer there is a beach at the lake, and you can rent a canoe here — or bring your own — so you can fully explore the estuary of the Gatineau River. Return to your car.

From the parking lot, turn right onto **Boulevard de la Carrière**. Just after you cross the tracks and rue Deveault, Carrière changes to **rue Jean-Proulx**. Continue on rue Jean-Proulx until it meets **Boulevard St-Joseph (Route 105 Nord).** Turn right here. This is actually a remnant of an old toll road cut along the west bank of the Gatineau River. Residents petitioned the government in Québec City for help with building a road in 1846. Most of the early roads were tolls — this method of funding roads lasted for approximately one hundred years. It was a user-pay system, where payments varied depending on the size of conveyance just like today's ferries: wagons and stagecoaches paid different sums, as did pedestrians.

After turning from Jean-Proulx, you pass through **Ironside**, formerly a separate village named after the Forsyth Iron Ore Mine, located west of here on Mine Road. This community, now absorbed by Gatineau, is the first of several old hamlets we'll pass through, all of which were deliberately settled approximately 7.5 km apart, being the distance a loaded wagon drawn by a horse could travel in a day. Stopping places (inns where man and beast could find rest) cropped up along the old river road, which were later replaced echoed by stations along the railway track.

The Forsyth Iron Mine lies inside the boundary of Gatineau Park, opposite Les Haute Plains near the old Samuel Pink homestead (see Gatineau Park ramble). Almost immediately after Ironside (look for the junction of St-Joseph with rue Freeman) you will notice a rise of land immediately to your left (west), known as **Mile Hill**. (Earlier it was known as Christy Wright's Hill, after Christopher Columbus Wright, son of Philemon, whose home used to stand at the hill's summit. A white home with a green trim now stands here on the east side of Highway 105.) Ottawa Ski Club members used to take the train (whose tracks you will flirt with during this entire ramble) here to Ironsides, disembark, and ski Dome Hill before continuing on to Camp Fortune, beyond Old Chelsea in what is now Gatineau Park (see Gatineau Park ramble).

Continue on Highway 105 north, passing rue Alonzo Wright and immediately east of it the **Alonzo Wright Bridge**. Its name commemorates the grandson of Hull's founder, Philemon Wright. Born in Hull in 1825, Alonzo inherited property on the east side of Gatineau River that his father Tiberius had leased to English emigrant William Farmer. When Farmer could not meet his payments, title reverted to the Wrights, and Alonzo took possession because his father had died.

Like his grandfather, Alonzo became a member of the Legislative Assembly of Lower Canada, a position he was elected to twice. He was also President of the Agricultural Society of Ottawa County, among other notable achievements. Alonzo eventually built a large residence on what used to be the William Farmer property, in Limbour, which still stands on the site of St. Alexandre College (see Lièvre River ramble).

Continue travelling north, until you reach **Chelsea**. Although the name originally derives from an English town, the New Englanders who came to settle this part of Québec named the village after Chelsea, Vermont. This town bordering the Gatineau River should not be confused with the original, "Old Chelsea," located 4 km due west via the Old Chelsea Road. This "new" Chelsea was created because of the railroad. The Chelsea railway station was a popular destination for people who were starting to build summer residences in the Gatineau Hills, such as those around Kingsmere Lake. People like the Alexanders and Murphy families of Meech and Kingsmere would pick up summer residents by horse and wagon, and later by car to take them to their summer lodgings. The Alexanders operated Meech Lake House; the Murphys operated a little inn and restaurant at Kingsmere.

Immediately south of the junction with the road to Old Chelsea there is a tumble-down picket fence surrounding an old home on the southwest corner. This is **Thomas Brigham Prentiss' home, store, and post office,** street number 461. Prentiss moved these operations here from an earlier site in Old Chelsea in 1843. As the years passed, outbuildings such as a carriage house were constructed, then two other structures were added to the original store and office. He completed a store on the north side of the street in 1860, then another dwelling place named "Yarrow Cottage" to the south. The little complex still remains at the southwest corner of the junction.

As with the Lièvre and other NCR waterways, the Gatineau's rapids were developed for hydroelectricity. The 1920s and 1930s was the era of dam building. From 1925 to 1928 the Chelsea Dam was constructed, flooding many communities, cottages, farms, and business ventures. What was spared, however, was any permanent flooding of the railway lines, although due to fluctuating water levels, particularly in spring, the tracks (notably at Wakefield) were submerged from time to time.

The story of the railway is one filled with frustrations and delays. The Ottawa and Gatineau Valley Railroad Company was incorporated in 1871, conceived as a route connecting Hull to Maniwaki. Landslides

Canadian Pacific Railway engine at Wakefield, Québec, during flood of Gatineau River, 1908. Collection: Frances M. Iveson. Notes: Man on cow catcher is shoving aside floating logs. NAC PA-122923.

caused by underlying unstable leda clay and other mishaps challenged the workers who built it. The Company's first Board of Directors included prominent entrepreneurs such as E.B. Eddy, Alonzo Wright, and John Maclaren. The first train steamed into Wakefield in 1892; a year later the tracks had been extended to Kazabazua, and in 1895 the first train pulled into Gracefield. Meanwhile, the railway's name changed: on 23 July 1894 it became the Ottawa and Gatineau Railway Company, but in 1901 it changed yet again to the Ottawa Northern & Western after it amalgamated with the Pontiac and Pacific Junction, which led west from Hull to Waltham. The train had still not reached Maniwaki, its original goal. The Gatineau Valley Historical Society's website explains, "The following year (November 1902) the ON & W was leased to Canadian Pacific for 999 years. Under CP's control, construction picked up. Grading was completed to Blue Sea Lake by April of 1903 with track laying being completed in June. Finally, in January of 1904, the rails were in place to the end of track at Maniwaki."[45]

Beyond Chelsea and the junction, the next heritage destination is on the west side of the road, the **O'Neill House**. It is a single-storey log cottage these days, but in 1850 it served as a stagecoach stop operated by Paddy O'Neill; later Arthur O'Neill operated a temperance hotel here. The temperance movement affected many places such as nearby Old Chelsea, causing quite a change in that town, which had previously been noted for its five lively stopping places, all operated by Irishmen. Not surprisingly, the temperance movement caused business in these establishments to rather severely decline.

Just north of the O'Neill House find the **Chelsea Pioneer Cemetery**, at **number 587**. A tiny white wooden sign with a broadaxe symbol (the logo of the Gatineau Valley Historical Society, which manages the cemetery) denotes that you have arrived: turn left here to enter a tiny parking lot. In the cemetery you will "meet" and be able to give your respects to such pioneers as Church, Meech, Alexander, Hudson, Trowse, Chamberlin, and other families. The land once belonged to the Church family; it was their private burial grounds from the 1820s until approximately the 1880s, when other neighbours and kin began to be buried here. There are fourteen grave monuments commemorating thirty-one individuals. Among these is Private Richard R. Thompson, the only Canadian to receive the Queen's Scarf.

Traveling north from here you soon find the second small community along the Gatineau, **Tenaga**. It derived its name — a Spanish word meaning "water tank" — from the days of the railway because after climbing Mile Hill, locomotives needed to refill with water. The village of Tenaga came about, however, because of the Chelsea power dam, the construction of which flooded several people's properties. Patrick Evans, the late historian of the Gatineau Valley Historical Society wrote that the Jeness, Coady, and Beatty families were among those whose homes were hauled out of harm's way at this time. Notes Evans, "The 'Tenagans' had at various times these amenities: a par nine hole golf course, tennis courts, a clubhouse, a tearoom (Blue Bonnie) a bowling green. The timber used in construction was that used in the building of the dam. They also achieved a swimming beach. The Road off the highway is known as Station Road. The Blue Bonnie was at the left as one enters. The inhabitants maintain their own roads — quite a hamlet!"[46]

Beyond Tenaga on the right-hand side of the highway is **La Boucanerie**, a smoke house that sells delectable foods such as local sturgeon fished from the Ottawa River near Fort Coulonge. Formerly the smokehouse was the Horseshoe Restaurant. Beyond it on the left is **Les Fougères**, a fine restaurant with an award-winning wine cellar. It is located at the junction to another road leading west to Old Chelsea. Stay on 105 Nord.

The next little community north used to be called **Summerlee**, but is now known as **Gleneagle**, the site of a golf course first created out of the undulating hills by Carson Cross in the mid-1900s. Proceeding north, you next arrive at **Kirk's Ferry**, so named because Thomas Kirk once operated a ferry that transported people, horses, and wagons across the Gatineau River. On the highway's west side is a parking lot and board-and-batten building, the former **post office and general store**. Pat Evans recalled it in its former glory when it was also a bustling telephone switchboard. He wrote that with "the old phones with a crank to twist and a button to press, one needed two hands."

Just north of here, you will sweep past a complex of barns immediately on the right-hand side of the highway: these are the **Brown Barns**, originally the homestead of Thomas Reid and Lucy Wright. In a letter dated Kirk's Ferry, 7 April 1888, penned to Miss Eliza Smith of Otter Lake by Bertha Reid, the writer notes, "The snow is going pretty fast here now and the stage went up on wheels today. I don't suppose you will be surprised to hear that school closed last Monday..."[47] The letter serves to remind us about former conveyances that plied the old toll road, which we now know as Highway 105. Perhaps this coach also stopped at the O'Neill House.

Cross Lumber Mill, Farm Point, July 1917.
Collection: Leonard Davis. NAC PA-110893.

Beyond the barns **Kirk's Ferry Road** descends east to the railway tracks and the river. If you wish, venture here just to remind yourself of both forms of transportation and if you time it right, possibly to get a good photo of the Wakefield steam train.

Farther north are the villages of **Larrimac** — primarily notable for its pretty sweep of golf course extending on either side of the highway — **Burnett,** and **Cascades**. Larrimac was named for Larry McCooey who developed the greens, which were originally kept at least partially cut by the grazing sheep owned by adjacent landowner Lacharity, who also owned a sawmill. Burnett was named for Irishman William Burnett, who came to Canada in 1839 when he was twelve.

Just beyond Burnett find **chemin Ramsay**. Although it leads to narrow and winding gravel roads servicing a small cottage community, it first crosses the railway tracks and passes alongside a farm on a piece of land jutting into the river. The brief diversion serves to remind us how the land was flooded by the dam, as well as showing us how every piece of arable land was cleared and farmed.

William Burnett, born 10 April 1827, Ireland, died 18 November 1903; buried in Wakefield cemetery, c. 1880. HSG 01638.

At the **traffic light** and **La Vallée Restaurant**, turn right onto **chemin River Road**. (When returning to Ottawa, you could connect here with the four-lane Highway 5 that appears ahead, on your left just beyond the lights.) Now, after an abrupt right-hand turn, you descend to the river. River Road wends its way along the undulating hillside of the west shore of the Gatineau. Houses snuggle between the river, railway, and road. Watch your speed and be alert for children, walkers, cyclists, dogs, and wildlife.

The Peerless Hotel at Cascades before the flooding of the Gatineau River, looking north. Train tracks were moved higher ground; buildings were demolished buildings prior to the flooding of the river in 1926 and 1927. HSG 00047–004.

Soon you drive through **Cascades**, a small community that used to be home to the **Peerless Hotel**. It attracted many vacationers who enjoyed picnics, country walks, strolls, and swimming along the river. Cascades originally overlooked a series of rapids that claimed the lives of many a riverman employed in the dangerous task of releasing logs from jams caught in the rocks. In her book *Wakefield and Its People*, Norma Geggie notes, "Elderly residents recall a small, fenced and wooden reserve on the hill above where markers honoured these nameless victims. Although evident in the 1950s, there is no trace remaining today."[48]

Levi Reid on scow at Farm Point, c. 1930. HSG 01319.

The next community is **Farm Point**. First you pass **Cross Quarry** on the left, once operated by Stephen Cross prior to being purchased by Alcan. Look northwest to locate a church steeple: this is **St. Clement's,** which we'll soon visit. Just now look for a watercourse and bridge on River Road, ahead. This is **Meech Creek**, the final outflow of Meech Lake in Gatineau Park (see Gatineau Park ramble). Cross it. Across the Gatineau River you will see a large barn and an expanse of green: these identify the **Mont Cascades Golf Club** built upon the old Levi Reid farm. At the water's edge, you can perhaps imagine a ferry crossing the river here, to the north side of Meech Creek. This is how everyone crossed the Gatineau before the era of bridge building.

Next, turn left on **rue St. Clement** into **Farm Point**, noting the community centre on your right, which used to be a school. Before that, it was the site of Lnwarn Lodge, built in the early 1900s as a holiday resort. It could accommodate up to a hundred guests who enjoyed tennis, golf, a dining room, and other facilities on the 50-acre site. Imagine the scene prior to the installation of the power dams: there were many islands in the Gatineau River at this point. Evidently a creative man, Freeman Cross built several little bridges, connecting them so that guests of Lnwarn plus others who stayed at his hotel and, presumably, the Peerless, could wander from island to island. This holiday community was submerged after the dam flooded the river valley here at Chelsea.

Ascend the hill and note the first left-hand turn down **chemin du Pont** (for residents only). The little bridge crosses Meech Creek. This property belonged to Freeman Cross, one of the eight sons of William Cross and brother to Stephen, who owned the quarry you just looked at. Late historian and columnist Pat Evans wrote,

> Looking for more revenue than he was provided by that farm, Cross aimed at a complex. As there was plenty of wood around he chose a sawmill, which led to the provision of power to run and light it and so came a dam. The generated power was available to the homes clustered around — for a price. This enterprising man also constructed a toy factory in which he used the scraps from his sawmill. It was running in 1918. Others seeing the potential built a couple of commercial enterprises, the Island View House and the Lnwarn Lodge, both of which were well endowed, offering all manner of services in the way of accommodation as well as entertainment — boating, swimming, golf, tennis, fishing; and this at the height of the depression.[49]

Freeman Cross's sawmill was located on Meech Creek and was accessed by this little road; the toy factory was located near the railway tracks.

Continue driving to the **Mission St. Clement Roman Catholic Church**, constructed in 1916. The quaint, simple church has a fieldstone grotto directly in front, containing a statue of the Virgin. Beyond it, kneeling in a tidy little flower garden, is another figurine.

Return down the hill to River Road. Turn left (north), and as you approach Wakefield you will pass the cement works of the **Maxwell Quarry**, opened in 1942 by Alcan to extract magnesium ore from the marble intrusion in the Precambrian rock. The mining ceased in 1968 and today the deep water-filled pit is home to the **Great Bungee Experience**. (Access to this attraction is from Highway 105.) Beyond the quarry, take special care: winterized, permanent cottage-like homes along the Gatineau's embankment crowd the road here. Soon on your right you'll find the red brick **Orange Hall**, identified by the sign below the gable, "L.O.L. No. 144," signifying "Loyal Orange Lodge." Below that, find the letters, "Y.O.B. No. 99," short form for the "Young Orange Britons," a less-recognized appellation.

Lnwarn Lodge on Island right of centre: all these islands submerged when height of Gatineau River rose after the dam was built. HSG 00441.

Now cross the railway track, pass by Rockhurst Hill, and enter **Wakefield**, named after a village in England.

The village sprang up here in a protected bay north of the Meech Creek and south of the Lapêche River's confluence with the Gatineau. Early homesteaders sought out watercourses, which served in winter as the best possible "highways" into the interior reaches. Later, rivers were useful for timbers that could be floated downstream to the Ottawa, and then to European or American markets. Waterfalls were popular spots for settlers to hang their hats, too, for the cascades provided power for saw, grist, and wool mills. Wakefield is topographically rich, being blessed with rivers and falls, so the settlement soon prospered. Scotsman William Fairbairn built the first mill on the Lapêche in 1834; the Maclaren family purchased it four years later. Even though Wakefield's prosperity took a beating after the mills closed in the 1940s after a series of fires, today it has rebounded due largely to its beautiful natural surroundings. The waterways and hills that were once valued industrial resources are appreciated now for their scenic beauty and recreational potential. The Wakefield of today is a thriving dormitory community for Ottawa and Gatineau, and is the centre of a flourishing artistic community.

Continue north on River Road until you arrive at a flashing light at chemin **Valley Drive**. Turn left and park for a moment or two. On your left (at the south corner of Valley and River roads) find a clapboard farmhouse, the **Robert Earle House**. It has been a restaurant since 1975 but was once the circa 1880 home of one of the region's well-known contractor-builders.

Across the street from it is a picturesque group of buildings known as **Place 1870**, once Earle's Agricultural and Farm Implement Shop, now a cluster of shops. Park here. Take the front entry (off River Road) and climb the steep, creaky staircase. If you're lucky, the antique shop will be open and, if so, enter it to discover an old stage where magic lantern shows once captivated all and sundry. Here, too, council meetings, dances, movies, plays, and all sorts of other entertainments amused locals and holidaymakers alike. The stage was last used in the 1940s. You can still see the painted screen that offers a rather bizarre image of Greek columns.

Return outside to get your car; return to River Road and turn left, passing **War Memorial Park** (overlooking the river) as well as interesting shops worthy of exploration. Watch for the shops beside the river: the one with the bay windows was the circa 1880 **Patterson store**, built by William Patterson. Park so you can enter shop, now so densely packed with "country-style" goods that it's becoming more difficult to appreciate its well-preserved interior. Built-in cabinetry and pressed tin is still evocative of days gone by. Patterson and his son George operated the stagecoach from Bytown and Hull to Alcove (North Wakefield). Both father and son often drove their coach to O'Neill House, which you saw just before exploring the Chelsea Cemetery!

Return to your car and drive north, noting the **Black Sheep Inn** on the corner of Mill Street. Arguably, this Inn is the NCR's most popular venue for live music. Musicians come from all over the world to play here, so you may wish to time your visit with a gig. A hotel has stood on the site for years: first it was home to Seth Cates' **Temperance Hotel** (1850s), then **Diotte's**, **Pearson's,** and now the Black Sheep. Cates also rented carriages to people such as surveyors and businesspeople who travelled the bumpy roads to other communities such as Duclos and Rupert to the west, or perhaps Low, or even Farrelton on the other side of the Gatineau, crossing first by scow. Cross Mill Street and continue north on River Road. (If you have time, consider visiting the Wakefield Mill complex and associated Maclaren's Cemetery half a kilometre upstream on Mill Street; see above.)

The **village centre** once was opposite the Black Sheep on the north side of Mill Street. This was the site of **Maclaren's General Store**, the prosperous outlet for all the Maclaren family's milled items, from woollens to millinery goods and flour, as well as notions and food. The shop thrived from 1850 to 1941 when the last of a series of fires destroyed the complex. This was the last straw for the family, who moved to Buckingham.

Continue north and almost immediately pass over the **Lapêche River** where, on its northern embankment, you find the 1850–60 **David Maclaren Manor House**, now part of the Gatineau Hospital. Both David and his wife Elizabeth Barnett are buried in the family cemetery, which you might wish to visit later. This house had an extensive garden and plenty of pasture for livestock. After the family left, they rented it to their mill managers, then sold in 1950 to the Gatineau Memorial Hospital.

On the west side of the railway tracks is jaunty-looking **Pot au Feu restaurant**, once the Wakefield Train Station (not its original location).

Drive past **Burnside Avenue** where you'll find the rambling Victorian Gothic bed and breakfast, **Les Trois Érables**, on a large well-treed and landscaped garden lot. Built in 1896, it was once Maclaren property too, because Ann Sully, James Maclaren's widow, owned it. It was the home and office of several of the local doctors — Dr. Hans Stevenson, then Dr. Harold Geggie and his three sons — and it also was where the telephone service was first maintained in Wakefield.

Beyond it, on the east side of River Road stands the **Wakefield General Store** operated now by the Nesbitt family, but started in 1923 by Rufus Chamberlin. Inside you'll find an old-fashioned look where groceries crowd the original shelving. A butcher offers excellent meats, making this a good spot to buy items for a snack or lunch, which you can enjoy at the nearby park. Once outside turn right (north) to drive or walk to the **Railroad Turnaround** and strip of park land where picnic tables await.

This park, opposite **Ormes' Bakery**, is the current end of the line for the Wakefield Steam Train. It is where the Wakefield Station stood between the years 1892 and 1930. After that time, the yard was used for marshalling logs. In the 1970s the tourist steam train started to use the original turnaround, where trains were disconnected from the carriages and turned 180 degrees on a hand-winched crank. These days the Wakefield Steam Train brings tourists to Wakefield, all of whom enjoy watching the engine being turned around and reconnected to the carriages, ready for its return trip to Gatineau.

After a break (there are washrooms nearby) continue driving but only just beyond the bend in the road; watch out for **chemin Gendron** on your right. Turn here and follow it towards the river to find parking in front of the **Gendron Bridge**. Built in 1915, the original covered (or "kissing") bridge succumbed to fire set by an arsonist on 11 July 1984. Its replacement represents a community project par excellence, showing what can be done when goodwill, determination, and volunteer talent are put to patient use. The committee held its first meeting in Wakefield on 13 November 1987, and one year later the Gendron Bridge celebrated its re-opening. If you are travelling here in summer, I'll tell you a secret: on the far side (east) of the bridge a tiny footpath descends to the Gatineau River and some fabulous bathing rocks. Join "Wakefieldites" for relief from a hot summer's day, although at time of writing there are no changing facilities available.

Return to your car, drive west on chemin Gendron to rejoin River Road and turn right, passing the **Vorlage** ski area. Almost immediately you come to the place at which it becomes the main highway again, Route 105. The bridge to the right takes Highway 366 across the Gatineau River, and connects to the Lièvre River (see Lièvre River ramble), the communities of Farrellton, Edelweiss, and Val des Monts, as well as the Laflèche Caves. But for this ramble, stay on the west side of the Gatineau.

We now proceed 5 km north to **Alcove**, called **North Wakefield** until the 1920s (watch for the sign announcing the hamlet). This tiny community represents the most northerly spot on our ramble, and really, in all seriousness if you blink and you could miss the little road leading towards the river. Actually, you may find it because of the strip of land opposite it, on the west side of the highway. This is where the daily commuter train that operated from Ottawa to Alcove starting around 1894 used to turn around for its homeward journey. These days it's astonishing to realize some schoolchildren used to hop on this train at 6:30 a.m. and head to Ottawa to school, then return at 6:30 or so in the evening.

Drive down the **Alcove Road** to its terminus, and park opposite the **Alcove United Church** (before the 1926 union, it was the North Wakefield Methodist Church). Built here in the 1860s, it is a plain front-gabled brick building with a modestly decorated shallow bargeboard and central finial. A projecting entryway of wood protects worshippers from the elements as they enter. Norma Geggie notes that it was built by dedicated volunteers who hauled the brick from Ottawa in horse-drawn wagons. As well, it used to front onto the main highway: yes, today's quiet "alcove" of a road once served as the main road.

Walk south to view the **James Pritchard Homestead**. He and his wife Judith Ferguson chose this spot to build their second home in the mid-1800s after arriving in this region from Northern Ireland in 1834. Sadly neglected today, the gracious lines of this clapboard home cry out for sensitive restoration. Look at its symmetrical front entryway: the doorway must illuminate the interior beautifully, because it is framed by generous sidelights and, above it, an Adamesque fanlight. Behind the home, accessible from a footpath behind the church, is the **Pritchard graveyard**, one of the NCR's several, little-known cemeteries.

The sloped ends of the Alcove scow allowed it to fit into the bank and passengers could disembark directly, though sometimes boards were put down, c. 1912. HSG 00072.

Retrace your steps back to your car. At the end of the road you will find a former shop and also a laneway, which leads to a slight depression in the land right beside the river. This is where the most-used scow on the Gatineau River used to ply its way back and forth, particularly occupied ferrying schoolchildren to the Alcove school. On Sundays it carried Presbyterians south to Wakefield or west to Rupert; Anglicans north to Lascelles, while the Methodists could simply stroll a few steps to their church. "People would whistle for someone to come and get them, or they would take a rowboat over to bring the scow back."[50] Geggie continued:

> This Municipally-operated scow was connected to a cable high overhead, except when the river was in flood in the spring. Then the cable was close enough to be reached by hand. A wooden stick hung from the overhead cable, while a rudder was manipulated to take advantage of the current to propel the ferry across the Gatineau River. The road north was considered so rough that in winter some people preferred to use an ice road along the river from Alcove to Farrellton.[51]

Winter 1910 at Tom Cooper's temperance stopping place, North Wakefield House (Alcove) located between Low and Kirk's Ferry. (Copy of NAC C-80115.) This from HSG 00269.

Ready to return to Ottawa? Drive back along Alcove Road to rejoin Highway 105 and turn left (south). After roughly 5 km, you meet the traffic lights marking the bridge over the Gatineau River. Turn right to climb the hill, then right again onto Highway 105 Sud (south). This section of highway bypasses Wakefield, taking you down the hill and over the Lapêche River just past the junction with Highway 366. On your right, **Parking Lot 17** provides access to trails in **Gatineau Park** and is an alternate place to park to visit the Wakefield Mill on the Lapêche River.

Proceed south, passing the Valley Road exit to Wakefield. Watch for huge piles of white rock marking the Great Bungee Experience located at the old Maxwell (Morrison's) Quarry. Continue south on Highway 105 past the upper part of Farm Point to the traffic lights. Here, turn right to join the four-lane Highway 5, which returns you to Ottawa via a tract of road that passes through a huge outcrop of Canadian Shield. Take a good look at the scant topsoil on its top, which serves as a good reminder of why settlers who tried to farm these Precambrian hills soon got discouraged, and left! There are also some excellent examples of wetlands along this road: look for beaver and muskrat lodges — if you're not the driver, that is! You'll be back in Gatineau/Ottawa in approximately 25 minutes.

OTHER PLACES OF INTEREST

Leamy Lake Park is located at the confluence of the Gatineau and Ottawa rivers, immediately east of Brewery Creek. In 2002 a grassroots environmental group saved the park from being developed into a golf course. The NCC manages this park, which has been the site of archaeological digs; in the 1990s I was "participated" in one. If you're interested in archaeology, enquire at the NCC Visitor's Centre to see if further digs are planned. Enjoy swimming in the lake; windsurfing and canoeing on it and on the channel to the Ottawa; cycling, rollerblading, and walking on the shared bicycle paths.

Wakefield Village Walk: Local residents decided to create a walk that takes hikers up the craggy rock of Canadian Shield to the Maclaren Cemetery. The trailhead is near the village centre. Great views become spectacular in early May, just before bug season, when the trilliums and other wildflowers blossom. Autumn is possibly the best time to appreciate the natural beauty here, thanks to the deciduous trees' palette of golds and reds that so beautifully contrast to the sweep of evergreens, such as white pine. Watch for pileated woodpecker… and white-tailed deer in the clearing near the cemetery.

Maclaren's Wool Mill, Wakefield, taken before the 17 May 1910 fire that destroyed the mill complex. The next-door gristmill was rebuilt; this was not; c. 1900. HSG P268.

Maclaren Cemetery, Maclaren House & Auberge Wakefield Mill Inn: Access these three historic sites either by parking near the mill on Mill Road, in Wakefield Village, or by finding Parking Lot 17 in Gatineau Park, just past the turnoff to Wakefield. The latter has a well-signed trailhead describing the way east to the Lapêche and Gatineau rivers. Descend, cross Highway 105 via a trail leading beneath an underpass, and walk alongside the Lapêche River to **Auberge Wakefield Mill Inn**, now a country inn, conference centre, and fine dining room (The Penstock Room). First built in 1834 by William Fairbairn, it was purchased and developed into a major mill complex (wool, grist, and sawmills crowded the river here) by the Maclarens. If you stay here, the rooms of choice overlook the pretty waterfall that once powered the mill complex.

Directly across the Lapêche River and falls you cannot miss **Maclaren House**, a red brick mansion probably built in the 1860s, sometimes called the "bachelor's house." John and James Maclaren may both have lived here, but John Maclaren and his wife Georgina Baird called it home until his death in 1874. I remember helping the Gatineau

Valley Historical Society decorate its front rooms, in the 1980s, when members operated a summer museum here. Long closed, now the house is part of the inn complex.

Beyond the house, walk up the gravel road to the **Maclaren Cemetery**, claiming the grassed summit of a farmer's field. Here you can wander amid a host of pioneer family gravestones, as well as the final resting place of former **Prime Minister Lester Bowles Pearson**.

Wakefield Steam Train: Catch a ride on an old steam train and explore Wakefield on foot. Dinner and sunset train rides are popular. Find out about departure times from the Gatineau station at 165 Deveault St. The round trip takes approximately five hours including a two-hour stopover in Wakefield. This is a seasonal operation.

Note: Wakefield brims with delights, such as **Les Trois Érables B&B, Chez Eric** restaurant, and **Radisson Outfitters** (where you can rent a canoe, or book a dogsled ride). In autumn, consider coming on the popular self-guided studio tour, **Artists in Their Environment**. Many artists' studios are near the village or river. If you enjoy music, don't forget **Black Sheep Inn**, where you can catch many live, eclectic musical groups.

Brewery Creek

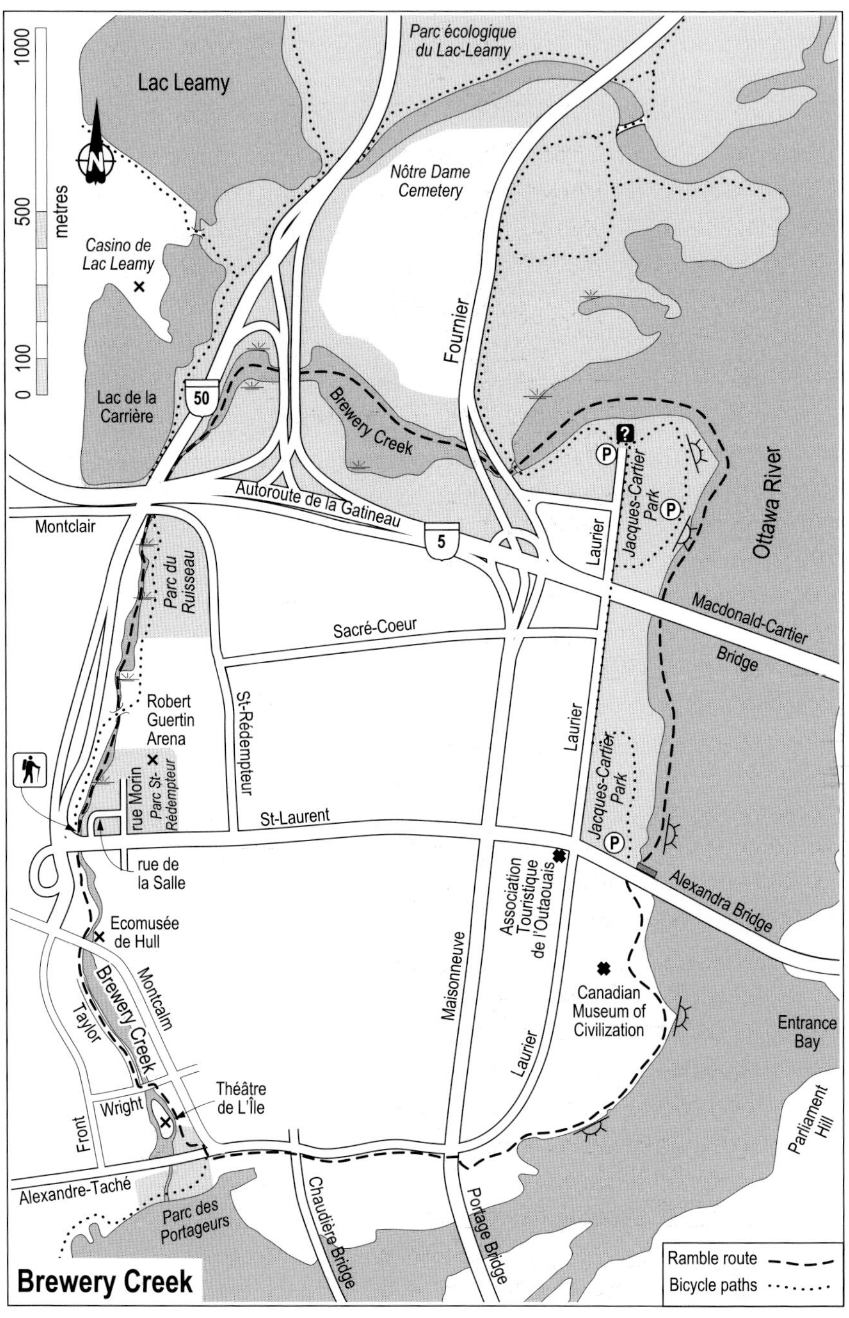

Brewery Creek, 1898. COA CA-1458.

You may not know Brewery Creek (Ruisseau de la Brasserie), which meanders its way northeast of its junction with the Ottawa, creating an island of old Hull. The creek lies immediately above the Chaudière Falls where rue Montcalm forms a T-intersection with Boulevard Alexandre-Taché at the Ottawa River. The creek was variously called Mill Creek and then Brigham's Creek, but the name Brewery Creek stuck after Andrew Leamy built his brewery near the Montcalm Street Bridge. All these names echo the creek's industrial use. The parks that define its start and termination immortalize the days of Paleo-Indian traders, explorers, Jesuits, and all others who portaged around the Chaudière Falls: Parc des Portageurs defines its western mouth, while Jacques Cartier Park is found at its eastern termination, where it rejoins the Ottawa.

You could not find a more historic circuit "paddle" of the Ottawa River than along this modest waterway. In fact, its human history starts in the mists of Paleo-Indian times. T.W. Edwin Sowter was an author and archaeologist who was born in Aylmer in 1860, fifteen years prior to the founding of the City of Hull. Sowter published his research in *Algonkin and Huron Occupation of the Ottawa Valley*. In his book, he suggests that

McKay's Mills, Rideau Falls.
Watercolour by Charles Erskine Ford, October 1851. C-116463.

natives paddled and portaged Brewery Creek as a natural bypass to the Chaudière Falls. His argument appears to make sense, particularly because archaeologists have unearthed pottery and other items from sites excavated alongside Leamy Lake, Jacques Cartier Park, and in an ossuary located on the site where the Canadian Museum of Civilization was built.

Champlain's journal tells us that he and his Algonquin guides portaged the Chaudière Falls when he paddled up to Allumettes Island in 1613. Therefore, Champlain walked sections of the very route you will explore! Moreover, nearly two hundred years after Champlain's time, Philemon Wright and his Massachusetts homesteaders settled along the creek in 1800. Six years later, Wright owned not just the land along it, but also the creek bed. Late historian and author Diane Aldred tells us that this calm-looking waterway was important to Wright's timber business:

> After [Philemon's] death in 1839, the rights to the west half of the creek were inherited by Tiberius Wright, and to the east half by Ruggles. Although it was not a fully navigable waterway, except at times of high water, the creek could be used for floating wood to the main river, and was, therefore, of interest to the lumbering Wrights. A towpath on the east bank allowed space for horses to pull rafts of timber through the shallow water.[52]

Later, industrialist E.B. Eddy purchased Ruggles' rights to the eastern side of the creek. Eddy had arrived in Bytown in 1851, whereupon he started a match factory that launched him into the lumber business. Buildings belonging to his complex still line the northern channel of the Ottawa River at the eastern edge of Parc des Portageurs and Brewery Creek.

Because of the rapids, mills sprang up. One of the first, a sawmill, belonged to Dr. Charles E. Graham, who resided on the east side of the creek at Montcalm. He sold his property to the City of Hull in 1888 and in 1904 the city purchased the west bank from the heirs of Tiberius Wright.[53]

Raft of J.R. Booth on Ottawa River with sleeping cabins, n.d. COA CA-0076.

In addition to a cluster of mills, Brewery Creek was a source of potable water for the developing city of Hull. In the same year that Dr. Graham sold his property to the city — and indeed probably because of it — the city built the first pump house immediately north of what is now the Montcalm Street Bridge. Here too we would have found Leamy's brewery as well as an axe factory. But the Montcalm pump house was soon inadequate for the city's requirements. In 1902, Hull's second water pumping station was built on an island in the middle of the mouth of Brewery Creek. Because the city's requirements outgrew this station's capacity, a filtration plant was built, which opened in 1968, and the island's pump house closed. Thankfully, heritage activists and culture enthusiasts recognized its value and in 1971 the handsome pump house was reborn as the Théatre de l'Île, a still-popular French-language playhouse.

View looking east from Hurdman's Mills along Bridge Street, Hull, Québec, October 1890.
Photo: William James Topley. NAC PA-27214.

Meanwhile, the creek's westernmost confluence with the Ottawa River also served as an industrial site on land now graced by Jacques Cartier Park. James and Allen Gilmour came to Bytown from Montréal in the early 1840s. In the period 1841 to 1853 they owned timber rights along the Gatineau River, and were felling trees as well as supplying goods for the lumber shanties — itself a profitable business. The brothers, along with partner John Hughson, purchased land at the mouth of Brewery Creek in 1874 and erected a large mill and office in 1893. Michael Davidson writes,

> In the mill, logs clamped to carriages would be forced by steam engines against high speed saw blades. The cut lumber was carried by horse drawn railcars and stacked over the area of the modern Jacques Cartier Park. It would be loaded onto barges from either the Hull wharf, then known as the ship yards, or their own wharf at the bottom of Brewery Creek.[54]

Canada Atlantic Railway freight yards, Chaudière District, Hull, June 1893. NAC PA-27927.

The fire that swept through Hull in April 1900 destroyed over two million board feet of the Gilmour and Hughson Company's lumber. Imagine the sight of the stacks of boards bordering the Ottawa at this period. In your mind's eye, picture the northern shoreline of the Ottawa — present-day Gatineau —totally obscured by giant piles of sawn lumber! After the fire, practically all of Hull was razed and not a single stack escaped the flames.

All of which returns us to the subject of water, the force that has shaped this region and so influenced its industry and inhabitants. Not only were residents of the twin cities of Ottawa/Hull eager for potable drinking water and power for their mills and other enterprises, they were also desirous of a constant, rapid source of water to fight fires. Just as ardently, they lobbied their respective municipal authorities, insisting that never again should stacks of timber be piled upon the riverbanks within either city.

Concerned citizens rallied and lobbied their political leaders, and eventually altered the course of development. Mills were moved beyond the city limits where unsightly, unsafe stacks were considered a lesser hazard. In 1933 similar public protests encouraged the Federal District Commission into purchasing the industrial lands at the confluence of Brewery Creek and Ottawa River. The Commission transformed the unsightly sprawl into Jacques Cartier Park.

But Brewery Creek was not simply an industrialist's haven. Remember the Scott home, built upon the western embankment of the creek? Although this mansion is by far the most stately home overlooking the watercourse, behind it, along quiet Taylor Street (the road directly overlooking the Théatre de l'Île and Brewery Creek immediately north of the Scott mansion), is a stretch of beautiful old homes. They are part of a piece of land called the "Village of Argentine," a name whose origin has been lost according to members of the L'Association du patrimoine du Ruisseau (Brewery Creek Heritage Association) to whom I spoke.[55] Around 1875, the enclave started to be known as "Eddyville." This appellation, which was used until the 1950s, appears more logical because of all the Eddy employees who lived in the vicinity. A decade later, in the 1960s, it was also called "Little Portugal" due to an influx of immigrants from that country. By 2003, however, I was told that there were possibly two or three Portuguese families left in this area; most have moved "on-island" — that is, further east, into downtown Gatineau.

Like the Scott mansion, most of the homes here were spared destruction in the 1900 fire. Baker William Feely however, lost his home, which was located where the homes at 6, 7, and 10 Wright Street are found. All of the buildings in this area stand on land originally deeded to Philemon Wright, which was sold in 1871 for housing development to such entrepreneurs as John Hanson, who owned the Hanson wool mill downstream. By 1881 there were almost thirty families dwelling in the Village of Argentine. One hundred years later, a new influx of residents moved in; professional and younger couples purchased the then-deteriorating homes, and started the gentrification process. Today the little enclave on Front and Taylor streets is a testament to their commitment to the heritage of old Hull, and it is they who now form the L'Association du patrimoine du Ruisseau.

Victoria Island, Ottawa, Ontario, n.d. (but prior to the Department of Public Work's construction of the Portage Bridge in 1973). Collection: Department of the Interior. NAC PA-43953.

Today, as we gaze upon Brewery Creek, it is almost impossible to imagine how this innocuous-looking branch of the Ottawa could possibly have been such a prosperous industrial site. Sure, the former functions and dates of some buildings — like the Théatre and the Ecomuseum — are carved on their facades jog our memories. But the parklands and homes now standing along the channel hide this quiet little creek's significant human history.

NATURAL HISTORY

Although we all know that Ottawa/Gatineau is blessed with many "secret" places to view wildlife, Brewery Creek remains unknown to most residents who don't even know it exists! Improbably, this little waterway remains a wildlife haven.

As you will discover while paddling, the creek is extremely shallow. This gives you ample opportunity to see how forces of geology over the millennia can affect the bottom of your canoe! While paddling, it will be impossible for you not to notice the flat sheets of limestone forming the base of the watercourse, which were laid down during the ages of sedimentary deposition, then uplifted and eroded to their present state.

Author exploring nature in the heart of the city on Brewery Creek.
Photo: E. Fletcher, 2002.

Bird watching is superb along the creek: the Ecomuseum of the Outaouais has a waterfowl feeding station located behind it, along with bird identification posters so it's a good place to start a birding trip. In fact, the creek has long been associated with birds. During 1944-45 Malcolm MacDonald served as British High Commissioner. A keen amateur ornithologist, he took particular pleasure in paddling across the Ottawa River in his canoe and slipping into the shelter of Brewery Creek. Surely he delighted in letting work stresses slip away while he paddled, observed, and took careful records of the birds he discovered here. His book, *Birds of Brewery Creek*, was published in 1947. It describes species that still visit the watercourse throughout the year. Let's dip into this journal, to read what birds he found in early May 1945:

> The forerunner of the swarms of May migrants was that charming little creature, the Ruby-crowned Kinglet. Early on the morning of the 3rd a flock of them appeared with the first rays of sunshine following several cloudy days. Except for the tiny Hummingbirds and two species of Wrens, the Kinglets are the smallest birds to be seen in Canada. There are two distinct species, the Ruby-crowned and the Golden-crowned. Each measures about four inches long, nearly half of which consists of tail ... The flock of Ruby-crowns stayed for only one day and then passed onwards to the coniferous forests where they nest. None of their Golden-crowned cousins looked in at the creek this spring, but they appeared on their return journey in the autumn.[56]

MacDonald spent much time along the estuary of Brewery Creek near today's Jacques Cartier Park, and he gives us a clear picture of the city:

> Nearby is a street of houses with street-cars and other noisy traffic. But the estuary of the creek itself is untroubled by these sights and sounds of a modern city's sophistication. The place has been mercifully by-passed by civilization and Nature there remains undisturbed. Amongst its woodland trees stand two or three small cottages inhabited by men who tend the log-rafts moored off shore in summer. Elsewhere on the bank is an abandoned sawmill consisting of an empty shed, a broken-down chute and the gaunt ruin of a tall chimney. Not far away are some oil tanks. Otherwise the estuary is untamed.[57]

Today, when we paddle through the estuary — or simply wander its shores by bicycle or on foot — we can still detect the foundations of the sawmill, but the other manifestations of human history are mostly gone. Nonetheless, most species MacDonald describes still pass by or are residents.

On a chilly November day in 2002, my husband Eric and I were thrilled to discover a flock of wood ducks. Though we attempted to drift closer, these shy birds soon flew off, declining to be photographed! That very cold day, there was a fluffed-up great blue heron perched in the reeds near Robert Guertin Arena, and Vs of Canada geese honked past, overhead.

What other birds are here? MacDonald's book reveals commoners such as the red-winged blackbird, northern flicker, and the grackle. He mentions less-common but still frequently seen species such as Baltimore orioles, yellow warblers, and killdeers, and remarks upon rare sightings, like this one, spotted on a September excursion:

> I continued to stare through my field-glasses at the trim body, slender neck, small heed and rapier-like bill of the delightful creature in front of me. It was a Northern Phalarope. ... Phalaropes have the forms of waders, but they are more than waders. They are also swimmers. Mr. Taverner says that they are "the only shore birds that habitually swim.[58]

Even in winter the creek offers us much, if we only have eyes to look for and interpret nature's clues. Search for paw prints in the snow. Can you tell the difference between a dog's print and a wild fox? Look for size of print, size of stride (length between the prints), and look for how the print "tracks." If it meanders "crazily" it could be a well-fed dog out on an amble, or a fox following the scent of a vole, mouse, or rabbit.

Look for wing prints in the snow, perhaps left by a blue jay that swept down to the snow to pick up a seed. Or perhaps the imprint is of a larger wingspan, such as that of a ruffed grouse. These birds burrow beneath the snow to stay warm and protected from predators such as red fox. When frightened, the grouse literally bursts out of the snow.

Common urban denizens such as muskrat, beaver, raccoon, skunk, and both red and black squirrels can be seen here. Watch for them all, whatever the season and remember: this is a paradise within the city. Please keep your dog on its leash, so it doesn't startle the animals that call Brewery Creek their home.

BEFORE YOU GO ON THE RAMBLE

Why go? Did you realize that the former city of Hull is an island? Brewery Creek was a former industrial site that serves today as a little-known canoe route through the heart of Gatineau. Whether you paddle, bike, or walk this ramble, you'll discover a surprising refuge for wildlife that's well worth your protection and enjoyment.

Distance: Almost 4 km of paddling plus 3 km of cycling or walking.

Modes of exploration: By canoe or kayak, bike, or on foot.

Getting there: Approximately 4 km long, Brewery Creek starts west of the Eddy mills on the Ottawa River and wends its way east through urban Gatineau, emerging in a broad estuary directly east of the mouth of the Gatineau, at Parc Jacques Cartier park. Start at the Robert Guertin Arena, located at rue St. Redempteur, corner rue Allard (north of Boulevard St-Laurent) in Gatineau (sector Old Hull).

Facilities: None at the trailhead but later on there is the Canadian Museum of Civilization and the Outaouais Tourism Office.

Of special note: Wildlife abounds here, as, unfortunately, does a troubling amount of garbage alongside the creek. Don't disturb the former, but consider removing some of the refuse if you want. Do not forget your binoculars and camera. If you're paddling, do remember that the creek is very shallow, so plan to do this trip when there is plenty of water coursing through it. (**Hint:** Ask staff at Tourisme Outaouais or City of Gatineau for draining/flooding times.) I have described this ramble as a very adventurous circuit route, but it only works as such if you put your bikes in your canoe and do a combination adventure as my husband Eric and I did. Note that if you follow in our paddle strokes, you must ask permission to tie your canoe at the Hull Marina. Otherwise, bike along the pathways that more-or-less hug the shoreline of the creek and then the Ottawa River. Whatever creative mix you use, this fun and highly unusual ramble along Brewery Creek simply shouldn't be missed.

Author paddling with mountain bikes — for a fun way of exploring Brewery Creek. Photo: E. Fletcher, 2002.

THE RAMBLE

Park at or near **Robert Guertin Arena** located off rue St. Redempteur on rue Allard (north of Boulevard St-Laurent). Portage your canoe to the creek immediately west of the arena and if you are doing what we did, place your bikes securely in the canoe. Push off downstream. Throughout the paddle, the person in the bow needs to be vigilant regarding water depth as Brewery Creek is shallow, at times being impassable. (Wear shorts or pants and shoes you don't mind getting wet, because you may need to get out and help nudge your canoe through the shallows.)

Northeast of the arena, the creek eventually wends its way to the Gatineau River estuary where it joins the Ottawa River. However, just beyond your put-in area at the bridge, the watercourse divides into a network of shallow channels. You'll have to select which one to try, and water levels will vary. As you go, keep your eyes peeled for heron standing statuesquely by the water's edge. Often they won't mind your presence if you are quiet, which offers ample opportunity for photography. Reeds, sedges, and grasses grow densely throughout the watercourse, providing hummocky islands for your feet should you have to rescue your canoe from the shallows. Step carefully and wisely; the trickiness of the first canoeing segment is lessened when the creek broadens.

It does this very soon; suddenly you're beyond the networked little watercourses, into a broad, shallow channel. Ahead of you is the overpass of the **Autoroute de la Gatineau** (to Highways 148, and 5). With it in view, pause a moment and look about you. Where shrubs and grasses grow along Brewery Creek these days, there used to be a community called "Creekside" from the mid-1920s through to the 1960s. Raymond Jolicoeur, City of Gatineau guide and historian, told me he remembers Creekside as Hull's version of a "favelas," or slum. The cluster of shack-like homes here had no running water or plumbing. They were all demolished and residents relocated in the mid-sixties, and so it is that when you paddle past today you won't discover any hint of Creekside.

Now you pass beneath the **Autoroute de la Gatineau**, one of the peculiar highlights of this ramble, and one that is missed if you choose to bicycle or walk this ramble. Paddling alongside the giant piers of concrete that are crowded by cattails, and with the reverberation of zooming traffic overhead, creates a truly bizarre urban canoescape. How utterly, utterly different this creek would have been thousands of years ago when native tribes used it to bypass the Chaudière! Still further ahead of you and on your left you'll spy the tall **Hilton Hotel**, located on **Leamy Lake**, beside the **Casino de Hull**. (We attempted to find one, but there is no water access to Leamy Lake from here.)

With the noise and concrete of the urban environment, you may be unprepared for the beauty awaiting you. On the east side of the overpass you emerge into such complete solitude and peace that the juxtaposition is startling. Dense stands of red and silver maple grow along the shoreline. This is a forested wetland habitat, characterized by soils that are wet throughout the year. If you paddle to shore and attempt to alight, you'll notice how mucky the soil is. Like much of Petrie Island (see Petrie Island ramble) the estuarine region you are now entering is flooded every spring. Therefore, it is a nutrient-rich habitat that is particularly sensitive to pollutants.

Before long, the broad channel narrows and you will scoot underneath another overpass, this time you'll paddle beneath the **Autoroute l'Outaouais**, (Highways 148, 50) heading east to Gatineau River, Buckingham, and beyond the NCR towards Montebello and eventually Montréal.

Brewery Creek broadens yet again. You see man-made "islands" of rubble used in logging days to assist in the management of logs floating downstream to the Gilmour and Hughson's mills at the confluence with the Ottawa. This body of water is where I saw most of the wood ducks, congregating for their migration south that chilly early November day. A bay extends to the southwest which you can explore, watching all the while for well-camouflaged species such as American bittern, or goldeneye in season. Watch, too, for muskrat and beaver lodges, and for the chewed trunks of trees left behind by our national rodent.

To your east there is a small neighbourhood community as well as the waterfront **Parc Desjardins** on an island created by Brewery Creek and the outflow of **Lac Leamy**. (Also nearby is **Nôtre Dame Cemetery**, in which notables such as Alexandre Taché, after whom Taché Boulevard is named, are buried.) This island is also part of the **Parc écologique du Lac Leamy** where archaeological digs were conducted in cooperation with Kitigan Zibi Anishinabeg Algonquin who live near Maniwaki. The next overpass is **Boulevard Fournier**. Beneath it, examine the western shore on your left. Through the trees you will be able to glimpse the foundation of an 1893 **sawmill** complex that once stood here.

The channel widens and you paddle into the **Ottawa River,** temporarily saying goodbye to Brewery Creek. Before you do, bundle up: the river forms an effective funnel here, so it can be suddenly quite cold or windy. Be cautious and stay close to shore. Whereas the current has so far been negligible, here you'll feel the pull of the current of this mighty river.

Immediately across from you is the curtain of the **Rideau Falls,** where in 1907 there was a spectacular conflagration during which the Edwards' mill complex was consumed by fire**.** Downstream (east) of it find **24 Sussex Drive**, residence of the prime minister of Canada. The building between them is the **French Embassy**, built on the former site of Isaac MacTaggart's distillery. To the right of the falls, upstream, is the former **City Hall**, now federal government buildings, and further west you'll recognize the **Macdonald-Cartier Bridge**.

Now that you've oriented yourself, turn right and paddle upstream, staying close to shore. Before you reach the bridge, look to your immediate right to see the green, grassy slopes of **Parc Jacques Cartier.** There are several areas here where you can land your canoe. Pull it onshore to stretch your legs, enjoy a picnic, or go on a short stroll. You can walk up the hillside into the park and its playing fields, veering generally to your right. Ahead of you, look for a stone building.

This is the **Gilmour and Hughson company head office** built in 1893 by stonemason Richard Lester. Look closely at the stones and you'll find fossils embedded in some of them. Actually, the more you look at this building the odder it seems: there are carvings to be seen, and whereas some of the stones are milled flat, others are rough-surfaced. Did Mr. Lester find inexpensive components such as the smooth stone lintels of the windows, and incorporate them higgledy-piggledy into this squat-looking office?

Weird carvings adorn the Gilmour and Hughson office.
Photo: E. Fletcher, 2002.

Behind it is the bicycle path. If you want to try descending to the waterfront (actually Brewery Creek here to the east) do so along one of the many casual footpaths. Amid the shrubbery and trees you might be able to find the **foundation wall** you saw while paddling up the creek in your canoe. Beyond the foundations find a pile of concrete anchors used to stabilize the logs awaiting their turn at the steam-powered sawmill.

Return to your canoe. While you paddle westwards along this shoreline, look for other remnants from the days of logging and milling, such as pieces of sturdy iron chain, or giant "eye hooks" upon which boats or logs were secured. Although less common nowadays, watch out for "deadheads" or logs floating just beneath the surface of the river.

Continue paddling, passing beneath the **MacDonald-Cartier Bridge**, whose traffic makes a surreal whirring mechanical noise on the open metalwork of the roadway — quite a contrast to the honking of Canada Geese you might have heard! You soon see the marina ahead of you, where you can probably tie up your canoe (ask permission before leaving it here, as I did). The marina lies below the gracious looking **Lady Alexandra (or Interprovincial) Bridge**. When built in 1900 to carry the train bound to Wakefield, Alcove and Maniwaki, it was the longest steel cantilever bridge in the world.

You now have a decision to make: you can certainly paddle further upstream if you wish, but be sure you have figured out where you can safely haul your canoe out of the water or you tie it up at your own risk. If you are biking from here as we did (or walking), then continue as described below.

Proceed up the paved roadway to **rue Laurier** and turn left, crossing to the south side of the street. At the corner of rue St. Laurent find the office of **Tourisme Outaouais**, the West Québec tourism association that also has a small shop selling local artisans works. Enter here if you wish to find more information about Gatineau and the NCR. There are washrooms, and helpful bilingual staff who can answer questions, and provide brochures and maps of the region.

Return to the south side of rue Laurier. Between the bridge and the 1989 **Canadian Museum of Civilization** find the paved combination bicycle and walking path that hugs the Ottawa River and cycle down here. Designed by Douglas Cardinal, the museum's curvilinear structure symbolizes the current and rapids of the waterway. There are many park benches along this embankment, from which you can gaze at the Entrance Bay locks of the Rideau Canal (see Rideau Canal ramble), and the back of Parliament Hill. Continue past several artworks, including **totem poles** and, to the rear and west of the museum, a sinuous Oriental **dragon**.

The nearby free-standing dishevelled-looking "tower" was once the **digester tower** of the old E.B. Eddy plant. This entire waterfront used to be peppered with the mills, factories, and outbuildings of Eddy's pulp and paper ventures, which have their modern counterpart in the

Scott Paper plant. After the 1900 fire, the industry of the twin cities of Hull and Ottawa shifted from sawn lumber to pulp and paper. Eddy and Booth were the two main industrialists at the Chaudière and in 1902 approximately 2,000 people in Hull alone were employed in E. B. Eddy's plants.[59]

Next stop along the route is the **Portage Bridge,** built in the early 1970s. The cycle path stops abruptly here: cross at the lights and proceed west along **Boulevard Alexandre-Taché** where you'll pass alongside the E.B. Eddy factory. Immediately past the traffic lights at rue Montcalm, turn left into **Parc des Portageurs** through some iron gates.

Cycle to the water's edge. A sculpture of two wolves and the hull of a boat grace the shoreline, through which you can see the city of Ottawa. In the foreground is the start of the **Chaudière Falls**. Conjure the image of how this ragged falls must have looked when unchecked! As well, imagine yourself in Champlain's company of Algonquin guides, watching as the natives performed their *tabagie* ceremony, during which they offered tobacco to the river spirits. Here you are standing in one of Canada's most historic spots, where Paleo-Indian traders, Étienne Brûlé and other French explorers, the Black Robes, coureurs-du-bois, and others passed on their voyages of discovery. Cycle still further west until you come to a little footbridge spanning Brewery Creek. A sign explains about the fire of 1900 and the industry that once lined the creek here.

Turn around and cycle back to rue Montcalm and Boulevard Alexandre Taché; cross at the lights and stay left, cycling up the little paved path through the little park. This green space was originally part of Philemon Wright's first property, and the grand house on the west side of Brewery Creek is where he built his first mansion in 1810, which was destroyed by fire in 1849. The present Gothic cut limestone residence was built in the 1860s for Richard Scott.

Cycle down to the little bridge that takes you to the **Théatre de l'Île**, originally the city of Hull's second water pumping station which found a new life in 1971 as Hull's French language theatre.

Return to the east side of Brewery Creek and cycle north to **Pont Wright** that spans the creek to its west embankment. Here the creek takes on a splendid look: old-fashioned looking lamp posts line both side of what has now become a grand-looking canal at this point. Once on the far (west) side, turn right to cycle north on **rue Taylor**. The little road was named in 1952 after a "giant of a man," J.C.F. Taylor who held various positions at E.B. Eddy Company, finally becoming its vice-president. His home was **6 rue Wright**.

The mostly clapboard, gentrified homes along the west side of Brewery Creek were all part of the land owned first by Philemon Wright and subsequently by his son Tiberius. Several of the properties along here and Front Street (the street parallel to Taylor, immediately to its west) were owned by William Feely, a butcher who invested in residential buildings. He owned the land extending from Taylor to Front, bounded on the north by the Presbyterian church. Several of his properties burned during the fire of 1900, with the exception of number 8 Wright Street, which was spared.

Number **18 rue Taylor** was built between 1871 and 1888, while neighbouring **number 16** dates from 1872. The latter is where Sabina Broadhead and her brother John William Broadhead lived. Evidently she caught the eye of neighbour Thomas H. Birk who lived at number 18, and they were married on 6 February 1911. **Number 30 Taylor** was built by William Plaxton, a contractor, in 1875. A year later he left Hull to live in Prince Albert, NWT, leaving the property to his godson, who was the same William Feely mentioned above.

This is the area of old Hull called "Village of Argentine," where most residents were employees of E.B. Eddy. Cycle to the end of Taylor and head left on **rue Montcalm** and left again on **rue Front** so you can view one of the old factories bordering onto Brewery Creek. Its brick façade still bears the original name: **Hanson Hosiery Mills**. It was founded in 1878 by New Englander John Hanson, who rebuilt after the original factory perished in the 1900 fire. Hanson Hosiery was the second largest employer after E.B. Eddy, in Hull. In the 1950s it was one of the first factories of its kind to incorporate nylon into its woollens: at the time nylon was a relatively new fibre developed during WW II. Hanson Hosiery closed in 1975, but in 2002 the building reopened. Now known as **La Filature, Inc.**, it is an artist-operated centre for the production of visual and media arts.

Return to Montcalm and rejoin the bike path you left, at the extension of rue Taylor. Now pass beneath the **Montcalm Bridge** which has a small section of the Eiffel Tower incorporated into in its fanciful decorations. Head north but first pause to note the **Ecomusée de Hull,** opposite you. (You can cross Montcalm Bridge and turn left on rue Papineau if you wish to visit the museum.) This old stone building was the 1902 **Château d'Eau**. It supplied Hull with drinking water and generated electricity for the city's street lamps. Here, at one time, the city's only water fountain beautified the property.

Otherwise, continue cycling north on the west side of Brewery Creek, watching for the next bridge, the **Boulevard St-Laurent overpass**. This marks the start of our ramble. On its far side note the dirt track up the embankment: push your bike up here, cycle across the overpass, then return to your vehicle, which you parked in the Robert Guertin Arena. Now you must return to the Marina, where you can retrieve your canoe.

Your tour of one of the most significant water routes of the capital region is now concluded: you have cycled, walked, and paddled a circuit travelled by adventurers for some 8,000 years.

OTHER PLACES OF INTEREST

The **Ecomusée de Hull** is dedicated to revealing the mysteries of the Outaouais Region's natural and industrial environment. "Eco" derives from a Greek word, "oikos," meaning "house." The museum itself is in the old water pumping station immediately north of the Montcalm Bridge. Because the NCR is a geologically faulted zone, the museum's simulated earthquake can be particularly interesting, especially for children. At the back of the museum is a bird feeding station where many species of songbirds and waterfowl gather.

Bicycle path connections abound here. A look at any good map will show the extent of the network, which goes west to Aylmer and beyond that village, to the Pontiac region of West Québec (see Ottawa River Loop ramble). Yet another path connects west and then north to Gatineau Park, along Promenade du Lac-des-Fées, while if you take the eastern bike path along Jacques Cartier Park, you can cycle north through Ironsides (see Gatineau River ramble) to Gatineau Park (see Gatineau Park ramble). As can be seen on our map, using the bicycle path to circumnavigate Brewery Creek takes you along the creek, but continues east into Parc écologique du Lac-Leamy before returning along rue Fournier to cross the creek into Jacques-Cartier Park.

Lac Leamy and the Gatineau River estuary: Canoeists and kayakers can use this ramble as a start to many happy hours of paddling. Get yourself a large-scale topographical map of the Gatineau River estuary so you can plan other adventures. You can paddle to Lac Leamy if you briefly slip downstream of the confluence of Brewery Creek and the Ottawa River, and do a loop, reconnecting to the Gatineau River. Just remember, please, that you will need to paddle back upstream, up the Ottawa River, where currents and cold winds can be challenging.

Kettle Island is a low-lying forested island wetlands that you can access by canoe from here, from Parc de la Baie, or from the Rockcliffe park area. It is downstream of the Gatineau River, opposite the National Aviation Museum.

At Montclair, you paddle Brewery Creek under the overpass, yet you are above the bicycle path. Photo: E. Fletcher, 2002.

Aylmer Road

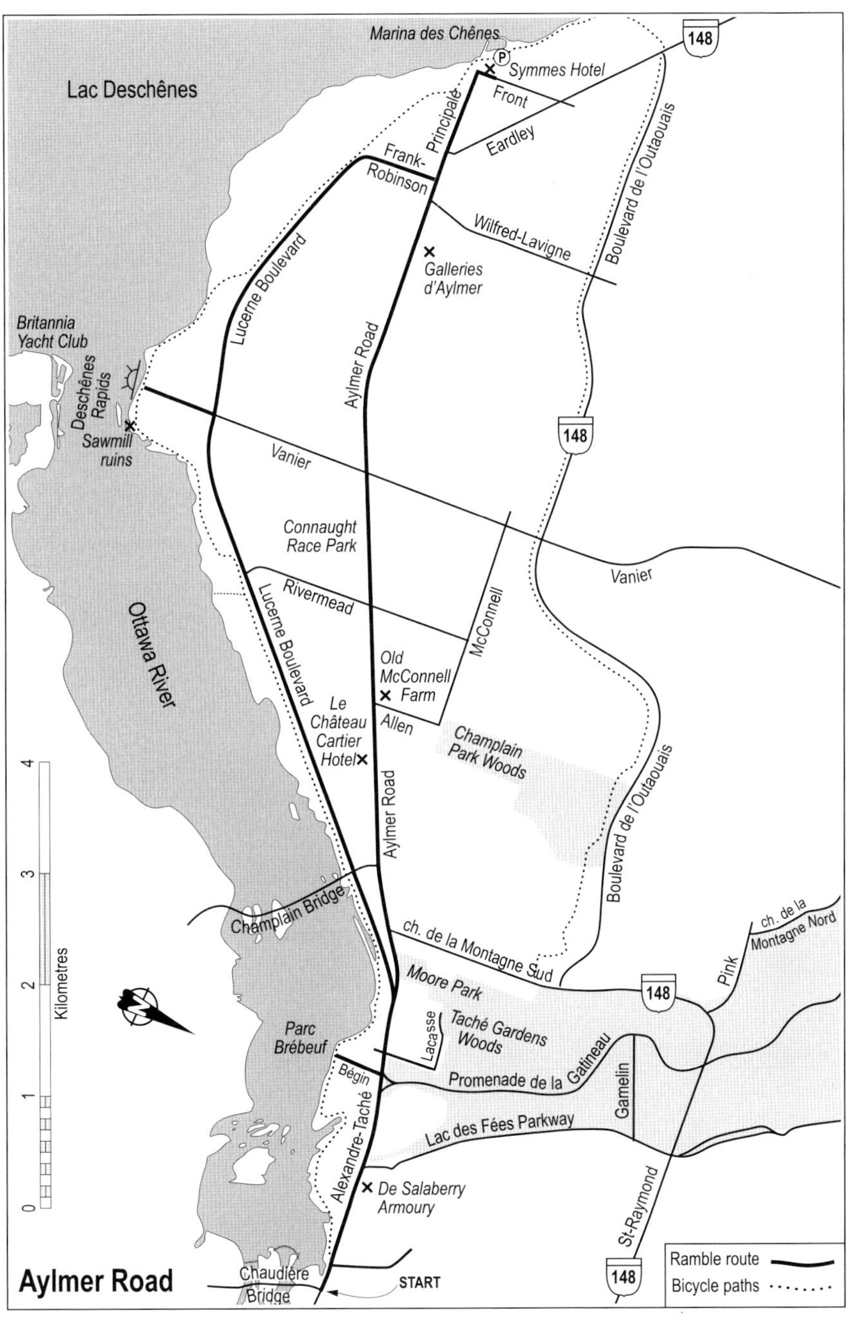

Marina des Chênes
Lac Deschênes
Symmes Hotel
148
Front
Principale
Eardley
Frank-
Robinson
Wilfred-Lavigne
Boulevard de l'Outaouais
Galleries
d'Aylmer
Lucerne Boulevard
Britannia
Yacht Club
Deschênes
Rapids
Sawmill
ruins
Aylmer Road
Vanier
Connaught
Race Park
Rivermead
Lucerne Boulevard
McConnell
Ottawa River
Old
McConnell
Farm
Le
Château
Cartier
Hotel
Allen
Champlain
Park Woods
Kilometres
0
1
2
3
4
Champlain Bridge
ch. de la Montagne Sud
Moore Park
Pink
ch. de la
Montagne Nord
Parc
Brébeuf
Lacasse
Taché Gardens
Woods
Bégin
Promenade de la Gatineau
Gamelin
Alexandre-Taché
Lac des Fées Parkway
De Salaberry
Armoury
St-Raymond
Aylmer Road
Chaudière
Bridge
START
Ramble route
Bicycle paths

Mystery at the Wake of Robert Conroy

The night that Thomas D'Arcy McGee was murdered on Ottawa's Sparks Street, 7 April 1868, just happened to be the first night of the wake of Robert Conroy, lumberman and entrepreneur of old Aylmer village. Everyone who was anyone attended the wake, which was held at the British Hotel, one of Conroy's properties that you can still see on rue Principale in the old part of the village.

At two o'clock in the morning, as the mourners chatted, drank, and ate in the finest of wake traditions, a knock was heard at the door. Folks looked about: who could that possibly be? Mary, Robert's widow, glanced at her sons, one of whom stepped to the door, opening it wide.

It was a nasty night, being wild and stormy outside. Three cloaked figures stood on the doorstep: strangers, all. Thinking they were business associates of his father, the son welcomed them into the cheery drawing room. The three claimed they wanted to pay their respects to the widow, the family, and the deceased. Only thing was, no one recognized them. They hung about for a while, yet hardly spoke to a soul, preferring to keep to themselves. Some said they glanced at the hour more than once. At half-past three they donned their cloaks and asked for their horses to be fetched from the stable, where the Conroys had ordered them watered and fed, as was the custom of good hosts. Off the three vanished, into the darkness.

Who were these strangers? No one knows. But folks said they were the real murderers of Thomas D'Arcy McGee. Why else would they have fretted over the time, except to be noticed, and to establish an alibi for murder?

Later, Patrick Whelan, an Irishman was hanged from the neck until he was dead for the murder of Thomas D'Arcy McGee. Did these three men watch him swing? Nobody knows ... and the identity of the cloaked strangers at the wake of Robert Conroy remains a true Ottawa Valley mystery.

After the amalgamation of Hull, Aylmer, and the other cities and villages into the mega-city of Gatineau on 1 January 2001, the village of Aylmer lost the uniqueness of its name. However, the stroke of a pen cannot wipe out a community with such a vibrant past and promising future. Many residents still lobby to preserve the village's name, so time will tell whether amalgamation will erase a peoples' pride of place.

The story of Aylmer is inextricably bound to the imposing rapids along the Ottawa River and to the founder of Wrightsville, Philemon Wright. In the early 1800s, Wright and his family owned much of the land extending west from the confluence of Brewery Creek and the Gatineau River to Aylmer. Even before he successfully floated the first raft of timber downstream to Montréal and Québec City in 1806, Wright realized a portage road was crucial to settlement. A road would serve as a bypass to the three rapids located upstream of the Chaudière Falls: the Petites Chaudière, Remic (named for Isaac Remic who had accompanied Philemon to settle here), and Deschênes rapids.

Late author Diane Aldred's seminal work, *The Aylmer Road, An Illustrated History*, gives a detailed, informative, and often amusing history of the original road. Its construction and then its maintenance posed difficulties, particularly for the earliest settlers who found the muddy, pothole-strewn bush road practically impassable. Aldred explains the system of statute road labour:

> In order to ensure that roads were built, the government instituted a system of statute labour that forced every landowner to "subscribe" a certain number of days of road work each year, according to the amount of land he owned along the route in question. Construction costs were reimbursed but the settler, himself, did not get paid for his time. He could send someone to replace him, but if he failed to honour his subscription, he was fined.[60]

The road was carved from the wilderness in a series of work bees. First, in 1802, a four-mile trail was built to Rivermead Road, followed three years later by an extension to the boat landing on Lac Deschênes. Other roads soon followed. Aldred notes:

> In 1808, a two-mile road was constructed directly south from the Main Road to the Deschênes Rapids, and in 1810, the first two miles of the Brickyard (Mountain) Road were built north of the Main Road, to link up with Samuel Benedict's farm. In creating the Main Road, the settlers had met several of their obligations to the government. They had improved the transportation system on the Ottawa River, they had opened up the country, and they had paved the way for more settlement. The farm lots on either side of the road became some of the most valuable in the district, and were very much in demand by the wave of new settlers that arrived in the district closely upon the heels of the first.[61]

The roadways were still little more than rough-hewn tracks. A year-round road was necessary, and so an all-season Britannia Road was built between 1817 and 1820. Ten years later the route had become the most important artery on the north shore. It linked a string of stately mansions with businesses, schools, churches, and cemeteries from Wrightsville (old Hull) to the marina at Lac Deschênes, and from there, extended northwest to Queen's Park.

The Wrights owned three significant farms on the road. The Columbia Farm lay north of the Chaudière; the Britannia Farm spanned the road where the Champlain Bridge is located; and the Chaudière Farm was at Aylmer, at the junction of today's rue Principale and Eardley, stretching north to the McConnell-Larimée bypass (Highway 148). People paid for the roads by tolls, and toll gates were located at the Britannia Farm as well as at the Union Bridge, built in 1828 to connect the north and south shore of the Ottawa at the Chaudière Falls.

In 1819 another New Englander, Charles Symmes, arrived in Wrightsville and within three years he was managing the Chaudière Farm for his uncle Philemon. Regarding the farm, author Enid Page writes, "ten people lived here — eight men and two women — and the village was made up of one house, two stores, and a hotel." Page notes:

> This small group of pioneers grew crops on 30 acres of cleared land. Most of the food came from the land and survival depended on a good harvest. Men and women worked hard to develop the village which became known as Symmes Landing. Soon several new families joined Charles Symmes and built their homes on lots and streets which he had laid out.[62]

Scenes at Queen's Park, Aylmer, n.d.
Photo: William Morell Harmer. NAC C-22672.

In 1822, Symmes had a falling-out with his uncle, so he purchased the land directly on the waterfront. Nine years later he built the Symmes Inn, which prospered, and was noted as one of the best inns in the Canadas. Symmes was busy: 1831 saw him build the *Lady Colbourne*, the first steamer to ply the Ottawa upriver from the Chaudière (steam ships had been in operation from Ottawa to Montréal since 1821).

River traffic was crucial to commerce, even though it was restricted to seasonal service. But exactly what type of trade goods were sent upriver? The answer lies in the nature of the lumber business at the time. Teams of men and horses headed into the hinterland to overwinter in remote shanties to cut timber. Every man and every horse required food and lodging, and so vast tracts of farmland grew produce that was sold to lumber companies to be shipped upriver. Pork and beans were mainstays of the shanty camps, and horses needed straw for bedding, hay, and oats for feed. How did these supplies get to the shanties?

Steamers were crucial components of a North American water route transportation infrastructure that supported the logging (and other) industries. All sorts of commodities were shipped, including the strong black tea sweetened with sugar, for instance, that sustained many a shantyman. Both these "ordinary" commodities required an international trade network to facilitate their delivery to the remote shanties.

In 1846 John Egan and Joseph Aumond founded the Union Forwarding Company, which operated steamships upriver from Lac Deschênes (Aylmer) to Quyon's Chats Falls. There, a horse railway was soon constructed to portage or "forward" goods across land to the Chats Lake. From here, steamers conveyed goods and passengers further west to Portage du Fort, and beyond. (See Ottawa River and Quyon rambles.) The steamers were extremely popular. "In 1841 the *Lady Colbourne* carried 6,480 passengers and over 1,000 tons of goods and supplies."[63] Passengers soon included tourists who exclaimed at the beauty of the wild river and the raging rapids such as those at Chats Falls at the upper end of Lac Deschênes.

Steamers reigned as the dominant mode of transportation until the railway tracks were laid down in the late 1800s. Rail promised year-round transportation for people and supplies, which effectively sounded the death knell for river traffic. Tracks were laid down on expropriated lands due south of the Britannia Road to create the Québec, Montréal, Ottawa, and Occidental Rail Road. In 1879 the first train pulled into Aylmer. In 1896 the Hull Electric Company lay tracks from Hull to Deschênes in that year, then from Ottawa via the

Hull Electric Railway Company Car #29 at Victoria Park, Aylmer, c. 1900. Collection: Andrew Merrilees. NAC PA-152234.

Interprovincial Bridge (Lady Alexandra Bridge) in 1902. The depot was near the Château Laurier Hotel. Soper and Ahearn, the owners of the Hull Electric Company, had developed Queen's Park, north of Aylmer on the waterfront, into an amusement park that was, of course, serviced by their streetcars. The tracks were transformed into present-day Boulevard Lucerne in the late 1950s.

Today's Britannia Road is sometimes called "The Upper Aylmer Road," to distinguish it from Boulevard Lucerne. The eastern stretch between the Chaudière Falls and Mountain Road (chemin de la Montagne) is Boulevard Alexandre-Taché, while the western section remains the Aylmer Road. It becomes rue Principale (Main Street) where it bisects the historic part of the village of Aylmer, west of Boulevard Wilfrid-Lavigne.

Lac Deschênes at Queen's Park, Aylmer. Collection of Charles Berkeley Powell. NAC C-5349.

NATURAL HISTORY

The waterfront — particularly at Deschênes Rapids — offers a superb opportunity to examine the layers upon layers of sedimentary limestone bedrock lining the north shore of the Ottawa. Look for shells and possibly trilobite fossils.

The shoreline varies, from a forested wetland with black ash and red and silver maples (all of which like to "keep their feet wet") through to the rocky, dry limestone shore at Deschênes and Wychwood where oak, basswood, and white pine flourish. Just west of the Champlain Bridge, for instance, the cycle path passes alongside a woods that is flooded every spring. At the water's edge along here you can observe many birds such as the green-backed and great blue heron and the northern water thrush. In summertime, and particularly in bug season (mid-May through end of June), large flocks of tree swallows swirl about the bridge. In the woods themselves, look for nuthatches, brown creepers, and both downy and hairy woodpeckers.

While exploring the woods and shoreline, it's easy to imagine how extremely difficult road-building was, thanks to the geology of the area. No wonder early settlers hated road work: the limestone bedrock is covered with clay soil in many sections. Because clay retains water, and is not porous like sand or sandy loam soils, the wetland forests mentioned above are kept moist if not mucky, year-round. Drainage poses difficulties to engineers even today, so it's no wonder that settlers found roadwork an endlessly repetitive task. Every spring would bring potholes to fill; and road traffic created further ruts. Come summertime, dust and stones hampered horses and made travel by stagecoach a bumpy and sometimes excruciating ride. Many a time passengers got filthy while pushing conveyances out of mud holes.

BEFORE YOU GO ON THE RAMBLE

Why go? The Aylmer Road started life as a "portage" around the three Ottawa River rapids that connected the earliest settlements of Wrightsville and "Turnpike End" (Aylmer) in the early 1800s. Because of its significance, business men, trades people, and ordinary citizens wanted to live along it. Travelling along it introduces us to heritage homes of distinction and recreational venues, and deposits us at Lac Deschênes, where the Ottawa River forms a broad, pretty "lake."

Distance: Approximately 25 km circuit from the Chaudière Bridge.

Modes of exploration: A drive is described, but this is can be a lovely bicycle ride if you avoid the rush hour (7:30 to 9:30 a.m. or 3:30 to 6:00 p.m.). Take your canoe or kayak to explore Lac Deschênes (you can put in near the marina). The cycle path is 14 km one way from the Chaudière Bridge to the Aylmer marina and Symmes hotel (see map).

Getting there: This ramble starts at the Chaudière Falls, at the corner of Montcalm and Boulevard Alexandre-Taché. Drive west to Aylmer, staying on the Aylmer Road (former Britannia Road) until its culmination at the marina (just beyond rue Front). Park your car here. A walk of old Aylmer passes some of the old buildings in the village.

Facilities: Shopping centres and all facilities exist along this route, including restaurants in Aylmer. At Lac Deschênes there is a marina, large parking lot, and, beyond the marina, a sandy beach and picnic grounds.

Of special note: This ramble is superb for cyclists or walkers because the NCC has created wonderful pathways that, generally speaking, hug the north shore of the Ottawa River, taking you from one community to another. Note that parts of this well-marked route can be flooded in spring. In winter it serves as an excellent cross-country ski trail.

THE RAMBLE

Start at the **Chaudière Falls**, accessed from Ottawa via the **Eddy Street Bridge** where the toll gate once stood at the Union Bridge. This is the heart of the most historic section of old Hull, for Philemon Wright first settled here in 1800, operating a farm called **Columbia Farm** here.

Turn left (west), onto the original route of the Britannia Road, here named **Boulevard Alexandre-Taché**. The tall brown brick office complex, **Les Terrasses de la Chaudière**, is on your right, occupying land once known as **Eddy's Corner**. The office blocks are built where Ezra Butler Eddy's private residence, **Standish Hall,** stood, which was destroyed in the 1900 fire. Eddy rebuilt a year later and, after his death in 1906, the home became a fine dining room and nightclub where some of the world's most famous musicians played, including Louis Armstrong. Standish Hall was demolished in 1951 after another fire.

The cut stone building on the south side of the road is a warehouse, a remnant of **E.B. Eddy's industrial complex** that used to cluster the falls. Travelling west, you immediately cross **Brewery Creek** and bypass **Parc des Portageurs** (see Brewery Creek ramble). (**Note:** If you are doing this ramble by bike, this is where you turn off the Britannia Road and head to Aylmer via the cycle path.)

As you cross Brewery Creek, note the mansion at **28 Taché** on your right-hand side. This is the **Scott home**, built in the 1860s upon land occupied by Philemon Wright's original home in 1810. Although the grounds are still lovely, the building itself was broken up into apartments in the 1960s. At the corner of St. Joseph and Alexandre-Taché boulevards is **de Salaberry Armoury**. Built in 1938, it was named after Colonel Charles de Salaberry who successfully battled the Americans at Chateauguay, Québec, in 1813.

The land rises here: it was always known as **Benedict's Hill**, after the settler David Benedict who built his homestead and operated a large farm here. Unfortunately, we've lost many of the original settlers' names: this neighbourhood was renamed **Val Tétreau**. On the south side of the road is **St. James Cemetery** (the actual church is located in old Hull, now Gatineau), operated by Beechwood Cemetery in Ottawa. Park nearby so you can enter the quiet, usually deserted cemetery where you can pay your respects to Philemon Wright and his wife, Abigail. The **Wright gravestone** is a granite obelisk: the tallest in the cemetery, atop the hill.

Still on the south side and on the top of the rise is the **Université du Québec à Hull**. As you descend the hill look right, to note a cluster of tall evergreens marking the "Y" in the road: this is the entry to **Gatineau Park.** In the midst of these spruce trees, look for a **milestone**, marking the first mile of the Britannia Road on land originally cleared by David Benedict.

Skead House in old Hull (now Gatineau) on Britannia Road. Built by lumber king David Moore in 1865, now a conservatory of music. HSG 01088.

Continue west. Behind a low stone wall and gracious lawn is a Jacobean style stone mansion, the **University of Québec's Music Conservatory**. The building has witnessed many transformations: it started life in 1865 as Riverview, home of David Moore Junior. It then, became Skead House after his daughter, Anna, married lumber king Edward S. Skead. After WW I it became the Homestead Inn nightclub and then, in 1939, started yet another life as the Joie-Ste-Theresa Orphanage.

Driving west you cannot help but notice a vast expanse of meadow where grasses and wildflowers blow on a summer's breeze. Atop the gentle rise is a picturesque white clapboard stable: the 1890s **David Moore horse barn**. Thoroughbred and other horses grazed these pastures until the mid-1980s. It was given to the NCC in 1973 by Mrs. Virginia Moore on condition they operate it as **Moore Park**. Unfortunately, we cannot take our green space legacies for granted. Local resident, tour guide, and historian Raymond Jolicoeur told me in spring of 2003 that the NCC is trying to sell the land for development.

The next home is now the residence of the **Italian Ambassador to Canada**, and because the neo-classical home is set well back from the road with a thick hedge shielding it from view, it cannot seen properly. This is the mansion built by the Blackburn family in 1924. The architect was John Pearson, who re-designed the Centre Block of Parliament Hill after it succumbed to fire in February 1916.

Following the Italian Ambassador's residence is the junction with chemin de la Montagne (Mountain Road), which connects north with the McConnell–Larimée bypass, Highway 148 west. That highway bypasses Aylmer, connecting with the Eardley Road, Luskville, and Quyon. (See Ottawa River, Gatineau Park, and Quyon rambles.)

Continue west, noticing next the sprawling greens of the **Royal Ottawa Golf Club**. This is our fourth example of recreational use of the land along Britannia Road (after Parc des Portageurs, Gatineau Park, and the horse barn at Moore Park). The golf club was first located at Strathcona Park in Ottawa's Sandy Hill. This is its third location and the present multi-gabled, sprawling Tudor-inspired clubhouse was the third constructed here, in 1932, replacing two others that — as you might have guessed by now — succumbed to fire.

On the left-hand side of the road, just before the Champlain Bridge, find a curved red brick complex of buildings resembling "wings." This is the **Jehovah's Witness Kingdom Hall** designed in 1991 by

Douglas Cardinal who is also the architect who designed Gatineau's Canadian Museum of Civilization.

Next is the **Champlain Bridge**, opened in 1928. The Honourable Thomas Ahearn, who served as Chairman of the Federal District Commission (1927–32), and who was also president of the Ottawa Electric Company, paid for the cost of its construction. This bridge would not have been constructed without Honourable Ahearn's intervention — and generosity.

Beyond the next few residences is a subdivision of elegant homes constructed on what were the extensive, exclusive grounds of **The Country Club**. The club started life as a single family home, built in 1907 for John Pipon Ashworth. One year later it became a posh club. In the late 1990s the club's popularity had declined; it closed and its property was subdivided and sold as a luxury housing development. At the time of writing Rockcliffe millionaire Marlen Cowpland is still in the throes of transforming the old clubhouse into her own private space. A large fence surrounds her property and, after seeing her home in Rockcliffe Park, it will be fascinating to see what she decides to do with this expanse of garden.

At **1210 Aylmer Road** find the cut stone **Ruggles Wright House** built in 1857. The house has served as home to many notables including Elbert Soper, son of Warren Soper, who was Thomas Ahearn's business partner. The original home was expanded in 1992: two wings now thrust out to the east and west.

Beyond it is **Le Château Cartier Sheraton Hotel** on the left and the **Club de Golf Chaudière** on the right. The hotel stands on land once used for the Chaudière Golf and Country Club. It was affectionately known as "The Chaud," infamous in the late '60s and '70s as a "watering hole" where young drinkers flocked after the bars in Ottawa closed. But in its heyday in the 1950s, dancers packed the Rose Room to groove to bands such as The Platters and to listen to crooners such as Tony Bennett and Frankie Lane. Time never stands still: in 1992 this châteauesque style hotel was built alongside the golf course. By the way, the end of the golf course marks the boundary of Philemon Wright's Britannia Farm!

Next, on the same side of the road, we come to the **Bellevue Cemetery**, where many early settlers' and residents' graves are found. Park if you can, possibly at the **Old McConnell Farm and Tea Room** (opposite, at the corner of Allen Road). In the cemetery, you will find that many older gravestones have been laid out flat on the ground in the shape of a Maltese Cross.

The **Old McConnell Farm**, opposite, is a charming white clapboard farmhouse with outbuildings, built circa 1850 for William McConnell, son of the pioneer of the same name. It started life as a modest structure, with end-gable chimneys and a central dormer window over the doorway, and a verandah that was rebuilt in 1930. The open farmland behind serves as a vestigial reminder of the farmland that once lay on either side of the road. Now a country shop and excellent little tearoom, it is owned by the NCC.

Proceed to **861 Aylmer,** the **Robert Stewart Jr. house**, notable because of its roofline, which, agreeably and unusually for this part of the world, curves around its eaves. The house was built in 1879 and has a long association with fine horses: Robert Stewart had a racetrack on which his thoroughbreds could often be seen, practising their turns around the oval.

We now pass **Rivermead Road**, once known as McConnell Lane because the brothers William and James McConnell owned property at the river's edge on the east and west sides of the road, respectively. (**Note**: Turn left, south, here if you want to see Rivermead Golf Course: yet another in a long list of greens located along the old Britannia road.)

Continuing west on Aylmer Road, you next pass by a large open space on the left: this is the **Hippodrome**, or **Connaught Race Park Jockey Club and Racetrack**. Diane Aldred tells us:

> The track was constructed by hand and horsepower during the winter of 1912. Six teams of horses side by side did the scraping and levelling of the ground. Dump wagons filled by hand with excess soil were hauled away by horses. Stone lifters winched up the embedded rocks, which were pulled out by two teams of horses and dragged away on stone boats. Six to eight teams pulled the roller that flattened and compacted the track. By June 1919, the track, a members lounge, a large grandstand and stables along the west side of the Rivermead Road had been completed.[64]

The next crossroads and lights mark **Vanier Road**, named after Governor General Georges Vanier. It was previously called Deschênes Road after the community and rapids of the same name. Vanier Road is a key artery of Aylmer that links with other important roads. To the south, it connects to the Deschênes Rapids so you can drive there if you wish to see them. To the north, Vanier Road eventually terminates at Mountain Road, which skirts the base of the Eardley Escarpment, the ridge forming the southern boundary of Gatineau Park (see Gatineau Park ramble).

Beyond the Hippodrome, on the north side of the road find **653 Aylmer Road,** the **Charles Hurdman House**, a stone Regency-style cottage with the same plan as Rivermead House we saw earlier. The Hurdmans were also in the lumbering business by the 1860s, and like E.B. Eddy, J.R. Booth, and the Wrights, were intimately associated with the Chaudière Falls. As well, Charles Hurdman is credited with being the first person to introduce the practice of using teams of horses in the bush, replacing the sturdy but far slower oxen.[65]

Next find **Woodlawn**, also on the north side of the road, another prominent stone home, erected by Richard McConnell. Like many homes along Aylmer Road, it was partially razed by the Great Fire of 1870, which not only devastated farmland and homes on the Ontario side. Sparks jumped the Ottawa River on strong winds and destroyed the homes, lives, and livelihoods of many Aylmer residents. It didn't stop here, either. The flames swept up and over the Eardley Escarpment, consuming settlers' homes up the mountain and as far away as Wakefield.

Continue on, now on the lookout for the Italianate red brick home on the south side of the road at **416 Aylmer Road**, the **Joseph McGoey House** (built in 1871). Delicate iron cresting grace its roof, and cut stone window surrounds further adorn this elegant home, which is situated on a long driveway. McGoey was related by marriage to the Wrights, and was part of Philemon's Gatineau Privilege (see Gatineau River ramble). Unfortunately, as of 2004, a dreary infill development of ordinary looking homes has now destroyed the once-beautiful stately grounds this home commanded. In fact, despite opposition from Aylmer's vigilant citizenry, the open spaces and wooded stretches of the village are under threat. I believe that unless Council "wakes up," that Aylmer's charming balance of heritage homes, greenspace, and new developments will have been irrevocably lost. To paraphrase Canadian songstress Joni Mitchell, will we *ever* learn not to pave paradise?

Just beyond yet another golf course, the **Club de golf Gatineau,** you can find **St. Paul's Cemetery** on the right (north). Next, on either side of **chemin Edey**, are parts of the former grounds of the **Samuel Edey Farm**. Edey was another New Englander, hailing from Vermont, who came here with his brother Moses in 1806.

The next traffic lights mark **Belmont Street** where there was a tollgate (removed in 1915). Farther along, extending to Avenue Frank-Robinson on the north side of rue Principale, was the **Wright Farm**. It's difficult to imagine, but the shopping centre, **Galérie d'Aylmer**, that inhabits the space today was once a bustling farm. Old photos reveal four greenhouses were located here: each was so large that a team of two horses pulling a plough were used to turn up the soil so that flowers could be planted. This was the Wright Floral Company and beyond it was the Wright-O Dairy with its long dairy barns punctuated by clusters of silos. Robert Wright had a private railway built connecting his greenhouses to the railway track along which Boulevard Lucerne now runs. On it he transported the coal that kept his greenhouses heated.

At the crossroads with Wilfrid Lavigne is the **Aylmer Academy, 170 rue Principale**, built on the Heaths family's farm in 1861. The tower and cloche-shaped cap were added in 1912. This was the village's first English-language high school where elocution, Greek, Latin, and the three Rs were taught.

Immediately west of **Boulevard Wilfrid Lavigne** stand two intriguing buildings. The smaller, more modest stone building is **Mount Pleasant**, once the home of John Egan, the lumber baron who founded both Eganville and Quyon, and who was one of the founding partners of the Union Forwarding Company. He built this cut stone residence in 1840, after buying the land from the Wrights. Egan was also Aylmer's first mayor, elected in 1847, who served as Member of Parliament for Ottawa County from 1848 to 1854. Robert Wright purchased Mount Pleasant in 1909 and operated his greenhouses from here. The second stone building immediately behind Mount Pleasant is the immense **Redemptorist Father's Seminary**, built in 1938 by the fathers who also used to farm on their property.

Beyond it, at the major corner of **rue Principale and rue Eardley** are several important sites. First, you will note an immense limestone neo-classical building at **120 rue Principale** on the left-hand side of the street. Today it is a library. However, from 1852 to 1897, it was **Ottawa County's Court House and Jail**, a fact that attests to the stature of Aylmer during those years.

Across the street is a pretty park with houses facing it: this was the **commons**, a feature of many English towns. These "commons" areas made perfect sense, for they were a central area in which farmers could bring goods to market and, on other days, provided a meeting place for citizens. Here in Aylmer the green space is known as the **Market Square**. It was previously called **Symmes Park**, laid out in 1843. The **War Memorial** to Aylmer residents who gave their lives in WW I was erected in 1921 and in 1992 it was updated to honour those who died in later wars.

Park your car so you can examine two residences facing the east side of the commons, on **rue Broad**. **Number 10** is the **Judge McCord home** built in 1842 for William McCord. How convenient it must have been for him to stroll over to the Court House where he worked! As of 2003, the home has been substantively renovated.

The John Murphy House, 12 rue Broad.
Photo: K. Fletcher, 2002.

Next door is the lovingly maintained **John Murphy House, 12 rue Broad**. Murphy was also able to walk to work at the Court House, where he held the position of Governor of the County Jail for twenty-three years. Later on, John Foran lived here; the fellow who built Green Park, the stone residence you saw earlier.

Back in your car, continue west through the traffic lights on rue Principale, looking now for **number 71**, the **British Hotel**. Charles

Symmes did not own the only hotel in town: competitor and businessman Robert Conroy built this stopping place in 1841. (The same Robert Conroy whose wake I describe!) He also operated a stagecoach business, where he conveyed passengers from Hull to Aylmer prior to their venturing further upriver from Symmes Landing. If you return on foot to examine the building's front façade, you can clearly detect the arched doorway where the horses drew their carriages through to the rear courtyard and stables. Today the British Hotel is the oldest hotel in Québec west of Montréal that is still in operation.

Murals on an old bank bring historic Aylmer alive.
Photo: K. Fletcher, 2002.

Diagonally across the street find the **Conroy-Driscoll house** at **72 rue Principale**. It was built in 1845 as Robert Conroy's residence, so from this we can guess he liked to oversee his operations! But he only lived here until 1855 when he moved down the road to Lakeview, which you'll soon see. The residence in front of you now is a fine, symmetrical stone house that, like many others of its era, sports chimneys at either gable end. These were a luxurious feature for their day, because it was difficult to keep homes warm with a single fireplace. From 1881 to 1962 members of the Driscoll family lived here; the first, Alfred Driscoll, was a son-in-law of Robert Conroy.

Next door, find **numbers 66 and 62–64 rue Principale,** which are fascinating examples of worker's homes. **Number 66** is the **Denault-Church** house built in 1870 as a single-family log house for a carpenter Ferrier Denault; the adjacent home is perhaps the first "double" erected in Aylmer, in the same year, built for **William and Hiram Inglis**. The brothers were bakers who baked bread in the western side of the house while living in the eastern half and second storey. Several other modest homes follow these: **number 58** was the **Ephraim Guimond** home built in 1870. Guimond was Charles Symmes' innkeeper prior to starting his own tavern here, eight years after building his home. One year later **Édouard Gravel** built his home at **60 rue Principale**. All of these buildings are constructed of square timber and variously covered with façades of stucco or clapboard, added in later years to "update" the look of what was considered an old-fashioned if not primitive appearance for a home and business.

Across from these find Robert Conroy's second home, **Lakeview**, now looking extremely sad in its life as a tawdry-looking bar at **61 rue Principale**. You can enter the parking lot to get a close-up, unimpeded view of its neo-classical, imposing presence. Greenhouses, stables, laundry, hen house, and other outbuildings once graced the property: all are gone, as are the gracious lawns. In her book *Discover Aylmer's Heritage*, Enid Page invites us to cast our minds back to the Conroy's days here: imagine how Mary McConnell Conroy, Robert's wife, once entertained guests while singing and playing the piano in the drawing room here. Long, long gone are the days when one of their ten children would perhaps recite a poem or two here to an appreciative family gathering.

Many of the fine homes we've seen so far have been constructed of cut stone, which was the most popular building material at the time because of its resistance to fire. But of course, only the wealthy could afford it, because it had to be quarried, cut, and hauled, prior to the structure being built by stonemasons. Brick, although expensive, was less expensive than stone, and when brickyards were developed, homes of distinction were erected from this material. We already viewed the McGoey residence and now, at **53 rue Principale**, let's look at the **George McKay Home.**

McKay operated a sawmill in Quyon (see Chats Falls ramble) before moving here and erecting this very lovely Queen Anne style home in 1903. Typical asymmetrical massing announces this style; also note the very lovely widow's walk, tastefully decorated with wrought iron cresting. Originally the home's grounds were defined by a wrought-iron fence.

Further south is an equally impressive home at **43 rue Principale**, though it is clapboard, not brick. It just goes to show, whatever the building material, a home can be built with beauty and grace, appropriate to its lot. If only modern infill developers could keep this in mind more often! This home was called **Castel Blanc** (White Castle) and was built in 1883 as **Dr. Woods' home**. He kept his office here, too. The home's dormer windows, which peek out from the roof, are prettily decorated with a gingerbread trim, as is the front gable of the home. Originally the bay window had iron cresting on it, but this has now been removed. Another most attractive feature of this home is the circular corner on the porch. It nicely balances the bay window, and its peaked roof sports a finial, as do the dormers, the gable, and the little pediment detail over the front door. All in all, this is a romantic-looking, finely designed home.

Next door, at **39 rue Principale**, stands a block of apartments. But they were not always so: they started life as **Ambroise Goulet's home** built in 1885. The home is an intriguing example of what can happen to a heritage dwelling — it was transformed in the 1960s into its current set of flats. Goulet was an "engineer who moved here from Québec in 1868 to work for the steamboat company. He did very well, and by 1881 he had bought a fleet of steamboats and was operating them himself. In 1888 he built the steamship *Albert*, which was named after Queen Victoria's husband. In its last years, until it was dismantled in Quyon in 1917, the *Albert* towed log booms down the river."[66]

The next brick home is located at **14 rue Principale**, the **Rajotte-Klock House,** built in the late 1870s for Alexis Rajotte, also a steamboat captain who was Treasurer of the Upper Ottawa Steamboat Company. James Klock, after whom Klock Road was named, lived here after 1881. He owned a stagecoach business carrying passengers and goods to and from the landing at Lac Deschênes to Hull and Ottawa, and places beyond.

During the 1980s and early 1990s, **Number 10 rue Principale** was the Aylmer Museum, but after it moved, this property, originally the **John McLean House,** has been boarded up. McLean worked for the Union Forwarding Company, so this too would have been an excellent setting for his home and office; the wharves at Lac Deschênes were only a few hundred metres to the west. Look closely at the exterior faux façade whose wood surface has been specially treated to look like stone.

Symmes Hotel, Aylmer.
From engraving by W.H. Bartlett, 1840. NAC C-002309.

Across from it is the heritage ***pièce de résistance*** of this ramble: the **Symmes Hotel**, built by Charles Symmes in 1831 and immortalized in print by W.H. Bartlett. Bartlett's famous engraving depicts the hotel and the adjacent wharf in deep winter, with a horse-drawn sleigh in the foreground. On the frozen bay of Lac Deschênes, immediately behind the inn, a dogsled speeds across the ice. In August 2003 this heritage building reopened as the Symmes Inn Museum, and as of June 2004 it will be open year-round as a museum reflecting the history of the City of Gatineau. In his book *The Ottawa Country*, late author and NCC historian Courtney C. J. Bond quotes an 1837 *Bytown Gazette* ad, which describe the Symmes Hotel this way:

> Situated on the Lake Shore, in one of the most pleasant parts of Lower Canada … from which the Steam Boat Lady Coulborne is constantly plying, to and from Fitzroy Harbour. The House, together with Stables and Sheds are recently new and very

extensive, and having undergone a thorough fitting up, is now very commodious and capable of accommodating a large number of customers.[67]

Although the landmark inn was destroyed in the fire that swept Aylmer in 1921, it was rebuilt. After that time, it served as an apartment block, the Aylmer Aquatic Club, and then in 1979 the Government of Québec restored it to its former glory.

Park at the **Marina des Chênes** in its large lot and stroll to the waterfront. (**Note**: Look left at the waterfront to see the **cycle path**. Those who have chosen to do this ramble on bicycle will emerge here via this path, having skirted the Ottawa River from Parc des Portageurs. Again, note that in early spring segments of this path may be flooded and covered with ice until the waters recede.)

In open water season, the marina's many sailboats jostle on the waves, creating a pleasant, nautical-sounding musical background that echoes the historic raison d'être of Aylmer as a wharf. Stroll around, taking in the view of the Ottawa River sweeping westward to the villages of Fitzroy Harbour and Quyon (not visible from here).

Laughing Gallery, Queen's Park, Aylmer, Québec, c. 1910.
Photo: William Morell Harmer, (1859–1949). NAC PA-106226.

Look to your right to find the shoreline curving along a protected bay; beyond the Parc des cêdres (Cedar Park) is a smaller bay called Baie Alexandria. This is Queen's Park, the termination of Soper and Ahearn's Ottawa Electric Company line, where there was a grand amusement park.

Stroll to the rear of the Symmes Hotel and walk left, staying behind it until you find the pathways leading into the delightful **Parc de l'Imaginaire**, an open-air art gallery started by local artist and community-minded spirit, Yvette Debain. Wander here, viewing the art as well as the fountain: its urn centrepiece has a fascinating history. In 1907, Lord Strathcona commissioned it while he was the Canadian High Commissioner to Great Britain, to celebrate the start of trade between Canadian and Japan. Turn right at the fountain to find a back garden with a saucy looking couple, perpetually "taking the bath" in an antique bathtub.

After looking around the park, you might like to meet the woman who started it all: Ms. Debain is also the founding director of the art gallery **Centre d'Éxposition l'Imagier, number 9 rue Front**, an enterprise she started in 1975. This, actually, is the building whose back garden is home to our bathing couple. To get there, simply walk to rue Front via the little footpath on the west side of the house.

The house beside the gallery at **number 7 rue Front** was erected in 1840 for **Ephraim Parker** and was later purchased in 1852 by **Archibald Lindsay,** who operated an axe factory at the rear, then a sawmill.

Return to you car at the Marina des Chênes lot. Follow rue Principale east past Market Square and turn right on Frank Robinson, then left on Boulevard de Lucerne. This wide corridor follows the route of the former Pontiac and Pacific Junction Railway line (subsequently the CPR). It used to transport iron ore from the Bristol Mine, west of Quyon, into Hull. Continue on Lucerne to chemin Vanier. At the southeast corner is the low limestone complex, formerly the Hull Electric Company car barn. Home to one of the region's finest restaurants, **L'Échelle de Jacob**, this important building started life as the Hull Electric Company barns, but was renovated by John Lurtz into apartments in the 1960s.

Turn left on Vanier towards the waterfront where a series of ruins awaits discovery. Park and stroll to the river front, where you can get right down onto the waterside, defined by jutting outcrops of layered sedimentary rock. Directly opposite on the south shore is the Britannia Yacht

Club: its sheltered marina was originally the western end of a canal built to provide a bypass to the Deschênes Rapids spanning the river here.

Walk downstream on the bicycle path, noting the many oak, pine, and mixed hardwoods and softwoods growing here. Use binoculars to identify the many birds on the water, the shore, and in the woods; this is an excellent bird watching area due to the many habitats. Soon you come to old ruins in the water, dating from the 1860s; arches and spans identify what was originally Robert Conroy's sawmill. It later became the power house for the Hull Electric Company, where power was generated to run the electric cars that went to Queen's Park.

Return to your car and drive back to Boulevard Lucerne. Turn right and proceed to the **Champlain Bridge**. If you wish, turn right here, or else continue on the north shore, now on rue Brunet, paralleling the cycle path. Turn right on rue Bégin and drive to the riverside **Parc Brébeuf**. The statue of Father Jean de Brébeuf stands dramatically against the backdrop of the Ottawa River, upon which he journeyed west to the Great Lakes in 1626 en route to founding Huronia. Undoubtedly Brébeuf portaged the Chaudière Falls and also this second portage around the Petit Chaudière Falls, as well as the other rapids of the Ottawa River you have seen.

Here too paddled the likes of Lalement, Verendryes, Brûlé, de Vigneau, Mackenzie, and Henry, as well as countless other missionaries, explorers, Hudson and North West Company men. Perhaps you can conjure their ghostly forms struggling along the shore, weighted down by their packs as they portaged these rapids. These Europeans all passed by here, from the days of New France through to the 1800s when the Britannia Road finally permitted travellers to bypass the tedious set of rapids. And before them for 8,000 years or more, Paleo-Indian peoples paddled and portaged this ancient trade and hunting route. A plaque erected by the NCC commemorates these courageous souls, and the portage route itself.

Follow rue Bégin north to Boulevard Alexandre Taché and turn right to return to the Chaudière Bridge, the start of this ramble. Appropriately enough, we conclude the ramble on what used to be **Philemon Island**, named for the man who was founder of Hull and the Ottawa Valley lumber industry. Today the island is no more: infill and roadwork eliminated it when Place du Portage was built. You can see where the watercourse was, however: look at the big steam pipes along this final stretch on Boulevard Taché!

OTHER PLACES OF INTEREST

Taché Gardens Woods is well worth visiting, particularly in spring when hepaticas fill the forest floor. This woods is important because it is one of the last areas left adjacent to the Britannia Road that maintains a tiny segment of natural forest cover. Here you can find the rare black maple, along with many shagbark hickory. Taché Gardens Woods is located immediately west of Gatineau Parkway and east of Mountain Road. Access these NCC-maintained woods from Lacasse Street, just west of the Gatineau Parkway and St. François Street in Gatineau.

Champlain Park Woods, also known as the Champlain Corridor, lies on the original Allen Farm. Access it via Allen Road, the first lights west of the Champlain Bridge off the Aylmer Road. Here the sandy loam soil deposited by the Champlain Sea eons ago offers an alternate type of vegetation to what you'll find in the Taché Gardens or the wetland forests immediately west of the Champlain Bridge.

Queen's Park was the site of an amusement park that has long gone. To view its location immediately north of a tiny bay called Baie Alexandria, itself north of the Symmes Hotel area, head north on the Eardley Road (Highway 148 West) towards Quyon. After the junction with Highway 148 (Boulevard de l'Outaouais) and the Alexander and Perry roads, turn left at chemin des Boulders. Continue, past the first right-hand turn to the shores of Lac Deschênes (the Ottawa River). This is Queen's Park. Return Queen's Park Road as it leads back to Aylmer via what becomes rue Beaulac (Beautiful Lake Road), which travels the original path of the electric rail.

Gatineau Park Loop

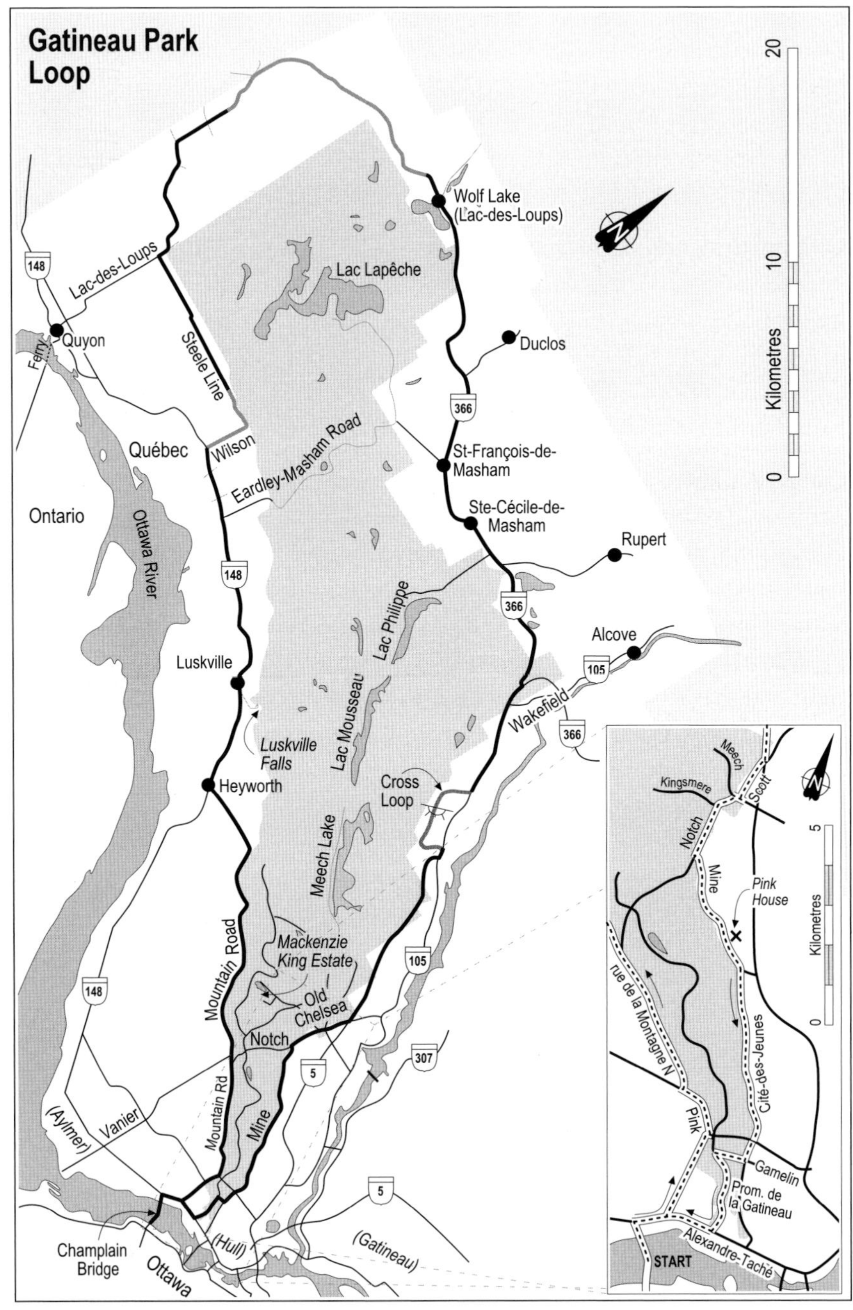

Blazing a Trail: The Earliest Roads

Here's another story first spun by Anson A. Gard in his book *Genealogy of the Valley,* his 1906 chronicle of his ramble along Mountain Road, where he interviewed every single resident. Many were the pioneer families who had built their homesteads there. Among those he met was eighty-something "Grandma Maxwell," who told the author how much her grandchildren loved to hear her tell of how the first settlers set to building roads through the virgin bush:

> *"Why children," she'd say, "we didn't have nice roads as you now have. Instead, if we wanted to go to some neighbours, one or five miles away we would have to follow what was called a blazed trail, which was made by cutting the bark of the trees, along a straight line. And the way they would make the line anyways straight was for some one to go to the point aimed at and blow a horn while the other fellow followed and chopped the bark, or if we'd start to make a 'road' to a neighbour's, each neighbour would blow a horn or shoot a gun 'till the direction was well known."* [68]

Nowadays, you would be forgiven if, like me, you wonder just how many neighbours shot one another in the process of finding that straight line! As we drive along the Mountain Road on this Gatineau Park circuit, try to imagine hacking through the forests like Grandma Maxwell recalls.

Poets in the Gatineau Hills

Poet Arthur Bourinot wrote many poems inspired by the Gatineau Hills. His mother sold Prime Minister Mackenzie King his first property at Kingsmere Lake in 1902. As you explore this circuit around Gatineau Park, you will drive along Mountain Road, which inspired his poem "Do You Remember," published in the chapbook entitled *Watcher of Men: The Selected Poems, 1947–66*:

Do you remember
That day in Early March
We went out the Mountain Road
Looking for pussywillows?
The sky was gentian blue,
The sun warm
As only a March sun feels,
Earth tangy with spring,
Birds on the wing,
Puddles on the road.

Just like the Confederation poets Archibald Lampman (who wrote his famous poem, "Heat" after climbing Mile Hill — see the Gatineau River ramble) and Duncan Campbell Scott, Bourinot loved the Gatineau Hills. Unlike them, he actually lived amid them at his Kingsmere Lake cottage whenever possible. Members of the Bourinot family still reside there.

HUMAN HISTORY

Gatineau Park's 36,131 hectares located a mere twenty-five minutes north of Parliament Hill represent the capital's beloved "backyard playground." Over 1.5 million visitors annually explore its paved parkways and networked hiking and cycle paths. But apart from a handful of interpretive signs, there is little to give us any hint of the human history of the park, of the voyageurs who paddled past, or of the 200 or so squatters and families who settled here, "up the mountain" in the late 1800s. Place names tell the story of this park whose lands started to be purchased by the Federal District Commission in 1937. After WW II, property continued to be acquired by its successor, the National Capital Commission, particularly in the 1950s and 1960s.

The place names in Gatineau Park recall the explorers who paddled the Ottawa and Gatineau rivers, as well as others who lived or passed through the area's woods and lakes. The park's name derives from Nicolas Gatineau, Sieur du Plessis, a notary from Trois Rivières who decided to shun his desk job and explore the river where he eventually drowned, well over three hundred years ago. Inside the park, lookouts and parkways recall famous names, as in Champlain, Étienne Brûlé, and Huron lookouts.

But what of the more obscure names that history books won't mention? How, for instance, did McCloskey trail get its name? Who were Pink, Meech, and Mousseau, after whom lakes are named? Who were the people who cut and maintained the first skiing and hiking trails?

It is tempting to say that some of the trails in today's park were first used by ancient trading peoples. To date, however, no archaeological remains bear this out, although local legend suggests that Ridge Road, the main arterial trail along the summit of the ridge, was a native footpath. To my knowledge, the only remnants of native life within the park's boundaries suggest that summer encampments existed along the beaches of the larger lakes, with Lapêche, Philippe, Harrington (Mousseau), and Meech being the most likely.

What was life like "up the mountain" after European contact? Who came here to hack down the trees and erect a first basic shelter from the elements, then pull out stumps, sow and harvest crops, and raise some livestock? For our answer, we must turn to scattered memories, to snippets of history in people's diaries, and essays delivered at historical society meetings.

Interestingly, it appears as though the top of the ridges were settled first, not the sweeping valleys. The reason was because, although more fertile land was available in the valleys, the ridges had fewer trees and were easier to clear and build upon to gain title within the prescribed time limit.

One of the first people to own a farm up the mountain was Reverend Asa Meech, who arrived in Hull from New England in 1815. By 1821 he owned a 200-acre farm bordering Meech Lake, which takes his name. He obtained rights to the land from Philemon Wright who, conveniently enough for this powerful fellow, was the government land agent. In November 1823, Wright described the Meech farm as having:

> One house, no barns, 24 acres cleared, six under cultivation, 15 horn cattle, 15 swine, 2 horses, 4 sheep, 20 days work on the road in the settlement, no saw mills, no labouring men, $50 expenses on the land.[69]

Asa Meech House on Meech Lake Road. Possibly the oldest structure in Gatineau Park, built by Asa Meech on his farm of 200 acres, c. 1821. Current house much altered. Photo 2001. HSG 02034.

As you can imagine, it was a considerable achievement to clear twenty-four acres of wild land and to have livestock grazing, and crops growing, all within two years. Note, too, that Meech performed his allotted twenty days of road work. As we learned in the Aylmer Road history, this onerous task was the responsibility of all landowners. Although they clearly benefited from a link connecting their remote farms to budding settlements, road duties were fraught with jealousies as well as technical challenges. Imagine working hard on the long stretch of road in front of your acreage, if your neighbours refused to do their fair share. Ah yes, it's rather like us, today, clearing snow on a shared driveway or sidewalk, don't you think?

Meech undoubtedly had assistance, evidently not from hired help, but from his sons and daughters who accompanied him here. When he first moved to Wrightsville, Meech and his second wife had eleven children, all of whom would have done chores. Tragically, in spring of 1822, his second wife and three children drowned in Brewery Creek, when a rush of meltwater swept away the bridge their horse and wagon

John Docksteader Meech (1825–1901) son of Reverend Asa Meech and Margaret Docksteader and his wife May Elizabeth Church (1836–1917), daughter of Gardner Church, c. 1890. HSG 00121–002.

was travelling upon. The Reverend took another wife, Margaret Docksteader, and together they had another ten children. John Docksteader Meech remained on the family farm until 1901. The homestead — although much altered — still stands south of the Meech Lake Road, but typical of the NCC, no sign marks its heritage significance.

Soon the Meech family had neighbours. In 1822 the Pink brothers — James, Charles and Samuel — along with their sister Isabella and her husband Alexander Moffatt arrived in Montréal from Ireland. They spent their first winter in Wrightsville where they took various jobs; James Pink helped build St. James Anglican, the first stone church in Hull. In April 1826, the two families decided to do what many immigrants did: join forces, clear some land, build their first log dwelling, then procure title for it. In this way, more work could be accomplished in less time. By autumn they had cleared a small farm, planted four acres of potatoes and one of corn, and completed their first log cabin. Pink Lake is named after this family (as is a road and cemetery south of the junction of Mountain and Vanier roads, where Moffatt and Pink family graves are located). The Alexander Pink house, built in 1873, still exists, though the farmland was developed into a housing subdivision in the 1980s. It is located near Mine Road, in Gatineau's Cité-des-Jeunes sector, near the old Forsyth Iron Ore Mine.

There were many French-speaking peoples who settled here, too. The lake we call Meech today might more properly have been called Lac Lacharité after François Lacharité, the first settler who actually built a homestead on its shores. His daughter Johanna married Irishman Patrick Farrell, a major landowner who erected a sawmill and dam by the lake. Upon the couple's marriage, Lacharité apparently gave the couple his home. Today, that much-altered dwelling stands beside Hope Bay, leased to descendants of the Hopes — and of course just like Meech House, no heritage sign identifies it, either.

West of Meech Lake is another body of water with a dual past. Lac Mousseau and Harrington Lake are one and the same; and in fact, for a while the lake was officially called "Lac Mousseau (Harrington Lake)." Today, however, it takes the French name. Louis Mousseau bought property here from James and David Maclaren of Wakefield in 1867. Nine years later his son Charles Mousseau purchased it, staying until 1905. And the name Harrington? The Hetherington family arrived from England in 1816. However, the land agent granting title to their 200-acre farm in 1827 misspelled the family name on the deed, inadvertently altering it to "Harrington." The error persisted, repeated by a surveyor named Driscoll who wrote "Harrington Lake" on his 1850 survey map of Eardley Township. To make matters even more confusing, the prime minister of Canada's retreat is in Gatineau Park, on Lac Mousseau, but the residence itself is always referred to as "Harrington Lake."

Families who lived in this area had a tough go of it, for the most part. But there were a few prosperous farms; Paddy and Mary McCloskey came from Ireland and settled immediately on the ridge directly south of Meech Lake, where they had twelve children. Along with help from neighbours Bradley and Marshall, this family cut the road down to the lake, which for years was called the McCloskey road, then the McCloskey trail. In 1966 the original McCloskey homestead was still standing, as was their son Richard's home, which was built out of sawn timber.

The McCloskeys left the mountain sometime around 1909. By 1915 most of the families who had been eking a basically subsistence-lifestyle had forsaken the top of the ridge. The topsoil there was scant, in places no more than a mere dusting over the Canadian Shield rock. Some accounts claim that after the land was cleared, the depth of topsoil eroded quickly. Whatever the reason, jobs in villages and towns seemed easier, and folks drifted away to seek a better life.

Nonetheless, it was not all a dreary hand-to-mouth existence. Colourful images remain of the life on the ridge. In detailed transcriptions, Sheila Thomson records snippets of people's memories of how life was. One person remembered the dog churn his family used when he was a boy. "The butter was churned in the cellar where it was cool. The long-haired collie dog worked the churn by walking around and around it. On a hot summer day, [the boy's] mother would go down and unfasten the dog, who would go over and get a drink of water, and then come back to be fastened to the churn again."[70]

Another old-timer recounted tales of dances at Dunlop's place located near the northeast corner of the parking lot on the Meech Lake Road. The McCloskeys' place seems to have been "the" place to be, because many family members and friends played the fiddle while others danced Irish jigs.

After hearing about all the large families in the area, it's not surprising to learn that there were schools along the ridge, too, as the community grew. One schoolhouse, called "the Tabernacle" was on Ridge Road, while a second was built near Mountain Road at a bend in the road that still bears the moniker "Hollow Glen." Yet another was Flynn's School. This is the one the McCloskey children attended:

a long four-mile hike northwest of the lake that took them an hour and a quarter to walk.[71] Come winter the children skied to school on skis fashioned from barrel staves.

There's a tale concerning work at a shanty somewhere near Lusk Lake (south of Lac Philippe), where a million and a half feet, or approximately 20,000 logs were cut and hauled out. Teamsters rose at 3:00 a.m. when it was pitch dark. "They used to make flares to see by — a bottle of grease with a wick in it, stuck in the snow. The logs cut in the Lusk Lake area were dumped into Harrington (Mousseau) Lake. The logs were floated down to Alexander's mill on Meach [sic] Lake."[72]

Lumbermen's Shanty. Alexander Henderson's portable photographic darkroom in front of shanty, Québec, ca. 1879.
Photo: Alexander Henderson, 1831–1913. NAC PA-149706.

Something else was happening in the Canadian Shield hills, too: mining. From Quyon's molybdenum mine to the mica mine at Pink Lake, to the Forsyth Iron Ore mine whose shafts lie in the woods near Mine Road, the ancient rocks yielded minerals. Mining ventures were started and two villages, Ironsides (see Gatineau River ramble) and Quyon, directly benefited from the industry. Various factors precipitated the closure of the mines, such as the relative difficulty of getting product to market, and today, due to the park's status, it is unlikely that minerals will ever be dug from within its boundaries again.

Although settlers and those eking a living from the hills left their homes here, others were moving in, purchasing land, and erecting summer cottages. By 1870 William Jeffs, the major landowner around Kingsmere Lake, had begun to sell off parcels of land primarily to Ottawans who sought refuge from summertime's torpid heat — and smells.

Former Prime Minister William Lyon Mackenzie King's long-standing attachment to the Gatineau Hills is well documented. He fell in love with the countryside after cycling to Kingsmere Lake from Ottawa on Thanksgiving weekend in 1900 with his good friend Henry Albert Harpur. It was the first of many happy trips. Two years later he purchased land upon which he built Kingswood Cottage overlooking Kingsmere Lake.

But King did far more than simply purchase a cottage lot or two. Kingswood was the first of several acquisitions. In 1924 he bought Moorside and later the adjacent lot known as The Farm, now the private residence of the Speaker of the House. King eventually amassed 500 acres of land for his personal use, all of which he donated in his will to the Government of Canada to be used "as a public park in trust for the citizens of Canada." Today the NCC manages both Kingswood Cottage and Moorside as national heritage sites within Gatineau Park, called the Mackenzie King Estate.

Simultaneous to King's acquisitions, recreational use of what is now Gatineau Park was becoming increasingly popular. The train from Ottawa and Hull brought holidaymakers to Chelsea and Old Chelsea, as well as taking them farther up the Gatineau River (see Gatineau River ramble). Local residents such as the Alexanders near Meech Lake and the Murphys at Kingsmere capitalized on this interest. They picked people up at the Chelsea train station and brought them to their respective hotel and inn. Meanwhile, cross-country skiing became a popular winter pastime, and in the early 1920s the Ottawa Ski Club purchased property that is now part of Camp Fortune. Teams of happy volunteers started cutting and maintaining ski trails and building lodges. Both trails and shelters were often given romantic-sounding names such as Petticoat Lane, Highland Fling, and Shilly Shally; others were given utilitarian names like George's Trail, Fortune Lodge, and McCloskey's Lodge. The latter three were named after people. Petticoat Lane was named because one of the female trail builders had a "petticoat" that she tore up to make slalom markers for a race. Highland Fling appropriately described an exhilarating run; the lodge named Shilly Shally evocatively beckoned you to linger a while beside its cozy wood fire.

But all are gone: the names are wistfully remembered by people like me who recall skiing past hand-carved wooden signs stuck in drifts of snow, pointing you onward. The NCC's current system of numbers and colours are oh-so-reasonable (particularly for cartographers), but are oh-so-dull, evoking nothing of the rich legacy of those who built the trails: the Night Riders of the Ottawa Ski Club.

Only a few vestiges of the human history of Gatineau Park survive. Pioneer roads linking the community, such as Ridge Road, McCloskey, and the road leading from the foot of Meech Lake to Wakefield still exist, but only as paths enjoyed by skiers, hikers, and possibly cyclists. The McCloskey farm was torn down, as was J.R. Booth's mansion, Opeongo, which used to stand on the Booth Road at Kingsmere. Northeast of Lac Philippe is the Healey farmhouse, and Herridge Lodge, being the Irish Cafferty family's first dwelling near Flynn Creek, is the oldest refuge in the park. These and several other buildings, such as the ruins of Thomas "Carbide" Willson's dam, generating station, and fertilizer production plant at the foot of Little Meech Lake still stand, but only just.

What are prospering, however, are the many private homes within Gatineau Park. The prime minister of Canada's retreat overlooks Lac Mousseau (Harrington Lake). The Farm at Kingsmere is home to the Speaker of the House. Former cottages on Kingsmere and Meech lakes are almost all winterized these days. According to the NCC's Gatineau Park Parkway Sector Plan (2000) there are seventy-one private homes in the Kingsmere community and eighty-two at Meech Lake.

Private ownership of land within the park remains a contentious issue, as does the ownership by the Government of Canada of Harrington Lake and The Farm. Suggestions from the NCC that lands within the park boundary, such as the Meech Lake Valley, be developed have met with vociferous opposition from local watchdog groups.

Around the park's perimeter, however, rural and urban municipalities, associations and private individuals alike promote new ventures or new usages such as horseback riding trails, snowmobiling, trailer parks, and campgrounds. The NCC is besieged by such requests for additional park services and access routes. From time to time, a Master Plan for Gatineau Park is researched and published, which incorporates public consultations into the planning process. The latest one ought to be published in 2004. To date, the Plan defines the park's three main roles within the context of the National Capital Region:

1. The park is a public space with a special status, developed and administered for the benefit of the public by the National Capital Commission.
2. The park is a natural area distinguished from the network of green spaces in the National Capital Region by the quality and variety of its resources.
3. The park contributes to the symbolic function of the Capital and to its green image, not only as a key element in the natural setting, but also because of its national attractions (e.g. Mackenzie King Estate).

So, in terms of human history, Gatineau Park symbolizes the transformation of a parcel of land from native people's hunting grounds, to pioneer homesteads, mining ventures, recreationalists' playground, private individuals' residences, and wildlife sanctuary.

Many pressures, many human wants and needs. Amid all of this, it is also up to the National Capital Commission — as well as to us all as individuals — to ensure that this park remains a viable habitat for its many wild denizens.

NATURAL HISTORY

Gatineau Park is a rich and varied habitat. Its southernmost "foot" penetrates into the urban landscape of the city of Gatineau, whereas its westernmost extremity north of Quyon extending northward to Wolf Lake is its wilderness sector. To the east it is bounded by the Gatineau River valley, to the south by the Eardley Escarpment rising dramatically from the Ottawa Valley rift plain.

Ancient Precambrian rocks such as gneiss and granite bedrock yielded minerals, but also created obstacles to settlers hoping to start prosperous farms. These mountains, once higher than the western Rockies, are now mere stubby roots of their former selves, ground down by eons of erosion, not to mention glacial scouring. King Mountain on the Eardley Escarpment now is the highest point along the ridge, at 344 m (1,129 feet).

The Eardley Escarpment's dramatic cliffs and wooded hillsides create a special micro-climate. Here rare species of plants thrive, while deer gather in "deer yards" in winter, enjoying the heat of the sun as well as reduced snow cover that makes foraging easier. As well, the ridge's craggy outcrops provide nests for raven, bald, and even golden eagles; all three species can be seen along the escarpment's western limit, particularly near Eardley-Masham Road.

You will see extremely varied vegetation along this ramble. Watch for dramatic white pines in the mixed hardwood and softwood forests of maple, birch, beech, and poplar along the Eardley Escarpment. On the north side of the park, look for alder crowding cattails in the wetlands near the Wolf Lake sector. And, if you venture out of your car or off your bicycle, depending upon where you are, you might find wild ginseng, leeks, or chanterelle mushrooms. Remember, please, that Gatineau Park's wildlife sanctuary includes all plants. Gathering of anything — plant, mineral, or other — is strictly forbidden.

Field of oats on an unknown farm in Rupert c. 1928.
(Copy of NAC PA-56323.) This from HSG 00257.

BEFORE YOU GO ON THE RAMBLE

Why go? Ottawans love Gatineau Park — but most people only know what's called the "foot of the park" close to Gatineau and Chelsea. Driving around this island sanctuary introduces you to old settlements, the gravelled back roads of Pontiac County, and some great views. The circuit also gives you an idea of how important it is to treasure our protected parks, because even in the more remote Pontiac region, development will always continue to encroach upon the wild and its denizens.

Distance: A 130 km circuit from the Champlain Bridge.

Modes of exploration: A drive is described. The circuit makes a good bike ride, but be aware of the approximately 15 km of well-maintained gravel roads along its westernmost sector.

Getting there: Head to Gatineau via the Champlain Bridge, then connect with chemin de la Montagne/Mountain Road. Your route includes Highway 148 Ouest (west), chemin Steele Line, chemin Lac des Loups (Wolf Lake Road), then Highway 366 Est (east) through the Masham villages to Highway 105 Sud (south) near Wakefield. I recommend a short detour on the picturesque Cross Loop road through the Meech Creek Valley before you take Highway 5 to Old Chelsea, then you'll take these roads back to the Champlain Bridge: chemin Notch, chemin Mine, Boulevard de la Cité-des-Jeunes, Boulevard Gamelin, Promenade de la Gatineau, Boulevard Alexandre-Taché, then the Champlain Bridge and back to Ottawa.

Facilities: There are dépanneurs (corner stores) periodically en route outside of Gatineau, but this is a remote ramble. Washroom facilities are limited. **Tip**: fill up with gas before leaving Ottawa.

Of special note: Be prepared with snacks and adequate clothing, too, should you set out in winter. Also, be aware that logging trucks still travel the more remote highways and byways, and gravel can sometimes be kicked up. Finally, be watchful for wildlife because, as in many parts of the region, deer can be a hazard. You might see these mammals, along with red fox, porcupine, skunk, raccoons, and even a coyote if you are fortunate.

Start by crossing the Ottawa River at the **Champlain Bridge**. Pass Boulevard Lucerne (Lower Aylmer Road) and turn right at the lights on chemin d'Aylmer (the "upper Aylmer Road"). (See Aylmer ramble.) Turn left (north) on chemin de la Montagne Sud, passing the exit west to Highway 148 and the big box shopping centre, then left again onto Pink Road, and right onto chemin de la Montagne Nord.

Chemin de la Montagne Nord (Mountain Road) skirts the base of the **Eardley Escarpment**, the landform whose natural formation provides a logical southern boundary for Gatineau Park. Along it you will find a scattering of residences variously built from the 1820s to the present day. First you pass several housing developments built between 1990 and 2004 before reaching the junction with **Notch Road**. (This road, which we will not take, marks the only access into Gatineau Park from Mountain Road; it runs north to the communities of Kingsmere and Old Chelsea.)

Notch Road is a modern demonstration of how imposing this ridge was — and still is — to human access. Imagine how arduous a trip it would have been for settlers to carry their sacks of potatoes or apples from their homestead on top of the ridge down to the market at Aylmer or Hull — or Bytown for that matter. This is exactly what the earliest pioneers accomplished. And of course, once their produce was sold, they still had the return trip to look forward to, this time up the ridge. "The Notch," and "Larriault's Hill" further west (now no longer open), were developed into trails and later on, into roads, because their routes followed natural folds or old watercourses in the ridge. Such crinkles in the "wall" of the mountain allowed the best footing and were more readily managed by engineers and road crews.

As you drive, consider life here in the early 1800s. Mail delivery, for instance. How did the community up the mountain get their mail? The post was delivered to Old Chelsea, so residents of this road first climbed the ridge however they could, then walked to the village, got their mail, and returned home. No wonder hotels and shops sprang up in that village; residents could linger, open their mail, purchase a few commodities, gossip, and then return on "shank's mare" — by foot.

Immediately beyond Notch Road is **Vanier Road**, which leads south to the Ottawa River at Deschênes Rapids. The home here, now a pony club, is a red brick house built circa 1870, which once belonged to Alexander Moffatt. According to journalist Gladys Blair, it used to be called **Moffatt Hall**. If you wish, park in the lot opposite it. Carefully cross to the north side of Mountain Road and just beyond the T intersection with Vanier, look among the trees for a rock with a bronze plaque. Mounted here on 23 September 1973, it commemorates the arrival of the Moffatts from Ireland in 1822.

In his 1905 ramble along this road, American author Anson A. Gard visited the Moffatt family, where he heard stories of the Great Fire of 1870, which swept from the south side of the Ottawa River up and across the mountain near here, all the way to Wakefield. Miraculously, not many people died, but many lost their homes and possessions. Imagine, while you drive, what you would have done if faced with such a conflagration, without today's conveniences of telephones or cell phones, and with no vehicle other than possibly a wagon, and frightened horse.

Proceed west, crossing Vanier Road. (If you turn south here, you quickly arrive at **Pink Cemetery**, at the corner of Pink Road. Here you can visit many settler's graves with family names such as Radmore, Pink, and Currie.) The cemetery land was donated by James and Agnes Pink in 1864.)

Continuing along Mountain Road, next look for a log fence on the right, marking the **Moylinny Farm** property. A photograph in the Gatineau Valley Historical Society's 1993 edition of *Up the Gatineau!* reveals that this fence was newly erected in 1970, being built by George Hetherington. Today, it serves to remind us of how early homesteaders depended on these structures not just to define property boundaries, but to contain livestock. Nowadays, farmers tend to use more practical — but far less picturesque — electric fences.

Moylinny is the original Joseph Hetherington farm, cleared by him in 1823. (George was his great grandson, and he left the family farm in 1970 — perhaps after building the fence!) The property straddles Mountain Road; the north side heads up Eardley Escarpment. This farm was razed by the fire of 1870. In his essay on his farm's history, Michael Reford wrote:

> In 1870 a great fire swept across the farm from the west. In two hours it burned a strip two miles wide and four miles long, going clear across the mountain and beyond Ironsides. Charred stumps of large trees burned in this fire could still be found in

the swampy bush a hundred years later. The Hetheringtons lost all their buildings and much else besides. But they carried on and built a new house of square cut logs.[73]

John Heyworth's home is today the Kingsway Golf Course, possibly the oldest building on the road. Photo: K. Fletcher, 2002.

Coming up soon on your left is the **Kingsway Golf Course**, the former **John Heyworth house**. He settled here in 1816 and his stone home is probably the one cited in the 1851 West Hull Census. Inside, today, there is a small **golf museum**, which you might be able to get permission to see. Beyond it, is **Larriault's Hill** at **Hollow Glen**. Today a cluster of homes marks the foot of what used to be a road up the ridge, used since the very early 1800s as one of the significant links to Kingsmere and Old Chelsea. It was closed in the 1950s after its precipitous descent (and perhaps careless driving) caused one-too-many accident.

Home in Hollow Glen below King Mountain. The road from here to Kingsmere Lake was closed in the 1950s. Photo: K. Fletcher, 2002.

Towering above Hollow Glen is **King Mountain**, the highest elevation of the escarpment and the site of one of Gatineau Park's most popular trails. Upon its summit is a cairn upon which is written, "Here was commenced the triangulation system of the Geodetic Survey of Canada, the basis of surveys for all purposes, topographical, engineering and cadastral." Dr. W.F. King took the first measurement here in 1905. Although you might think this is who King Mountain is named after, others say the name was used earlier, perhaps referring to early settler John King who homesteaded on Kingsmere Lake. Others say the mountain earned its name simply by being the highest point of land. A thirty-foot cedar cross once stood upon its summit, erected by Father J.E. MacGuire, parish priest of St. Stephen's Roman Catholic Church in Old Chelsea between 1888 and 1891. Long gone now, the cross was originally covered with tin so that it would reflect the sunlight. Apparently it could be plainly spotted from Parliament Hill when conditions were just right! The cross survived for a decade or so before toppling over the cliff.

Beyond the foot of King Mountain and, beyond Hollow Glen, watch for some of the oldest homes on the road. One is a **log home** of squared timber and dove-tailed joinery at the corners. Another home's façade is shingled. Watch, too, for a couple of old **carriage houses** beside these homes. These are important heritage reminders of how all homes would have first appeared along this road.

You have now left the municipalities of West Hull and Chelsea, and are entering the easternmost sector of the Pontiac region of West Québec.

At the abrupt right-angled turn in Mountain Road, you leave the escarpment to travel down a straight stretch that connects to **Highway 148**. Known as **Young's Corner**, there used to be a school here, right where the road pulls away from the ridge. In appropriate weather, this is now a favourite hang-gliding location. Watch for the graceful "sails" of hang gliders as they navigate the updrafts along the ridge. It is precisely these updrafts that appeal to turkey vultures, various hawks, golden and bald eagles, and ravens. As you continue westward keep your eyes peeled for these birds.

Farms line either side of the road along this straight stretch. After the white and red pine were logged from here, and after horses hauling stone boats full of rocks and stumps cleared the land, farms grew from a scant few acreages of potatoes and beans to the "spreads" you see today.

Turn right at Highway 148: this corner and its residences is the former community of **Heyworth**, named after John Heyworth and family. It still appears on some maps, fooling unsuspecting travellers into thinking they might find a gasoline station here.

Proceed west towards Luskville and Quyon. This northern stretch of the Ottawa River was sparsely settled in the early 1830s and you can see this is still the case today. Farms here raised crops used by workers in the lumber industry to sustain both horses and men during the winter months. After the main stands of timber were felled, and despite other industries such as mining creating temporary employment over several decades, the farms proved to be increasingly less viable and many people drifted away looking for employment elsewhere.

The highway soon turns into an "orphaned" four-lane stretch, apparently as a corrective to the many turns and hills of the old highway, or perhaps more likely because a mayor lived along here! You pass by **Luskville**, whose earliest buildings are actually located immediately south of the highway where you'll see the spires of **Saint Dominique Roman Catholic Church,** built in 1884. This community was first settled by English-speaking settlers and is named for Irishman

Joseph Lusk, who was a significant landowner here. The Lusks built Ghost Hill farm located east of here (see Ottawa River Loop ramble). Thanks to the Lusk family's intervention, the 1877 **Hotel de Ville –Town Hall,** located at the corner of the highway and **chemin Hôtel de Ville**, on your right, was saved from demolition in the 1960s. (**Note:** chemin Hôtel de Ville leads to another great diversion: **Lusk Falls**, a popular hike in Gatineau Park and also where you can horseback ride along the base of the ridge. (See Other places of interest.)

After Luskville, the highway reverts to its normal two-lanes. Now look for the cut stone house on the right, standing prominently amid a cluster of white pines. It was the **Captain D.C. McLean residence**, dating from the 1850s or so. As you continue west, note the homes, farms, and outbuildings on your left, built on top of a terrace (or beach head), the geological feature that marks the recession of the Champlain Sea. The elevation affords residents a superb view of their fields of corn, hay, or other crops, or cattle, below. Some barns were built below the rise of land, providing a natural wind break shelter for livestock.

You now pass **Eardley**, named for a village in England, well marked by a road that crosses the highway. To the left, it descends the terrace slope to farms and cottages fronting the Ottawa River. Many years ago, there was a cheese factory behind the dépanneur on the highway here. To the right, the **Eardley-Masham Road** bisects Gatineau Park. (**Note:** you can cut this ramble shorter by following this road to Ste-Cécile-de-Masham. En route, you would pass Ramsay Lake, a most unusual landform of the region. It is a peat bog like Mer Bleue — see Mer Bleue ramble. Be aware, however, that the road is mostly gravel and can be rough in the spring and winter. There are no services along the route.)

Check your odometer here, because you will need to turn left after 3 km onto chemin Wilson Road, a gravel road heading north to the Eardley Escarpment. (**Note:** you can avoid gravel roads if you want, by continuing on Highway 148 west. Turn right (north), at the second turnoff to Quyon, at chemin Lac des Loups. This junction is marked by a Stinson's Gas Bar on the left and Stanton's garage and restaurant on your right, called "Restaurant Restaurant Restaurant" a name inspired by Quebec's French language police.)

The Wilson road ends abruptly at the foot of the mountain, connecting with **chemin Steele Line**. The Gatineau Trail Rider's Association horseback riding trail is located at the end of the road. (**Note:** Riders must get permission from this club to use the trail.)

Turn left on the **Steele Line** and proceed carefully; the gravel road continues for about two kilometres. This entire road is an excellent place to spot wildlife, including black bear, which — much to the farmers' chagrin — enjoy dining on corn crops planted in the fields here. At the hydro cut, look for raven's nests on the towers, red-tailed hawks, and both bald and golden eagles.

Farms line this road that bears the name of the Steele family, and many belonged to them at one time. **John Steele** was born in Yorkshire, England in 1799. He had served overseas in India, where he was blinded in one eye. Because of this, he received a discharge with pension from the army. Steele emigrated to Canada, arriving in Almonte by riverboat in 1841. After marrying Sarah McKenny from Pakenham in 1842, the couple moved to what is now known as the Steele Line, settling on a property described as a "half-cleared farm." Steele paid for it with half of his pension. He also received the timber rights to lots north of the farm — property now within Gatineau Park. The Steeles had five sons who also settled "the Line," so it is no wonder that today this rural road bears the family name.

The Mohrs were the first settlers to homestead north of the Ottawa River near Quyon. John Christian Mohr was a Swedish immigrant who arrived in 1831 and built a house close to the river. Other Mohrs farmed along the Steele Line. Although the large Victorian brick house on the south side of the Steele Line was built for James Thomas, it became a Mohr home. After passing the house, decrease your speed to negotiate the abrupt S-turn in the road that once marked the little community known as Steele. As you can see, nothing remains of its schoolhouse and church.

After it are two cattle operations: both beef and dairy cattle graze in the lush pastures. These farms mark the last livestock operations of any size along this ramble, because as we start heading farther north the soil cannot support such herds.

At the junction with **chemin Lac des Loups** (Wolf Lake Road) turn right. Veer left on the paved road as you approach the hill, bypassing **chemin Swamp**. Sand and gravel pits are clustered on either side of the road, remnants of glacial till and deposition from the Champlain Sea. Be on the alert for large sand and gravel trucks.

After passing the entrance to the Municipality of Pontiac's landfill, you drive through a landscape that was ravaged by a fire that started in that dump and swept into Gatineau Park in 1988. The conflagration prompted an immense effort from the joint forces of Quyon's volunteer firefighters, NCC, volunteers, and provincial firefighting teams. It took almost two weeks for the blaze to be completely extinguished. The regrowth you now drive through is an excellent example of succession, the process by which various stages of vegetation reclaim the land.

Watch for the sign on your left marking the former site of **St. Brigid's Church** (1888–1959) and **cemetery**. Only the latter remains. Beyond it is a Y in the road, once the site of the Town Hall of North Onslow Township, through which you are driving. Bear left, remaining on the paved road as it curves its way in a northwesterly direction.

Continue on Wolf Lake Road, driving through land that is increasingly challenging to farm, because of the sandy, rock-strewn soil. The intersection with **Henderson Road** is marked by farm buildings on your right and, bereft of its church, you'll discover tiny **North Onslow Cemetery** whose grass is still well maintained. Continue straight ahead: in winter this is a good place to find large flocks of snow buntings or, in February, to spot horned larks in the stubbled cornfields. Immediately beyond them, watch out: the pavement ends and gravel begins at the next hill. The road curves here a bit; at the top of a rise you'll find a road, the **Twelfth Line**, heading left (west). Ignore it, remaining on the main gravel road, the Wolf Lake Road/chemin Lac des Loups, which forms the westernmost boundary of the NCR at this point. If you are nervous about the gravel, remember that this is a well-maintained road that is kept clear for school buses. It is well sanded in winter; well graded in good weather.

Remain on this road for about thirteen km, wending first along a mixed landscape of open pasture, then entering a pretty, albeit remote sector of lakes rimmed by forested hills. Eventually the road joins with **Highway 366** in the community of **Lac des Loups (Wolf Lake),** the NCR's most northwesterly village.

St. François d'Assise, an imposing Catholic church constructed of cinder blocks, dominates **Lac des Loups** at the corner of **rue Pontbriand**, opposite the grey brick **École Ste Thérèse**. Enter the church, if possible, to see its stained glass windows, which commemorate both English- and French-speaking families such as Foran, McCann, O'Hearn, Joanisse, and Legros. This mix is typical of this area of West Québec, despite what separatists would have you believe. As well, in Ladysmith and other communities further west of here, there were significant German and Polish settlements. After checking the interior of the church, you might wish to investigate the cemetery outside, where simple metal crosses mark several graves.

St. François d'Assise looking chilly on a winter's day outside the church at Wolf Lake. Photo: E. Fletcher, 2002.

Proceed along Highway 366, noting the carriage house on the left amid the farm buildings. Soon you find a sign indicating Masham is 13 km ahead, Wakefield 17 km. Pass by the cottages along **Lac des Loups** (Wolf Lake). As you drive here, take particular care because the road is extremely narrow: there's not much space between lake and craggy outcrops of Canadian Shield. We are now entering what is known as the "Masham" area, a community comprised of several settlements incorporating that name. Watch for a farm on your left where pheasants are raised. You soon pass a major intersection with **chemin Duclos** on this northern route, which leads to the northerly community of Duclos (3 km) and East Aldfield (11 km) beyond. This is a spectacularly pretty route, but for now continue on **Highway 366 Est**.

The next community is **St. François-de-Masham,** marked by a bridge spanning the **Lapêche River,** on your right. This is the northern terminus of the **Eardley-Masham Road** that you passed earlier on Highway 148. It leads south towards the remote **Lac Lapêche** picnic and overnight camping area within Gatineau Park.

Note the remnants of mills on the Lapêche River downstream from the bridge. Take a tiny detour: turn left on **chemin du Moulin**, noting the small park, picnic table, and play area for youngsters. Cross the river, turn right and immediately pull into the little parking lot here, the yard of **L. Martineau Portes et Chassis**. On either side of the **Lapêche River** you can see old foundations of sawmills known as the **Masham mills.** They were once a going concern, now they are forlorn and mostly forgotten reminders of this community's past prosperity.

Return to the main road and proceed right (east), to what used to be called **Ste-Cécile-de-Lapêche**, a mission founded in 1843 to serve the Irish and French Catholics living here. There are a cluster of administrative buildings, along with another immense Catholic church, which was built of cut limestone in 1913. A decade later this parish altered its name to **Ste-Cécile-de-Masham**. For the most part, it seems as if the twenty or so families who lived here during the 1840s slowly migrated north from the corridor created by the lakes of Meech, Philippe, and Mousseau (Harrington) in search of arable land.

M. Bertrand's gristmill (right) and Dufour's sawmill (left), Ste-Cécile-de-Masham, Québec, c. 1870–80. NAC PA-123699.

These hills imposed hardships on its earliest settlers, who had a particularly difficult time. Homesteaders carved wooden clogs as footwear, and black bears were troublesome intruders, devouring crops such as corn and apples. There was no talk of protecting such wild beasts back in pioneer days: bears were considered a dangerous nuisance and were either trapped or shot on sight. People used all parts of the kill including the fat, which was rendered and used for insect repellent and candles, among other things. Wherever possible, people grew produce or made things to sell at markets in nearby Wakefield, Hull, and as far away as Bytown. One manufactured item sold at market item was potash, or lye. This was made from wood ash, a by-product created while clearing the land.

Imposing symmetrical stone façade of the 1913 church at Ste-Cécile-de-Masham. Photo: E. Fletcher, 2002.

At **Ste-Cécile-de-Masham** there is a sign pointing to a covered bridge: take this road, another access into Gatineau Park, this time leading to Lac Philippe and the Lusk Caves. The tiny bridge crossing the Lapêche River at this point is the first example of a "kissing," or covered bridge, on this ramble. (They took the name "kissing" bridges because unchaperoned couples could steal a kiss as their horse ambled along, pulling their wagon through the sheltered bridge!) This one was built in 1958. On the far side of it, turn left on **chemin Schnobb** (named after a German resident) and left again almost immediately, onto **chemin Brazeau**. Here you pass a farmhouse immediately on your right. Go slowly; do you see the hand-made replica of the covered bridge you just drove through?

Turn right at the main road and proceed to the junction of **Highway 105 and 5** — rather unhelpfully, this highway takes both numbers here. Turn right here, so that you are travelling south towards Gatineau and Ottawa. (Maniwaki, the community that is home to the Algonquin First Nation's community of Kitigan Zibi Anishinabeg, is to your north.)

Pass the exits to **Wakefield**. The white marble pit on your left is **Morrisson's Quarry**, where those of you who are far braver than me can try bungee jumping. Can you see the tall tower? That's what you jump from, into the former quarry's water.

As you approach the buildings clustered at the top of the hill at **Farm Point**, watch closely for your next right turn onto **chemin Cross Loop**. (You can bypass this 5 km pretty gravel road completely if you wish: simply proceed south).

The road traverses the **Meech Creek Valley**, a highly controversial and beautiful "hidden valley" where expropriations of farmland occurred while powers that be mulled over whether to build a zoo here. Cross Loop wends its way past a series of farmhouses; you will note most are on the left-hand side. This is because farms on the right were expropriated by the Société d'Amenagement de l'Outaouais (SAO) in the early 1970s. Beyond the pastureland, woods define the boundary of Gatineau Park. This stunning valley has seen decades of controversy; the SAO (and sometimes the NCC along with the Municipality of Lapêche) didn't just conceptualize building a zoo here. Other development ideas included an old-time heritage village, a development of estate homes, and a golf course. Fortunately, these concepts perished on the vine. The Meech Creek Valley remains a fertile "secret" valley that acts as superb buffer to, and guardian of, Gatineau Park.

Who once lived here, and cleared this pretty valley?

William Baldwin's farm used to stand at the first easterly bend in the road (past chemin Cafferty), on the left-hand side just under a kilometre from the highway. In her book *Wakefield and Its People*, Norma Geggie wrote:

> In 1840, William Baldwin was granted 200 acres on which he erected a house. The grant was in recognition of his service in the 8th Regiment of Foot. A later brick farmhouse which belonged to the Baldwin family sat in the clump of trees to

the left. In the 1960s 'Morningside,' a residence for the elderly, was established in the brick house and offered accommodation to six to eight women.[74]

Beyond it, on a knoll, is the Baldwin graveyard.

Across from Baldwin's farm is a gated lane marking the former site of the Mulvihill family's farm, Brookdale, built in the 1860s. Geggie's book notes that this became a home for needy children; as many as thirty were cared for here.

The covered bridge spanning Meech Creek on Cross Loop.
Photo: E. Fletcher December 2002.

A kilometre from here the road dips and you pass through the second and last covered bridge of this ramble, built in 1935.

The Cross barn raising at Meech Creek Valley,
in Farm Point in 1916. HSG 01348–002.

This road is called the Cross Loop for good reason, for three other Cross family farms existed here prior to the land being expropriated. The red brick house and barn located at the junction with **Pine Road** was built in 1915. The barn you see here on your right was built by Wyman Cross and others in a "raising bee" in 1916. Wyman's son, Stan Cross, wrote about the raising:

> The sand and gravel used in the concrete for the basement was scraped from sand bars in the Meech Creek with a team and scraper and mixed by hand on a sweat board, seven parts sand to one of cement. No reinforcing iron was used.
>
> Likewise, the hemlock trees, required to make the 10x10 foot frame and the sheeting, were felled from the farm bush lot immediately to the west and sleighed, on the ice, down Meech Creek to the F.T. Cross mill at Farm Point, for sawing.
>
> ... In later years, father would periodically get the urge to expound about his barn-building experience but he never seemed to comment on the materials used in its construction. He preferred to recall the fifty-two friends, neighbours and

relatives who arrived to help with the Concrete Bee and a week or so later with the Raising Bee.... He would refer to the Caves, Reids, Clarks, Stevensons and Bradleys who farmed on the East side of the Gatineau River at Farm Point, and how they had to cross the river with their horses and buggies on a scow or ferry and then journey the three or four miles to the bee site.[75]

Albert Cowden and his team of horses at his property on Pine Road in Cascades, ca 1935. HSG 01577.

If you wish, before turning left onto Pine Road you can explore **Cowden Road**, straight ahead of you. There is superb bird watching here, particularly in spring when returning migrants such as American redstart, indigo bunting, and other uncommon birds can be found. The NCC-maintained Parking Lot #16 is at the corner here, offering ample parking. The trail into Gatineau Park's woods beyond is Trail #50; it connects to the Trans-Canada Trail, eventually leading west to Wakefield or south to Gatineau/Ottawa.

Otherwise, turn left onto **Pine Road** to rejoin Highway 105/5 and turn right (south) onto it. After less than a kilometre, turn right again at the traffic lights to connect with **Highway 5 Sud** (south) to the twin cities.

Highway 5 is perhaps the very best place in the National Capital Region to view the Canadian Shield bedrock. It, along with the beaver-pond-strewn wetlands and mixed bush you see here, illustrate the difficult landscape with which First Nations peoples, explorers and European settlers had to struggle. Beneath the highway, also note large culvert-like underpasses built expressly for wildlife so they can cross beneath the traffic. Also, look ahead of you to catch the first glimpse of Gatineau and Ottawa.

Take the first exit to **Old Chelsea** and turn right onto **Scott Road** where you'll soon come to the **Gatineau Park Visitor's Centre, Museum**, and offices on your right. There is no admission fee, and there is a small gift shop as well as toilets. Pause here if you wish.

Otherwise continue, passing **Gerry and Isobel's Country Pleasures** (local artisans are featured here in their gift shop; there is also a tearoom, and outdoor equipment rentals are available, too, for items such as skis and snowshoes). Next you pass the **Old Chelsea Gallery**. Both are located in old homes built in the early 1800s. You are now at the corner of Scott Road and the Old Chelsea/Meech Lake Road. Find a place to park here, and take a brief break. The junction of these roads is very historic.

Gilmour's Gatehouse, moved in about 1926 from Chelsea to Old Chelsea at corner of Scott and Old Chelsea Road. Now is L'Agaric Restaurant. Photo dated 1975. HSG 00111–002.

L'Agaric is a restaurant on the northeast corner of the crossroads, but it used to be the toll house, where tolls for road maintenance were charged for every conveyance and pedestrian passing by. Immediately east of it is a **general store** and **patisserie** (a delicious place to visit), and east of these is the **Chelsea Restaurant**. Stroll over to check out its door. Notice something odd? The main doorway space is on the left; however, to its right there is a second, far narrower hinged door. This is a rare example of a "hoop door." The right-hand side of the entry was opened to provide enough space for a lady wearing a hooped skirt to pass through.

Old Chelsea looking west, c. 1900. Edmond's Post Office on left, beyond is Dunn's Hotel (flat top roof). HSG 00109–001.

Opposite this restaurant, find the historical marker leading to the **Old Chelsea Protestant Burying Ground**. Beside it, on the right, is the flat-topped, pressed-tin-clad former **Dunn Hotel**, one of five stopping places, or inns, owned by Irishmen in the mid-1800s. This one also served as the village post office, to which those settlers on Mountain Road would have walked. Cross the street carefully and enter the cast iron gates into the cemetery. Directly ahead of you is the grave of the **Reverend Asa Meech**, after whom Meech Lake was named.

There's lots to do in Old Chelsea, so plan to visit another day because we should continue our circuit. Return to your car and proceed right (northwest) on **Meech Lake Road** for a moment. Almost immediately after its intersection with Scott Road, you pass over diminutive-looking **Chelsea Creek**, once the site of many mills. Now turn left onto **Kingsmere Road**, passing the **Old Chelsea Picnic Ground**, and turn left again at the next road, **Notch Road**. Pass **Dunderosa** golf course on your left, and at the stop sign 1.5 km beyond Kingsmere, turn left again onto **Mine Road**. It follows the park boundary on your right. As you approach the new subdivision on your left, watch for **rue Quartz**. Turn left, then right at **chemin Galène**, and right again onto **rue Granite** to see the original **Alexander Pink farmhouse** at **number 5**, now beautifully restored amidst the new homes.

Return to Galène and turn right, staying on this crescent-shaped road to rejoin Mine Road. All the streets in this Cité-des-Jeunes subdivision are named for minerals, and Mine Road is so called because opposite this enclave of homes is the **Forsyth Iron Ore Mine**, now inoperative and well hidden from view by saplings and raspberry canes.

At the intersection with **Boulevard des Hautes-Plaines** (and its access to Highway 5), Mine Road becomes **Boulevard del la Cité-des-Jeunes**. Several institutions on the right-hand side of the road back onto the park, including the **École Sécondaire Mont Bleu, Campus Gabrielle-Roy de l'Outaouais CEGEP** (with its associated log building, **La Cabane en Bois Ronde**), **Heritage College**, and the **Asticou Centre**. Cross **Boulevard St-Raymond**, and directly after **St. Rédempteur Cemetery**, turn right on **Boulevard Gamelin**. On your left is the **Lac des Fées (Fairy Lake) amphitheatre** and ski hill, a very popular spot with families during wintertime. There is a spectacular view of the cities of Gatineau and Ottawa from here.

You soon reach the termination of rue Gamelin. On your right is another entryway into Gatineau Park with an information kiosk, parking lot, and an easy pathway called **Pioneer Trail**. To return to Ottawa, turn left on **Promenade de la Gatineau**, directly opposite the park entrance and drive south to connect with Boulevard Alexandre-Taché, where you'll turn right. Immediately on your right-hand side is a clump of tall spruce and pine marking the **Britannia Road milestone.** It was erected here in 1820 on the Benedict Farm, marking the mile from then-downtown Hull along that road. As well, there used to be a tollgate immediately east of the milestone. The Federal District Commission purchased this land from descendents of the pioneering Benedict family in 1948 to build the parkway you have just driven upon.

Now proceed west along Alexandre-Taché until you reach the Champlain Bridge, where you can turn left at the lights and return to Ottawa.

OTHER PLACES OF INTEREST

Note: User fees apply in Gatineau Park. Contact the park for current rates.

Bicycling and skiing: Ask for a Gatineau Park summer hiking and biking trail map and winter ski and snowshoe and hiking trail map. Find out how to best access the various trails and remember that not all trails are open to shared activities. (For the unique guide to Gatineau Park's human and natural history, as well as a description of 25 hiking/ski trails, see my book, *Historical Walks: The Gatineau Park Story*, 3rd edition, Fitzhenry & Whiteside, 2004.)

Luskville Falls is accessed at chemin Hôtel de Ville at Luskville, along the four-lane stretch of Highway 148. There is a delightful picnic ground here and an excellent, though vigorous, uphill scramble to the disused fire tower at the summit of the ridge. Also here **Luskville Falls Ranch**, the only **equestrian stable** authorized to take you on horseback through designated trails in Gatineau Park. For horse lovers, this is a must. Owner Pierre Lapointe is a member of the **Gatineau Hills Trail Riding Association**, and has been instrumental in building and maintaining a trail for horses that skirts the base of the ridge. It crosses the Eardley-Masham road and terminates at the Steele Line.

Lusk Cave is a marble cave that you can fully explore in Gatineau Park. Entry to Lusk Cave is from the north at Ste-Cécile-de-Masham.

Mackenzie King Estate includes Moorside and Kingswood, the former prime minister's beloved retreats that are part of the 500 acres he bequeathed to the people of Canada in his will. Both sites are operated as museums; Moorside has a tearoom as well as a collection of King's collection of architectural ruins picturesquely dotted about the garden-like setting.

Champlain Lookout and **King Mountain** are two lookouts (and hikes) that offer superb view of the northern limit of the Champlain Sea, and today's flat Ottawa Valley. An absolute must-see.

Rupert farm scene shows men stooking hay; in background, team of horses with hay binder, barns and road in background, c. 1900. HSG 00821

Duclos and **Rupert** are two interesting villages north of Ste-Cécile-de-Masham. You can take an adventurous back roads circuit to explore these, then end up in Alcove and Wakefield.

Lac des Fées: This is a super tobogganing hill in winter, perfect for families. Also in spring-summer-fall, there are good cycle paths around here, along the Lac des Fées Parkway.

Pioneer Trail. It takes roughly twenty minutes or so to walk this short circuit. Interpretive signs tell you about the original homesteader, Samuel Benedict, who was farming here in 1801. Of interest here, too, is the well-explained concept of succession, whereby plants of different kinds take root and grow in various "waves" while the landscape changes from cleared and worked farmland to mixed woodlands. Trees such as basswood, white pine, and sugar maple are identified, along with their uses, on this easy walking trail. For example, wood from the American linden has a clear white colour, and is free of knots, making it prized by sculptors. There is ample parking here, as well as an information kiosk (staffed in the summertime), and outhouse-style toilets.

Ottawa River Loop

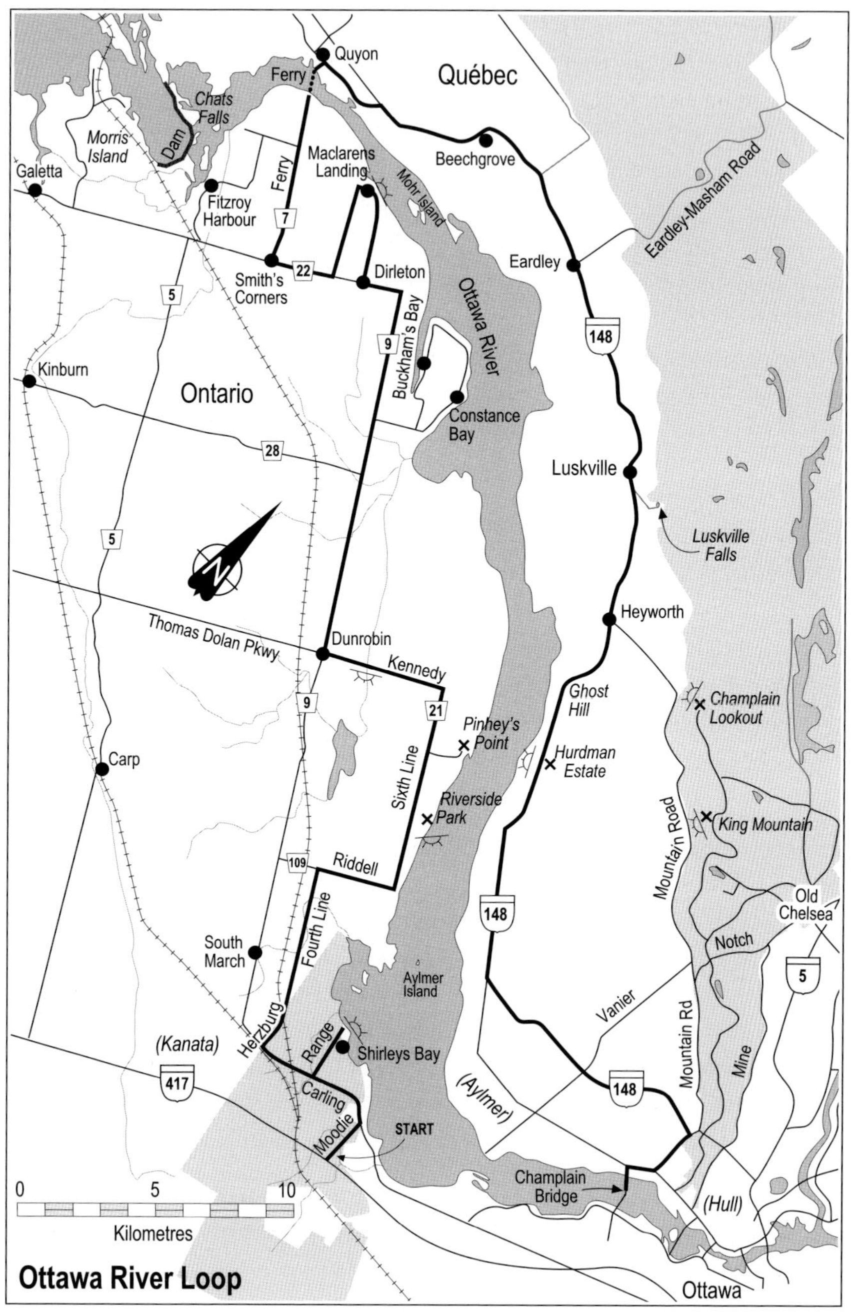

The Great Fire of 1870

When my husband's parents lived on a farm in Kinburn, they became fast friends with an elderly farmer-neighbour. Like many of the Valley's finest, he was a talker, and did not shy from telling us all a thing or two. Norman kept us amused with his first-person tales of "the fire of '70." It took a while before we realized he wasn't talking about *1970*, but of the Great Fire of 1870. This fire, he claimed, was the cause of the "chicos" (burned trunks) of cedar trees still standing in their cedar woods.

A long drought had plagued the land during that summer of 1870. By August, parched land was tinder dry, and on August 18, the winds sprang up. No one could remember where the fire started, but soon the conflagration consumed the countryside of Fitzroy, parts of Lanark, Huntley, Gloucester, and Nepean. Borne on the wind, sparks leapt across the Ottawa River crossing through Hull (now Gatineau) and burned their way over "the mountain" (Gatineau Park) towards Wakefield.

American raconteur, author, and tourist Anson A. Gard, wrote many an interesting note concerning the fire in his book, *Genealogy of the Valley* (1906). People who lived along the Eardley Escarpment described fleeing flames in their horse-drawn wagons. Others with their tongues firmly planted in their cheek recounted how they'd dined on baked apples for the duration of the winter, which cooked on the trees while the fire swept through.

Tall tales or truth, the Great Fire devastated both town and countryside. Harry and Olive Walker describe Ottawa on 18 August 1870:

> *About four o'clock a fierce gale arose, springing from the southwest; it grew so dark that lamps were lighted in the city ... Then clouds of ashes began to fall in the streets, and the dense smoke got hotter and still hotter and more blinding, and people at length began to realize that the terrific gale had fanned the flames into frightful proportions, and at the moment were travelling at the rate of five miles an hour and spreading in every direction. In the township of Gloucester an area of ten miles was in flames ... Hundreds of people passed the night in the river, seeking safety in the water. Some saved themselves in wells and root houses.*[76]

Country people poured into the city the next day, thinking they would find shelter there. Over 2,000 fled along Richmond Road, attempting to flee the flames, seeking refuge in the Ottawa River. Meanwhile, 2,000 men from the Chaudière mills marched out towards the west end of the city to extinguish the fire. Others prayed for deliverance at churches.

The population of Ottawa was 21,000: possibly all but the youngest feared that the city — if not their lives — would be lost. Nevertheless, the fire threatening Uppertown was extinguished, thanks to firefighters, "able-bodied men," and troops who cut the dam holding Dow's Lake waters from the lowlands.

Mrs. Braddish Billings documented terrors in the countryside amid the conflagration:

> *Throughout the whole time people were on the move from place to place in search of shelter and safety; women were on foot, with terrified children clinging to them, picking their dangerous steps among the patches of burning ground; while some, to save both themselves and their horses, mounted and galloped at breakneck speed over fields of fire... The punk-dry fences acted like powder trains, and invariably conducted the fire to the farm buildings.*

A Spooky Tale of Ghost Hill

While driving west along Highway 148, the river views are breathtaking. Soon, however, you will come to a lonely looking stone church with a broken-down fence at the top of a hill, at Braun Road. This is St. Augustine's. As the road slips away from the church, you find yourself descending Ghost Hill toward Breckenridge Creek. Dense woods crowd either side of you, which soon give way to a wetland at the base of the hill.

It is one thing to descend the hill these days in a comfortable car. During the 1800s however, you would have been on shank's mare (foot), or perhaps in an ox- or horse-drawn wagon. Imagine the cart creaking and groaning, and you, the driver, dozing at the reins. After a long day at Symmes Landing (Aylmer) or the Wrightsville (Hull) markets, perhaps the horse could pick its way home along the lonesome stretch of roadway hewn from the dense woods.

One such night, exactly such a scenario was in progress...

Suddenly, the horse started in fright and the driver, awakened from his slumber, shrieked: *"What was that?"* A horrific apparition galloped toward him, bellowing. Was it man, or a beast? It had the head of a cow and the body of a man — or, was that the body of a cow and the head of a man? Without thinking, the driver picked up his gun and fired at the ghost.

It dropped to the ground, felled with a single shot. Whipping out of the cart, the driver ran to the figure. Bending over it, he cried aloud. There, shot dead, was his best friend who for a lark had dressed up in the hide of a calf to scare the life out of him, on a dark and lonesome night ...

This is but one of the tales of Ghost Hill. Here's another ...

The Armenian Peddler of Ghost Hill

In the early days of settlement, many country folk earned a fragile living going from door to door, selling this and that. One such fellow was an Armenian peddler, who had a horse and cart. Resembling a rag picker, he would sell his wares to whomever he might. Perhaps it would be a needle or some metres of cloth, a kettle, or something pretty. This particular peddler, however, was rumoured by some to have a bag of gold hidden on his person.

Such rumours have a habit of getting themselves about, and before too long the peddler heard some ruffians were scheming to rob him. Thinking to thwart their evil plot, he buried his little bag of coins beneath a tree along the winding road down Ghost Hill. He continued along, believing he could talk his way out of any attack.

Alas, such was not the case. Instead, he was accosted, and his attackers demanded the money they just knew he had. Searching him, they found nothing and, angry at defeat, they murdered the Armenian.

Now, would that be tall tale or truth?

The details slip and slide, but one day the late owner of Ghost Hill Farm, Elizabeth Hay, told me that when workers were widening the road they knocked on her door one day. There, in their hands, was a little bag of old coins.

Ghost Hill Will-o'-the-Wisp

Elizabeth Hay also told me of a possible origin of many of the ghostly sightings on the lonesome stretch of wooded road beside her heritage farm.

As a young woman growing up on the farm, Hay sometimes worked at a little shop in Breckenridge below the hill. A village once stood at the little creek at the bend in the road where Highway 148 abruptly curves west towards Luskville. One day she was asked to hasten to the marsh below the farm before it was too late. "Too late for what?" she might have wondered, but off she went.

There, hovering above the waters of the marsh bobbed the fantastical-looking and seldom-seen will-o'-the-wisp. Created by marsh gases, people describe these phenomena as looking eerie in the falling light of an evening's approach.

Will-o-the-wisp or ghostly apparitions? Who can say? Nevertheless, the frequent sightings on Ghost Hill cloak the stretch of roadway with mystery and intrigue. As for Elizabeth Hay, did she see any other marsh gases in her lifetime? None, she told me: this was the only one. Perhaps the far more frequent sightings of ghosts are true, too. Who can say for sure?

HUMAN HISTORY

This western ramble from Ottawa brings you along Ontario's southern shore of the Ottawa River, following the waterway as closely as is possible, to Fitzroy. Here you'll cross to Quyon, in West Québec, and drive east along panoramic Highway 148 towards Aylmer, Gatineau, and Ottawa. Wherever possible, pause to appreciate the many splendid views of the Ottawa River.

The southern section of the ramble introduces the townships of Nepean, March, Torbolton, and Fitzroy. Although the first Europeans paddled the Ottawa in the early 1600s, settlement did not begin here until the early 1800s. The establishment of Philemon Wright's community of Wrightsville at the Chaudière Falls and the development of Aylmer preceded settlement here.

This is true despite the Crawford Purchase in 1783, with which Carleton County was surveyed and purchased from the Mississauguans (see Settlers on the Ottawa chapter). Indeed, it was only after the War of 1812 — in 1819 — that Torbolton, Fitzroy, Huntley, March, and Goulbourn townships were added to Carleton County. Britain was keen to claim and protect her colony from American incursion. Accordingly, lots of up to 1,000 acres were granted to military men who had served in the Napoleonic Wars.

One such lot was granted to Captain John Benning Monk in 1819 (the lot is clearly shown on a map of March Township, dated 1863). Monk, who was born in Nova Scotia, saw active service in these wars and eventually built a stone mansion, Beechmount, overlooking the river. We can all be wryly amused by the name of his first log dwelling, which he all-too-descriptively dubbed "Mosquito Cove." In 1820 he married Elizabeth Anne Fitzgerald. Her family was from Bessborough, county Kilkenny, in Ireland. Her family's origins might have been the reason the Monks' new neighbour, General Lloyd, called his home Bessborough. Lloyd was granted 1,600 acres immediately north of the Monks — and married one of his neighbour's sisters. The link between the Monks and Lloyds was not confined to their military background and intermarriage. Nature and fate had something else in store for their beautiful mansions: both were destroyed by the Great Fire of 1870.

One of the next arrivals to this area was Englishman Hamnett Kirkes Pinhey. Born in Plymouth, England, in 1784, he had exhibited such impeccable loyalty to the Crown that King George III personally commended Pinhey for acting as His Royal Highness' messenger during the Napoleonic Wars. Pinhey was also an extremely successful merchant and ship owner. In their book, *The Carleton Saga*, Harry and Olive Walker wrote:

> … he ran the French blockade of the Channel. While Napoleon was stabling his cavalry in all the Capitals of Europe, Pinhey speaking French and German, undaunted travelled by coach the roads of war. Knowing his contacts, the British Government utilized his proffered services as a blockade-runner and bearer of dispatches to a Prussian General, 'conscious that thereby my personal safety was much endangered'. Which it was. On one occasion he was captured, with the final prospect of facing a firing squad. But he talked himself out of it and actually 'wangled' a French passport to Berlin.[77]

Despite his not being a military man, Pinhey's obvious loyalty and capabilities were rewarded. He was granted 1,000 acres fronting the river, located upstream from present Shirleys Bay, and eleven or so lots south of the Lloyd and Monk properties. After returning to England to wrap up his affairs, he brought his wife and two children, Horace and Constance, back with him to Canada.

He called his new estate Horaceville. One might be forgiven for thinking nearby Constance Lake, Creek, and Bay were named for his daughter, but this appears incorrect. Research suggests the name derives from an Algonquin chief named "Constaw." Today, Pinhey's draughty-looking mansion still overlooks the river, though most of the outbuildings have not survived the ravages of time.

As people like the Monks, Lloyds, and Pinheys settled in and started to build estates, they hired servants, stonemasons, gardeners, and labourers. Pinhey alone hired twenty-five labourers. For some, life on the south shore was rather grand. There are tales of balls and dinners at which VIPs like Lieutenant-Governor Lord Dalhousie and Bishop John Strachan were entertained. Just west of what would become the capital of Canada, at least some of the inhabitants of March Township were living the high life.

North of March, Torbolton Township has quite a different tale to tell: a story of native settlement and Iroquois ambushes. Constance Bay once served as a seasonal stopping ground for native peoples, just like estuarine delta of the Gatineau River (see Gatineau River and

Brewery Creek rambles). Even today we can still appreciate why it would be a favoured stopping place.

The bay is sheltered by a long spit of sand (called Big Sand Point) that thrusts into the Ottawa River. North of it is a projecting point of land and a sheltered deep inlet known as Bucham's Bay. Many creeks drain into Constance Bay, most notably Constance Creek flowing northwest through a wide marshland from Constance Lake. Because of the game found here amid the rich wetlands, and because of its sheltered situation alongside the river trade and transportation route, Constance Bay was a logical spot for early native peoples to rest, catch game, feast, dry, and otherwise cure food for the winter, and to bury their dead.

The documented evidence of native bones indicates that Torbolton's Constance Bay was a burial ground habituated not only by nomadic Algonquin, Huron, and Iroquois, but also by their ancestors. In fact, it is likely that this entire "nub" of the Ottawa River extending east of Chats Falls, the mighty rapids west of Fitzroy Harbour and Quyon, was a resting place in Paleo-Indian times. It makes sense that they would pause here, downstream of the rugged portage that bypassed the falls.

"March [Township] on the Chaudière," with log rafts on the Ottawa River east of Pinhey's Point. At rear is St. Mary's Church; foreground shows post office. Steel engraving by W.H. Bartlett as published in Canadian Scenery, Willis and Bartlett, London, England, 1842. From author's private collection.

There are also documented native burial mounds on the Québec side at Indian Point, also known as Mondion's Point. (See Chats Falls ramble.)

In fact, as mentioned previously (see Trade along the Ottawa and Gatineau River Loop chapters) this entire stretch of the Ottawa has been a subject of archaeological research since the late 1800s. T.W. Edwin Sowter was an archaeologist who was born in 1860 in Aylmer. He distinguished himself by documenting several findings in the capital region, made in the early 1900s. He did considerable work at Constance Bay, as well as some along Brewery Creek in Hull (see Brewery Creek ramble). Others who worked here included Dr. Edward van Cortlandt, W.J Wintemberg, J.F. Pendergast, Clyde C. Kennedy and, more recently, Dr. Gordon Watson.

What did these archaeologists and scientists find? Shards of pottery. Arrowheads. Tools. And bones. Here's what Sowter wrote in 1917, after scouring the stretch of shoreline extending from Big Sand Point to Constance Creek:

> The beach at this point for about 150 yards in length and 20 yards in width from high water mark was strewn with fragments of pottery, flints, arrowheads and shards of earthenware. It would appear that here the red hunters [sic] made their campfires and appeased their appetites with roast clam.[78]

Because this was such a prime spot to rest, no doubt there were battles and skirmishes here; canoes laden with trade goods would yield "easy pickings."

It is helpful to put all of this in context, because it is difficult for us now, in the twenty-first century, to realize how much traffic plied the waters here in the 1600s. Archaeologist Clyde C. Kennedy wrote:

> After the Iroquois had driven the Algonquins out of the Ottawa Valley and had virtually destroyed the Huron nation in 1647–1650, the Outaouais (Ottawa) Indians from the upper Lake Huron-Lake Michigan region became the predominant Indian fur-traders travelling the Ottawa River. ... Great flotillas of canoes, sometimes with hundreds of Indian and French paddlers and traders, and later the traders of the North West Company and the Hudson's Bay Company, travelled the Ottawa. Most of the canoe traffic was simply the result of the demand in Europe for hairs from beaver skins, used to make felt hats. But missionaries,

explorers, coureurs de bois, lumbermen, scientists and settlers used the river as a highway to their quests.[79]

This brings us to the story of one particular ambush here on the Ontario side, reputedly at Constance Bay. The year was sometime in the mid-1600s. The Iroquois lay in wait for a group of French and Algonquin. Sowter "read" the story told in the artifacts and bones that he found. This is his interpretation of what happened near the mouth of Constance Creek, known as "Pointe à la Bataille":

> A great many years ago an expedition of French fur-traders, together with a number of friendly Indian, possibly Algonquin and Huron allies, went into camp one evening at Pointe à la Bataille. Fires were lighted, kettles were slung and all preparations made to pass the night in peace and quietness. Soon, however, the lights from other camp fires began to glimmer through the foliage, on the opposite shore of the bay, and a reconnaissance presently revealed a large war-party of Iroquois in a barricaded encampment on the Wendigo Mound at Big Sand Point. Well skilled as they were in all the artifices of forest warfare, the French and their Indian companions were satisfied something would happen before morning. ...
>
> Towards midnight, the attacking party left Pointe à la Bataille and proceeded stealthily southward, in their canoes, along the eastern rim of Sand Bay, crossed the outlet of Constance Creek and landing on the western shore of the bay, advanced towards Big Sand Point through the pine forest ... The attack was entirely successful, for it descended upon and enveloped the sleeping camp like a hideous nightmare. Many of the Iroquois died in their sleep, while the rest of the party perished to a man in the wild confusion of a midnight massacre.[80]

So it was that concerns about war, territorial protection, and ambushes compose part of the fascinating history of this western sector of the NCR. This terrible natural disaster waged its own kind of war upon the region, destroying many log cabins through to estate homes. It lasted from August 7 to 23, and at least one source claims that the fires extended to Québec's Saguenay Valley.[81] Whatever the authenticity of that claim, here in this sector of the Ottawa Valley, a wall of fire extending over 11 km swept Fitzroy Township in an easterly direction towards Ottawa, travelling up to 16 km an hour, leaving entire herds of livestock roasted in the fields. There are many tales of heroic battles with the flames: some people were burned alive in their attempts to save their homes and animals. Others lived, but had to rebuild their lives completely. Still others returned to find their homes spared while their neighbours homes were razed.

As people fled, they gravitated towards the Ottawa River, where some piled into boats, seeking safety. Others cowered by the shore seeking protection from the cliffs of layered limestone at the water's edge.

Author inspecting cliffs where children sheltered from the Great Fire of 1870, Pinhey's Point. Photo: E. Fletcher, 2002.

In actual fact, the story of this fire returns us to Pinhey's Point. Come nightfall during that conflagration, a huddle of refugees sheltered, terrified, below the cliffs on the point. Standing on this shoreline today, we can try to imagine the scene. A bucket brigade is credited with saving the estate from being destroyed, while at night, wrote Harry and Olive Walker in *The Carleton Saga*, a different scene emerged:

> Under a high overhanging bank at the riverside, between thirty and forty homeless men, women and children spent the night.

> Some of the refugees from the back townships had brought beds, and on these, children were put to sleep while the rest of the desolate assemblage spent the night in fitful slumber broken by fears of the pursuing flames. The night was pitch dark with the inky blackness broken only where the flames roared high against the Western sky or where the wind caught up the burning embers and hurled them blazing through the air. It was a fearful night and many thought the end of the world had come.[82]

After the fire was spent, homes had to be rebuilt, including General Lloyd's Bessborough and Monk's Beechmount manor homes. August is not far away from winter's snows, and particularly after a summer drought when the harvest yield would have been less than usual, people would have had a hard time feeding themselves because not only the crops, but also livestock perished. In addition, the fire is credited with destroying the last great stands of pine in Fitzroy, Torbolton, and March townships.

Although this history has largely concentrated on the Ontario side of the Ottawa, the Great Fire of 1870 connects us to the Québec side, as do the native encampments that also existed on the northern shore. The islands in the Ottawa River — Mohr Island and Aylmer (or Lighthouse) Island, for example — were used by ancient peoples. Champlain makes a reference to Mohr Island in his journals, noting its beauty, and archaeologists Sowter, Kennedy, and others spoke of the ossuary (place where bones of the dead were laid to rest) on Aylmer Island.

NATURAL HISTORY

The sand dunes of Constance and Shirleys bays, the extensive wetlands of Constance Creek, and the outcrops of rocky ridges that extend like fingers parallel to the river in these townships are physical features arising from the retreat of the glacier and the changing levels of the Ottawa River. As the kilometre-high Laurentide Ice Sheet melted, its retreat left piles of detritus, and ground-up rocks in the form of moraine were strewn along this shoreline. As the Champlain Sea rushed in to submerge the depressed and scoured landscape, its currents and depositions further influenced today's topography.

Buckham's Bay, in Torbolton Township, forms a narrow inlet in the Ottawa River. Once, it would have been an "island" in a much bigger Ottawa River, as would all of the ridges you will travel over. The sand banks on the eastern shores of Torbolton, March, and Nepean townships were deposited as the Champlain Sea withdrew.

We can imagine how vast the Ottawa River once was, particularly along Highway 148 east of Quyon. Here the road travels along the top of a long terrace that more-or-less parallels the ridge of the Eardley Escarpment (see Gatineau Park ramble). This terrace is an old beachhead, marking the shoreline of a much larger Ottawa River that flowed into the Champlain Sea from the receding ice sheets to the north. Just past the four-lane section of the highway as you drive east toward Aylmer, you suddenly descend from this terrace onto the "Luskville Flats." To the south is a brackish bay whose shallow waters offer good opportunities to spot wetland and open-water species of birds. The road then twists and turns, first crossing Breckenridge Creek, a watershed originating in Gatineau Park, which courses through the lowland plain below the Eardley Escarpment. Highway 148 crosses it, then immediately runs up Ghost Hill. This is an outcrop of Precambrian rock: its northwesterly face is a prominent geophysical landmark (it can be spotted clearly from Champlain Lookout and Western Lodge in Gatineau Park). Woods cover its slopes: to the left of the highway there are hemlock trees amid the mixed woods, whereas the right-hand side features a swamp, then a mixed hardwood forest.

BEFORE YOU GO ON THE RAMBLE

Why go? This is a spectacular circuit drive of both the south and north shores of the Ottawa River, which introduces you to a varied topographical region of ridges and wetlands, villages, and heritage homes. Views of the river are breathtaking, and the short ferry ride to Quyon is always fun.

Distance: This ramble is 113 km from its start at Moodie Drive and Highway 417 to the Champlain Bridge.

Modes of exploration: I have described a drive. This is an awesome bike trip, too, but note that the route through Quebec traverses Highway 148, which isn't very bike-friendly.

Getting there: To start, head west on Highway 417; exit at Moodie Drive and go north to Carling Avenue to Shirleys Bay, then to Pinhey Point Road and the estate. Next explore Constance Bay and, via Dirleton and Galetta you continue to Smith's Corners, identified by the Pinto Valley horse farm. Next is the ferry across the Ottawa River to Quyon, then Luskville, Breckenridge, Ghost Hill, and the old village of Aylmer, now Gatineau, before crossing at the Champlain Bridge to return to Ottawa.

Facilities: A variety of village-type shops, restaurants en route.

Of special note: The circuit as described is only possible when the seasonal Quyon Ferry is open, usually mid-April to end of November. Take binoculars so you can look at the topographical features, check out the islands, and, while you cross on the ferry, look west towards the Chats Falls (see Chats Falls ramble). When exploring the Pinhey Estate you can wander the property, but the point of land in the river, due north of the mansion, is an extremely fragile environment that is off-limits. If you wish to explore this fascinating point, take your canoe, portage it down to the shore, and put in.

In fact, this ramble is ideal for canoeing. You can put in at Shirleys Bay and many other spots along the river. But remember: the Ottawa is a large river and winds can play havoc with your body temperature, as well as your ability to paddle. Many nearby watercourses, such as Constance Creek, Bay, and Lake are easy to paddle, however.

THE RAMBLE

Start at the western segment of **Nepean** (part of Ottawa West). Drive west on Highway 417, which you exit at **Moodie Drive**, driving to **Carling Avenue**. You pass the Bell-Northern/Northern Telecom research centre, then the **Crystal Bay** golf course.

Along Carling, the road veers abruptly west. You drive past by the NCC's 4 km Trail Number 10 (explore it another day) and its Parking Lot Number P2, as well as Davidson's Side Road. Turn right at **Range Road** and proceed to the riverfront **Shirleys Bay Park** to view the sweep of the Ottawa River at the broad, lake-like reaches of **Lac Deschênes** (Oak Lake). Across from you is Aylmer, and east is Britannia Bay, Ottawa's former amusement park and dance hall, now a fine beach and recreational area. In front of you is a public boat launch, so you can wind sail, kayak, or canoe from here. (The Department of National Defence area is on your left, however, so take care not to paddle into that area that is cordoned off by a series of buoys!) This is an outstanding area for bird watching, particularly during spring and fall migration. To your left is **Innis Point** where the rare alvar environment can be found (see Natural history section of the Mississippi Mills ramble).

J.R. Booth house near Shirleys Bay. COA CA-17501.

You cannot explore much of this area because a large segment of this sandspit and shallow bay is DND property. Do, however, take a stroll or drive along the mostly deserted roads immediately east of here: this was **Shirleys Bay Village**. Properties here were bought by the NCC in the late 1950s as part of the move to create the Greenbelt in this western sector of the capital. The intention was to develop a park of 900 acres or so near the DND and Northern Electric Company research centre. By 1961 the present DND research centre, Connaught Rifle Ranges, and DND reserved lands had been set up.

Return to Carling and turn right, proceeding under the **CNR railway track**, and turn right again at **Hertzberg Road**, the easternmost boundary of **Kanata**. You now leave Nepean behind and soon pass

Sandhill Road. Immediately you again cross the railway tracks, and then drive along what has become the **Fourth Line** — a country designation for a road. On your right is a fence marking the DND property. Roads on the opposite side of it are sandy, a cattail wetlands extends as far as you can see towards the Ottawa River, to the north.

Continue on the Fourth Line until its termination at **Riddell Road (Route 109)** where you turn right, then left onto **Sixth Line Road (Route 21)**. This pretty country road bisects the original 1,000-acre lots granted to the military men and likes of Hamnett Kirkes Pinhey.

Watch now, on your right for the **YMCA Bonnenfants Centre.** Immediately beyond it turn left into the parking lot of **Riverside Park**. Park and stretch your legs on a very pretty trail descending through a forest of basswood, ironwood, maple, and cedar, among other trees. You briefly emerge onto a clear space (to the right a trail goes east to the YMCA). To the right of a storage building in front of you, the trail continues its descent to the river. A flight of wooden stairs leads through a very interesting section of the forest. Look for windfalls (uprooted cedar trees) here, and see if you can spot the new growth trees that are actually branches of the former trunk, now stretching to the sky, forming trees in their own right. The root mass of the original tree sustains this new growth. Before emerging onto the rocky beach, and while still on the steps, examine the cliff face closely; it's composed of thin layers of shale.

At the base of the staircase two large slabs of limestone form the last two steps to the rocky beach. Look closely to discover carvings of two feathers on these. This pebble and rock beach is fascinating: you can gauge the normal water level from the "line" of larger rocks, driftwood and other detritus along the shore. Here, tenacious plants cling to the cliff face in an extremely exposed environment. Opposite you, look at the Québec shore: this is where you'll be driving on your return route. To your right spy **Aylmer Island** with its lighthouse and, at close right, **telecommunications towers** near the DND Shirleys Bay property.

Return to your car and continue west on the Sixth Line Road to **Pinhey's Point Road**. Turn right to enter the **Pinhey Estate**. In summer, this is operated as a museum complete with interpretive signs and exhibits inside the main building. However, the grounds can be explored all year round. Hamnett Kirkes Pinhey started building Horaceville in 1821 and completed the settlement circa 1840. In 1826, he wrote a letter to a friend in England, noting that melons were ripening in his hothouse frames as well as in the ground. "The grain," he wrote, "[was]

Britannia Boat Club outing to Pinhey's Point, 1910.
COA CA-3379.

from half a ton to three tons per acre, [and] according to the soil, we are now cutting, and the wheat, oats, barley and peas next month."[83]

In its heyday in the mid-1800s, Horaceville included neighbouring Old St. Mary's Church (now private property), a sawmill and gristmill, barns, silo, lime kiln, ice house, powder house, among others, as well as a terraced garden cascading down the hillside towards the river. (The low cliffs at the riverfront are where people sheltered from the 1870 conflagration.) Beside the manor house, only a few other structures remain today, and even the stone manor house seems in constant need of repairs. Nonetheless, we can still tell this was a prosperous concern for some time. Pinhey died in 1857; his wife predeceased him by five years. Both are buried in the churchyard next door, which Hamnett Pinhey had built in 1828.

Returning to your car, walk beside the ruins of the fort on the manor's east side. In their 1985 booklet, *Guide to A Heritage Tour of March*, the March Historical Society explains: "Pinhey built a stone fort complete with flag staff and a battery of small cannons which were fired on ceremonial occasions and to greet arriving dignitaries. The grounds were terraced to the river for vegetable gardens, flowers and orchards with rose bushes and fruit trees brought from England."[84]

Return to the Sixth Line and turn left. Close by, find an immense driveway leading to the former property of Captain John Benning Monk, **Beechmount**, destroyed by the 1870 fire. It became entrepreneur Michael Cowpland's estate in the late 1980s. In fact, many of these former estate lands granted to veterans of the Napoleonic Wars are the expensive estates of today's high-tech elite. Next pass the "new" (1909) **St. Mary's Anglican Church** on the right-hand side of the road. Beyond it, another shared laneway marks the original property deeded to **General Lloyd**. You might be able to see the ruins of Lloyd's home, **Bessborough**, also destroyed by the Great Fire.

At the end of the Sixth Line turn left at Route 129 (Kennedy Side Road). This road is the northern border of March: to the right (north), is Torbolton. On your left is a stone home, the **Rolston house**. The Society booklet explains that it might have survived the 1870 fire, though it also could have been rebuilt. Regardless, its central gable over the front door is a classical design of pleasing symmetry. Next to it is the **Kennedy farm**, originally built by James Payne after the Great Fire. It was first constructed of logs, now covered by siding. Now you cross a bridge over **Constance Creek,** here thickly lined by dense mattes of cattail. This is a superb spot to canoe and bird watch (to your left, (east), the creek continues to **Constance Lake**).

When you reach the Dunrobin Road (Route 9), the brick building on your right is **Younghusband's store**. The March Historical Society booklet notes, "Younghusband's store, which has operated continuously since 1854 and until June of this year [1985] was still in the same family; and the former Gold Medal Cheese Factory, across the Dunrobin Road on the [right]. This was opened in 1910 by an association of 24 farmers, who continued to run it until shortage of milk forced it to close in 1952." That building is now an apartment. The church on the southwest corner is the 1895 **St. Paul's Anglican**. This is the second Anglican church we've seen; there are three in this vicinity.

Turn right, proceeding northwest on the Dunrobin Road through flatlands now used largely for horse farms. Interestingly, the 1,000-acre properties granted to the military elite proved far more fertile away from the riverfront. These "back acreages" were occupied by the estates' labourers and other settlers; ironically, they got the best land. A rise of land lies ahead: it's a sandy and rocky outcrop of moraine deposits, once an island in a much-broader Ottawa River. At its base is the Constance Bay Road. (There you can turn right to explore **Constance Bay** and **Buckham's Bay**: see Other places of interest.)

We take roads for granted these days. But let's look at the Walker's book, *The Carleton Saga*, again, as a means of reflecting on how far we've come. The Torbolton Road (Third Line) was called "Purgatory Road," the authors say.

> The pioneer John Buckham, who lived at the farther end of it, was the first to drive a team over it ... Not to be outdone by a mere husband, Mrs. Buckham, as a young bride, was the first woman to ride over the road on horseback, in proceeding to shop at Bytown. The return journey was a nightmare as she frequently had to dismount, letting the horse flounder through sloughs and creeks while she navigated across on fallen timbers to remount her blown horse to finally reach home and a distracted husband.[85]

Proceed on the Dunrobin Road, which presents no such challenges to us these days. Shortly it becomes heavily wooded on either side and long lanes through the trees denote today's new estates. Turn left onto Route 22, the Galetta Side Road. You soon pass by Dirleton, where the Scottish settlers of Torbolton built a Presbyterian Church, as well as a school in the mid-1800s.

Turn right here, to take a look at **Maclarens Landing**, named for the same David Maclaren family of Scotland who purchased William Fairbairn's mill on the Lapêche at Wakefield in 1844. As its name suggests, this was an old wharf that served the steamships such as the *G.B. Greene* and others plying Lac Deschênes from Aylmer to Fitzroy Harbour. The Maclaren home still stands here at the landing west of the main beach: it is a frame home built circa 1840.

Return to the Galetta Side Road and watch for the ferry signs to Québec. At **Smith's Corners** (Pinto Valley Ranch) turn right and drive to the wharf on the Ottawa River. This is one of the narrowest channels in the river. Beneath its waters are shifting sand bars and devious, strong currents. Although the beach on the north shore of the river, at the confluence of the **Quyon River** looks appropriate for swimming, avoid it: people have drowned here as recently as the summer of 2002. To the west, beyond proper view, are the Chats Falls and Fitzroy Harbour (see Chats Falls ramble).

You are now travelling the waters that the steamers used to ply. The *G.B. Greene*, *Emerald*, and *Ann Sisson* travelled here, along this body of water known as Lac Deschênes. Famous people have travelled here: late author and historian S. Wyman MacKechnie wrote about the year 1860, when British Royalty visited Mrs. Mary Beane, proprietress of a stopping place (now demolished) on the shore of the Ottawa River at Quyon:

Albert Edward, Prince of Wales, while visiting Canada came on a cruise up the Ottawa River on the Ann Sisson, the boat in service at that time. Evening was approaching and the royal party decided to remain overnight at The Quio [former spelling of Quyon]. There was only one hostelry, an inn at the river shore catering mostly to lumbermen and local river travelers. The proprietor, an elderly Irish lady by the name of Mrs. Beane, was not the least bit flustered at the prospect of entertaining the future King of England. She sent out and borrowed some silver, china and linen, to supplement her own supply, and the royal entourage was duly accommodated in her establishment."[86]

At the ferry docks at **Quyon**, you have arrived in the **Pontiac Region** of the Outaouais. Drive straight ahead passing the fairgrounds on your right (there is a country fair here during the Canada Day weekend) to connect with **Clarendon Street**, the original Highway 8 that serviced the Pontiac. On your left is **Gavan's Hotel**, a well-known tavern in the valley. Turn right on Clarendon, passing the **War Memorial** on your left. Directly beyond it is a **spring** where locals like me gathered during the ice storm of 1998 to get potable water and exchange news. Above the hill is a residence and you'd never guess, but in the mid-1900s it was one of the best-known dance halls in the Ottawa Valley, attracting many bands from Upper New York State. Beyond the hydro cut, which crosses the Ottawa River to your right, and extends over Gatineau Park on your left, rejoin Highway 148. Turn right (east).

On your left, you soon glimpse the **Eardley Escarpment**. Here the highway wends its way eastward through bush lots, homes, agricultural fields, farmhouses, and their outbuildings. At **chemin Hammond** you drive across the overpass, over the old **Pontiac & Pacific Railway** line (1886). The tracks were torn up a few years ago and despite momentum from some of us to turn it into a bike path that would be part of the Trans Canada Trail, many landowners objected, particularly farmers. Unfortunately, this sector of railbed extending from Wyman (northwest of Quyon) to Aylmer remains a "blank spot" on the cycle routes of the NCR.

Note the flatlands north of the highway: this is where **Mountainview Turf Farm** grows and cuts sod for lawns, parks, and golf courses. To the south, you view the Ottawa River in the distance. **Mohr Island,** opposite the community of **Beechgrove** (south of the highway), is beyond view from here, but this island is where settler John Christian Mohr purchased

G. B. Pattee near Mohr Island, Ottawa River, with Eardley Escarpment (southern ridge of Gatineau Park) at horizon, n.d. COA CA-18452.

property circa 1840. He built a home and a sawmill on his farm, and overwintered his horses on the island that bears his name.

Now the highway ascends to the top of a rise of land; to your right, the flat valley extends to the river. To your left, more or less flat land extends to the Eardley Escarpment. You are now travelling on what would have been the bottom of the Champlain Sea, and the terrace on your right would have been the shoreline of a much larger Ottawa River. Just imagine how mighty it would be if it still lapped against this terrace; its depths would have covered the land you drove through on the river's Ontario shore.

If you have been on the Gatineau Park Loop ramble, this next section of highway will be familiar — albeit in a reverse direction. Pass the **Eardley-Masham Road** entryway leading to Gatineau Park's **Lac Lapêche** sector and the **Masham** villages to the north, then proceed through the community of **Luskville**, marked by the four-lane stretch of highway. Back on two lanes, watch for a white church on your left: this is the **Eardley United** (once **Methodist**) **Church** where you can find graves of many pioneering families such as the Lusks. This hamlet was once called **Heyworth**, but is now unnamed. Note that it still appears on some maps at the junction with **chemin de la Montagne Nord** (**Mountain Road**).

After passing Heyworth, you are again on a "new" stretch of highway. Highway 148 dips down the terrace slope onto the "Luskville

Flats" and here you can really see the old shoreline. You are now approaching **Breckenridge Creek**, situated beyond the next bend. It is hard to believe, but quite a sizeable community once lived here just west of the creek, with mills and at least one store. **Breckenridge Station** was here, too, one of the Pontiac & Pacific Junction Railway's stops, (as were Luskville, Eardley, Beechgrove, and Wyman).

Before the railway, mail was delivered to communities up the valley: either by a rider on horseback or by stagecoach. After 1886, the Pontiac and Pacific Junction Railway (still called "Push, Pull, and Jerk" by locals) and subsequently its successor, the Canadian Pacific Railway, delivered the mail. If a community of homes existed but wasn't close to a station, mail was dangled from the carriage on a metal arm, and dropped off, literally. Later, Breckenridge and Luskville won contracts as post offices, and the communities of Heyworth and Eardley disappeared. Still later, when automobiles took over, Breckenridge closed and Luskville remained as the only post office between Aylmer and Quyon. Luskville was still operating in 1989, when I moved to the region, but the post office closed there soon afterward.

Immediately beyond Breckenridge, Highway 148 passes a wetland sanctuary (look for wood ducks here) and ascends **Ghost Hill**. The name derives from supernatural happenings, whether imagined or real, that legend says occurred here. Certainly, it is a spooky place on a foggy night, and we can all imagine how eerie it would have seemed while clip-clopping along on a horse and wagon, with the wetland's mists obscuring views and muffling sounds.

The house at **Ghost Hill Farm** sits atop this hill of legends, hidden from view. It's a pretty limestone home, built in 1880 by Isaac Lusk, the youngest son of Irishman Joseph Lusk, who settled in West Québec in 1820. Luskville, Lusk Lake, and Lusk Cave take his name. The Lusks and their descendents have dwelt here for all but a few years in the 1920s and 1930s when the home was rented to tenant farmers.

At the top of the hill at the junction of **Braun Road**, find **St. Augustine's Church** to the north, erected in 1874 from rough-cut stone. The late local author and historian Diane Lusk Aldred was the last person married here. The parish has moved to Aylmer, and the church is privately owned.

Beyond St. Augustine's, Highway 148 regains its elevation on the terrace and grand views can be seen to the south. On your left you'll find the **Charles Hurdman** white clapboard farmhouse built in the mid-1800s with its former carriage house and sheds. Directly opposite it, on the other side of the highway, is the farm's main sawn plank barn: we can all sympathize with what a nuisance it must have been when the highway divided their property, forcing the owners to watch carefully for traffic before crossing to the barnyard to do their chores.

The adjacent property is an immense new stone mansion erected in 1997. The main twin-chimney central block is flanked by two wings, immediately followed by a large horse barn and fenced paddock. This restored heritage barn was built circa 1880 and is well known in the area because no nails were used in its construction. At the corner of **chemin Elm**, look left to see the 1875 **Orange Lodge,** now a private residence.

Nearby is a stone house reminiscent of the Symmes Inn (see Aylmer ramble). Built of cut limestone, it has an unusual two-storey verandah. This is **Hurdman Heights Estate**, built in 1860 by James Hurdman after the French-Canadian style, which sports a slightly bell-cast eave. The Ottawa River broadens here, affording the mansion atop the hill a spectacular view upriver to Quyon, and across to the Pinhey Estate of Horaceville, which we've already explored. Hurdman built here three years after Pinhey died, but he would certainly have known of the English manor house across the river. The interior of Hurdman Heights has been renovated by the present owners, but some original details remain: the central exposed beam in the living room features a stylized view of the estate, along with hounds pursuing a stag over undulating countryside towards the river. Family legend says an itinerant artist painted it, possibly in exchange for a warm meal and bed.

Beyond it, on the right (south) side of Highway 148 find two buildings, now private homes. The first was the **Eardley School #1**, the second the **1875 Methodist Church**. Both stand on land first granted by letters patent to Ephreim Sanford on 22 August 1806.

Ahead of you, past the uphill bend in the road is **Stoneleigh Farm**. I'll quote from the owner, Mo Laidlaw, who privately published a useful booklet entitled *Heritage Highway — the scenic route to the Pontiac*. She writes that her home was:

> settled in 1844 by William Maxwell Herdman (1819–1881). He married Mary Moffatt (1828–1891), whose family had settled in neighbouring Hull Township (now Aylmer) in 1822. ... the one-and-a-half storey stone farmhouse with a veranda on three sides, built about 1864 to replace the original one-and-a-half storey log house. There's also a barn dating from 1880. Note the decorative trim on the veranda. On the right

are several barns including one made from round logs dating from about 1870. This is now the Jamie Laidlaw farm.[87]

Note that Laidlaw spells the Hurdman name "Herdman," which she claims was the original spelling of this Wesleyan Methodist family. She adds, "Henry Herdman Sr. emigrated from Ireland to New York City in 1811, and then moved to Hull Township (now Aylmer) in 1818 with his wife Elizabeth Maxwell Faris."

Past Stoneleigh, at a bend in the road, look right. Set back in a copse of trees locally known as "Foran's Grove" you might glimpse another stone house, the **Michael Foran home**. According to family historian Rita Foran, the home was erected in 1871 on a prosperous 200-acre farm that produced potatoes, peas, corn, barley, and oats. The limestone for this house and the two Hurdman homes we've just seen (Stoneleigh and Hurdman Heights) was quarried from the same location in Aylmer. In an interview, Mr. Ossie Foran told me that "The original roof was made of cedar shingles, 27 inches wide — cut by hand with a draw blade. I know because in 1923, my dad decided to put on a steel roof. He told me to get up there and measure. I walked along the central roof beam and it's 32 feet wide."

Continue driving, passing **Terry Fox Road**, the boundary between Eardley Township in the Municipality of Pontiac (which we've been driving through since Quyon) and Aylmer, now part of the City of Gatineau. Here Highway 148 also bears the name **chemin Eardley Road**. As you continue, the road becomes increasingly built up, although some farms do remain. On the left-hand side at **400 Eardley Road** is a complex of barns, several are plank and one is log, all stained red, built circa 1870. Beyond them, on the right-hand side, see if you can spot **255 Eardley**, which was one of the earliest houses built here (1840).

At the junction of Highway 148 and the **McConnell-Larimée bypass** (also called the **Boulevard des Outaouais)**, turn left and drive to its termination. As you do, note the housing developments encroaching on the countryside. At the end of this four-lane autoroute, turn right onto **chemin de la Montagne Sud** and follow it south to its T-junction with **Boulevard Alexandre-Taché** (also known as the Upper Aylmer Road, or chemin d'Aylmer). Turn right and immediately get into the left-hand lane so you can turn left to cross the Ottawa River at the **Champlain Bridge**.

OTHER PLACES OF INTEREST

Shirleys Bay: Although we do visit this bay, you may like to revisit so you can explore by canoe. Actually, to explore this area fully, buy yourself a copy of the NCC's *National Capital Greenbelt All Season Map* because there are many trails to explore here, including Trail #10, a 4 km path for skiers or walkers.

"City of Ottawa" road gang, possibly near Shirleys Bay, n.d. COA CA-17000.

Constance Bay is really a destination unto itself, particularly for canoeists and kayakers. Here you can explore the riverfront and sandy point on a good half- or even full-day trip. The Big Sand Point mentioned above is today simply referred to as "The Point." The dunes have been vastly reduced in size because of years of "mining," during which sand was hauled away for manufacturing cement, among other purposes. For years naturalists and outdoors enthusiasts have paddled Constance Creek, enjoying its wildlife and broad cattail and bulrush wetland. To get there, turn right from Constance Bay Road onto Allbirch Road and proceed to the river.

Buckham's Bay is a diversion just north of Constance Bay. It is accessed by turning left onto Allbirch Road, then left on Bishop Davis Drive, which eventually turns into Bayview Drive. You can thus circumnavigate this ridge of rock thrusting out of the Ottawa River, and appreciate the still, calm waters of the deep inlet "channel" to the west.

Smith's Corners: Horseback riders may enjoy renting a horse at Pinto Valley to explore the rocky outcrops of Canadian Shield. If you do this, just think about how difficult this land would be to farm.

Pontiac Artists' Studio Tour is an annual event that takes place on the second and third weekends in June. The self-guided tour takes you along the back roads of the north shore of this ramble, and extends westward beyond the NCR, providing another good way of getting to know the region.

View towards Eardley Escarpment from Pinhey's Point.
Photo: E. Fletcher, 2002.

Pinhey's Point and Bessborough: If you are canoeing, you might wish to paddle by this area to view the estates from the water. Be mindful of the strong current, and of private property stretching along the shore.

Chats Falls Canoe Trip

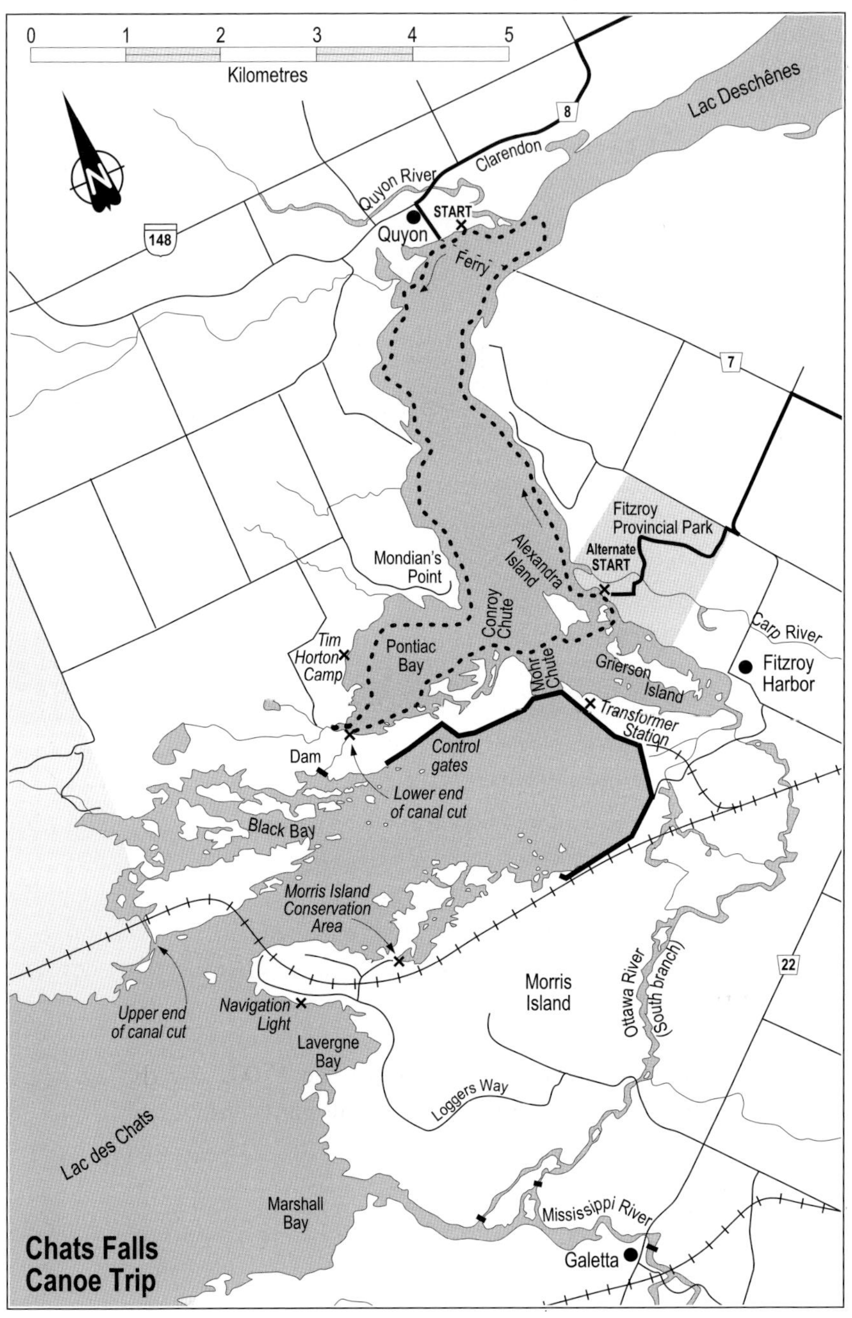

Portaging Chats Falls. Steel engraving by W.H. Bartlett as published in Canadian Scenery, Willis and Bartlett, London, England, 1842. From author's private collection.

As far as we know, in the year 1609, Étienne Brûlé was probably the first European to venture to Chats Falls, once a raging set of rapids extending three kilometres through wild bush and jagged rocks. Champlain was next to follow in his paddle strokes, documenting his journey in his diary. After Champlain's trips to Huronia on Georgian Bay in 1615, the French began to use the Ottawa River more and more. These explorers' journeys marked the beginning of the fur trade, as a result of which the Ottawa became a heavily travelled waterway shared by the Iroquois, Algonquin, Huron, and other native peoples with their new partners, the Europeans.

The steadily increasing river traffic of the 1700s saw the earliest beginnings of settlement in the region. Some hardy individuals cleared riverfront parcels of land and established rudimentary stopping places, perhaps raising a pig or two to supply fresh food to passers-by, and perhaps providing a rough bed or shelter away from the damp. In 1786, French settler Joseph Mondion built a supply depot and cleared a small farm overlooking Pontiac Bay, where he lived for fourteen years. By

1800 he had sold his property to Forsyth, Richardson and Co., which operated a fur trading business in Montréal. He might have been more-or-less forced to sell, because he apparently sold liquor to the voyageurs; an activity that was supposedly forbidden. There is no further record of Mondion, and by 1821 the Hudson Bay Company operated a fur-trading post here called Chats House. According to Courtney C. J. Bond:

> A new set of buildings was made in 1828. John McLean, Charles Thomas, and Cuthbert Cumming served there and in 1836 Chief Factor John George McTavish made his district headquarters at the Chats House. The next year the post at the Chats was closed and the buildings sold.[88]

What sort of items did these posts stock? Joseph Bouchette commented in 1832 that Hudson Bay agent Charles Thomas kept "a store supplied with the articles most in demand by the Indians and other traders: broad cloths, blankets, beads, ammunition, spirits." After the Chats House, Thomas became an agent for the Hudson Bay Company at Golden Lake on the Bonnechere River watershed.

By 1814, Philemon Wright had purchased land at Chats Falls and soon a timber slide was built so sticks of timber could bypass the rocks en route to Bytown. Logging soon ruled, and the fur trade dwindled in economic importance.

As the lumber barons' shanties penetrated further west and north, so did commerce along the Ottawa and other river systems. Increasing and urgent demands upon transportation systems forced an end to the era of the canoe, because of the volume of supplies and machinery required by the teams of men, horses, and equipment in the lumber shanties, not to mention the needs of settlers who were starting to homestead the region.

In the 1830s, a bustling community called Pontiac Village had sprung up at Pontiac Bay, west of today's Quyon, approximately 50 km west of Gatineau. The community grew along the northern shore of the bay at the base of Chats Falls. Everyone had to portage around its fury, and this didn't involve getting out of a canoe and walking along a roadway. Goods and supplies needed to be hauled past swamps and over rugged and inhospitable terrain. Therefore, as the promise of industry blossomed along the Upper Ottawa, so did two schemes for how to bypass the falls.

Enter the Union Forwarding Company. This group managed the forwarding of goods, supplies, and people up the Ottawa River via a combination of steamers and land conveyances. At Pontiac Bay they envisioned and then built the "horse railway." First a path was cut through the bush and rock and , after tracks were laid, two horses could haul goods and passengers on carriages between Pontiac Bay and Union Village, a forwarding settlement located above the rapids, on Lac des Chats. Concurrently, other entrepreneurs were planning their dream of a Grand Canal up the Ottawa River, which would transport goods from Montréal to the Great Lakes. A canal would eliminate the need to unload and reload passengers and goods

So it was that here, right at Chats Falls, two major visions for a navigable Ottawa River were born, had their day, and died. Both schemes were killed by the advent of the railway.

Today, Pontiac Bay is home to the Tim Horton Voyageur Camp for children. A handful of cottages stand opposite it, perched on an outcrop of Precambrian rock. The once-mighty (and still impressive) falls is now controlled by a generating station and dam built in 1931. In the relatively peaceful waters immediately below present-day Chats Falls, there are no historical signs to tell the story of the portage, the Grand Canal, or horse railway. Nothing whatsoever is noted: Canadian history slumbers here. So it is well past time to tell curious people what happened here, and why.

In 1846, John Egan and Joseph Aumond's Union Forwarding Company operated steamships travelling upriver from Aylmer to Chats Falls, and from there up Lac des Chats to Portage-du-Fort. In that year they launched the *Emerald*, a 140-foot-long, 19-foot-wide double-decker steamer with a paddle wheel on either side. The company introduced another brand-new vessel in September of the same year, the *Oregon*.

But goods and people portaged around the Chats Falls on the Ontario side of the river. Passengers disembarked on Victoria Island across from Fitzroy Harbour (now part of Morris Island since the dam blocked the rapids that flowed around its south side). Bypassing the 12-metre-high falls by crossing the island on a dirt road, both goods and people then reboarded little boats called "bonnes" or "buns" that could navigate the smoother waters above the falls. But the river fell an additional 8 feet (2.5 m) in rapids at the site of today's railway bridge, so a second portage was required between Lavergne Point and Lavergne Bay on Morris Island. Finally clear of the falls and rapids, everyone — and their goods and chattels — could board a second steamer (such as the *George Buchanan)* to travel upstream towards Portage du Fort on Lac des Chats. Along the upper Ottawa, the process was repeated many more times.

No wonder the entrepreneurs of yesterday dreamed of a bypass system.

Portages must have been exhausting, yet even that network of conveyances was astonishing for its day. But the Union Forwarding Company wanted to improve the speed and efficiency of transporting goods and people overland. How could this be accomplished? They decided to construct a "horse railway" to go

> over swamps, where some rock and earth fill but mainly log trestles were built, and through the tough rock of the Canadian Shield where expensive rock cuts were necessary to keep the right-of-way level. It was a laborious task hand drilling the granite gneiss and pink syenite that lay along most of the railroad right-of-way. (Pneumatic drills did not come into use until 1867.) As the line neared Lac des Chats, drillers found their task a little easier, for here the bedrock was the softer, white, crystalline limestone.[89]

Author exploring the old cut of the horse railway.
Photo E. Fletcher, 2002.

Pontiac Village sprang up as a hamlet to house the workers, and a similar settlement, Union Village, rose up on Lac des Chats. Passengers disembarked from steamers such as the *Emerald*, and the *Ann Sisson*, then clambered into the roughly 6-metre-long carriages or loaded their goods, then two-horse teams hauled them 5.6 km through the woods, swamps, and rocky outcrops. Once at Union Village, when the waiting steamer was full, off it went westwards for the 32 km voyage to Portage du Fort, almost a day's excursion.

On 12 June 1847, the editor of *The Packet*, Bytown's newspaper, wrote about the new horse railway:

> The Union Railroad ... is a work of vast consequence to the people on the banks of the Ottawa. When it is considered that Messrs. Egan, Aumond, and Wright caused this improvement to take place, and that it has cost some thousands, ought we not to wish we had many like them. ... The land through which it passes is very uneven, and the cost of levelling has been a principal item in the outlay. ... On landing from the Emerald (at Pontiac Village) you enter the "reception room," mount a flight of stairs, and take your place in the cars. The baggage, etc., is drawn up by machinery, and at a signal the cars start ...

Today, the point of rock against which the *Ann Sisson* docked still thrusts into Pontiac Bay, west of Quyon. But no remnants of the horse railway remain visible right here.

Although efficient, the horse railway was doomed by the advance of the "iron horse" railway. By 1886, the Pontiac and Pacific Junction was operating along the north shore of the Ottawa, bypassing Quyon but stopping just north of that village, at Wyman.

But the horse railway wasn't the only project envisioned to bypass the Chats Falls. Another far, far grander and competing scheme had been envisioned in the 1830s: the construction of a Grand Canal to link the Great Lakes to the St. Lawrence via the Ottawa River.

Prominent entrepreneurs of the day included the tireless promoter Charles Shirreff (who lived on a 3,000-acre land grant near Fitzroy Harbour), as well as John Egan, Ruggles Wright, Nicholas Sparks, and others who promoted a navigation route along the Ottawa River (then called the Grand). Their petition was submitted to none other than Lieutenant-Colonel John By, who built the Rideau Canal. Charles

Shirreff's son Alexander was one of the engineers By employed; hence, the Shirreff father and son were, in fact, the first promoters of the Grand Canal scheme.

But the British Government did not back the project; after all, the Rideau Canal was costing more than they had anticipated. They probably felt they did not need yet another venture to balloon out of proportion in a vast and, to them, unknown land.

Nonetheless, the vision of a Grand Canal gained momentum. The argument for a canal was economic. The Upper Ottawa River was sparsely settled, but the stands of red and white pine were deemed "unlimited." Rapids presented major obstacles to any kind of trade; the rocks and swirling backwaters damaged the timbers and, hence, profits. Canals would assist the safe conveyance of goods and people along the water route.

In 1836 Sir Frances Bond Head, the Lieutenant-Governor of Upper Canada, toured the Upper Ottawa in January in the company of canal promoters. He evidently supported the canal's merits and recommended a survey. So in 1837 one of our greatest Canadian explorers, David Thompson, got involved with the venture as surveyor. Like the promoters, Thompson wondered whether a series of canals could be

Mohr's Chute, Chats Falls with two children, n.d.
Photo: William James Topley. NAC PA-9389.

constructed to link Lake Huron to Montréal, via the water network of the French, Mattawa, and Ottawa rivers.

Still, no funding materialized and the concept languished on the back burners of political will. But like many good ideas, it was kept alive by keen minds who recognized opportunity when they saw it. Enter lumberman John Egan, founder not just of Eganville but also of Quyon. Between 1845 and 1854 Egan was MPP for the County of Pontiac in Québec's Legislative Assembly. He joined with Montréal entrepreneurs to urge the government to fund the Grand Canal. Finally, £200,000 was designated specifically for building a canal linking Lac des Chats (from Union Village) to Lac Deschênes (at Pontiac Village on Pontiac Bay).

This money was used to blast and dig a canal that still exists. Historian and author Clyde Kennedy's words as published in 1970 remain true today:

> Visitors to Pontiac Bay today can see the enormous problem faced by the canal workers who had to drill the syenite rock of the Canadian Shield by hand. The great cut made there between 1854 and 1856 may still be seen; a block dam was built across the upriver end of this section of the canal when the Chats Falls Generating Station was built in 1931.[90]

Kennedy reveals that it was much easier to dig the western end of the canal because there the rock was "relatively soft white crystalline limestone."

The canal promoters were soon dealt a serious blow, however. The General Report of the Commissioners of Public Works for the Year 1856 was singularly unimpressed with the cost of the project. Work ceased. Some people wanted the project permanently stopped; others such as Walter Shanley, who was now the surveyor for the canal, expected it to continue. Shanley was experienced: he was director of the Bytown and Prescott Railway, and an ardent proponent of the canal. He not only considered the scheme to be an economic boon to industry, he also believed an unimpeded route extending from Lake Huron to Ottawa would prove a significant tourist draw for Americans as well as Canadians.

But despite one other channel being cut at Allumette Island's Culbute Canal (1873–76), opponents of the venture dealt the Grand Canal scheme its death blow. In 1876 they built a bridge connecting Allumette Island to the mainland precisely where the steamers would need to negotiate the canal. Several years of petitioning by local residents ensued and eventually the bridge was removed. But it was too little, too late. Although a swing bridge was erected in 1880, steamer traffic had enjoyed its supremacy and was doomed: railway technology replaced it.

Chats Falls, 1906. Collection: Department of Public Works. NAC C-4911.

The era of canal building and the great scheme of the Grand Canal was dead. In 1889 the Culbute Locks were abandoned. Without a complete network of canals and locks, the Chats Falls canal was also doomed. As noted above, when the Chats Falls generating station and dam was constructed, the upstream end of the canal was "dammed" by a block dam.

History does have a habit of repeating itself, doesn't it? Although not a canal scheme, we have our present day Walter Shanleys who strongly believe in the importance of tourism along the Ottawa. Over a hundred years after the Grand Canal scheme died, the navigation of the Ottawa River is still a going concern. In 1993 the Ottawa River Navigable Waterway Corporation started to develop a system of bypasses, using trailers to tow boats around non-navigable sections of the river. Their ultimate objective is to develop an 800 km navigable water route from Montréal to Lake Temiskaming. Now the river is open to craft of a certain size from Arnprior to Lake Temiskaming via a series of bypasses. The lower Ottawa, however, from Chats Falls to Ottawa remains, as of 2004, without a bypass sections. Environmentalists such as the Ottawa Riverkeepers Society, as well as local residents have formed a citizen's lobby group, opposed to the creation of a bypass here.

NATURAL HISTORY

Chats Falls is tame now, at least in comparison to those early years when the rapids and falls raged unchecked before the dam was built in 1931. The rugged outcrops of Canadian Shield that proved so costly for canal builders to blast create a spectacular series of islands and dramatic shoreline to explore today. Because of the construction of the dam, the rocks that were once part of the falls are now exposed directly north of it. The mixed hard- and softwoods you see along Pontiac Bay include stunted specimens of oak, as well as red and jack pine, all of which cling tenaciously to sparse topsoil. There are also some wetlands here, where red and silver maples grow, enjoying having their "feet" kept wet due to fluctuating water levels, particularly in spring.

Many water birds can be found here such as common loons and mergansers, lesser scaup, grebes, common goldeneye, as well as great blue heron. In addition, for several years ospreys have nested near Fitzroy Provincial Park. Of course you'll probably see herring and ring-billed gulls soaring overhead or bobbing on the water's surface. Along the shore, use your binoculars to search the water's edge for the scurrying movement of spotted sandpipers.

Plant species abound; take along an identification book while you're paddling so you can identify species while "on the water." You'll find duckweed among more stagnant stretches along with feathery-looking water millfoil. Look too for the pink flowered plant called water knotweed, and the white water lily.

BEFORE YOU GO ON THE RAMBLE

Why go? This is a little-known part of the NCR that possesses immense heritage importance. The horse railway and Grand Canal are unmarked but are of major Canadian historical significance. Fitzroy Provincial Park is a super place to camp, and you can use it as a base from which to explore.

Distance: Quyon is 55 km west of downtown Ottawa via Highway 148. The paddle is roughly 11 km.

Modes of exploration: Drive to Quyon (or Fitzroy Provincial Park) and then canoe to the Chats Falls. Sailors will enjoy sailing from Britannia Bay here, but remember that "Quyon" means "sandy bottom" and sailors know that shifting, submerged sand bars can be hazardous here.

Getting there: Leave Ottawa via the Champlain Bridge and turn left onto Boulevard Lucerne (Lower Aylmer Road), driving through Aylmer, connecting to Highway 148. Pass Breckenridge, Luskville, and Eardley, then watch for the first exit to Quyon, marked by a ferry sign. Turn left onto what becomes Clarendon Street in Quyon and proceed to the ferry docks via Onslow Road. Park at the "Beach Barn" or Lion's Hall, (no fee as of spring 2004) and put in your canoe at the docks. Paddle west to Chats Falls.

Facilities: Quyon offers a bakery, and a gas bar/dépanneur (corner store); Fitzroy Provincial Park has campsites and outhouses, and check for their summer family programming.

Of special note: **Special Caution:** Historically, anyone paddling close to Chats Falls understood that the waters posed a serious risk. Nowadays, it's easy to completely forget this because on a nice summer's day, the waters appear calm. There is, however, a very good reason why the exposed rocks along the shoreline are not covered with lush vegetation. It is because the dam controls the water level of the Ottawa River. The dam's control gates can suddenly open to release a large volume of water; the tranquil scene can become turbulent and currents can change quickly. This does not mean that Pontiac Bay is unsafe: after all, nearby Fitzroy Provincial Park has a boat launch. It does mean that you should take care. Do not boat or swim or wind sail any closer to the dam than the hydro buoys that are placed there to warn you of the potential danger. As well, do not swim off the Quyon docks as there is a dangerous undertow here at the mouth of the Quyon River.

THE RAMBLE

At the **Quyon boat launch** or **beach** immediately left of the **Quyon Ferry docks**, put on your lifejacket and other gear (sunhat, sunscreen etc.). To your left is the confluence of the Quyon (locally known as the "Quio") and Ottawa rivers. Notice the sandbanks at its mouth and look for great blue heron here. (**Note:** However attractive it appears on a hot day, please do not swim here. A young girl and her father drowned in the strong and unpredictable current during the summer of 2002.) Instead, paddle right, upriver, immediately passing the ferry docks.

Because this is one of the narrowest channels in Lac Deschênes, it was a perfect spot for early settlers to devise a ferry to transport them across to Woodridge, also known as Mohr's Landing, on the Ontario side. It was named after John Christian Mohr, a Swedish immigrant who settled 2,000 acres at Beechgrove, downriver some 4 km or so from Quyon. An island in the river opposite his land takes his name: Mohr Island. (This is where Champlain camped at least once, and he mentioned the biting flies. Today, campers still complain about the mosquitoes that emerge immediately after sundown: beware!)

One of the first ferries to operate at Quyon was a platform affair powered by two horses, called a "horse tamper ferry." Today's very different ferry accommodates about six or seven regular sized cars, though you may see a trailer of cattle being transported on it, bound for the Galetta stock auction.

Paddle past the ferry dock. You cannot miss the limestone church on your right; the most prominent feature identifying Quyon from afar. This is the **Roman Catholic Church of the Holy Name of Mary**. The Quyon Millennium Booklet notes the symbolism behind the church being oriented on an east-west axis:

> The symbolism of the directions is powerful: the west symbolizes the world of darkness and death because it is the place of the setting sun. The east is the place of the new day, the rising sun. Therefore, in the church, we face east, the place of Resurrection, and turn our backs to the west, or the world of death.[91]

Continue paddling west, beside the cottages in this quiet bay. Watch for loons, great blue herons, and mergansers here in these shallow, reedy waters. Also on your right, note another channel emptying into the river. Today this is known as Knight's Creek, but it also marks the place where John Egan's men cut a bypass channel to the Ottawa River. Egan had decided to build a sawmill at Quyon in 1846. He could not locate it at the "Quio" River, because of the sand bars. Logs could not navigate the shifting shallows, so the founder of Quyon built a dam just upstream and had a channel cut to the river at this point — then spent some £40,000 building a state-of-the-art sawmill. (Today the site has a feed mill adjacent to the ruins of the old dam.)

Continue paddling for a while. There are many more cottage communities alongside the north shore, as well as dense wetland woods mostly of red and silver maple, rather like the woods on Petrie Island, and at the confluence of Brewery Creek and the Ottawa River (see Petrie Island and Brewery Creek rambles). Particularly in spring migration, there are many waterfowl here, and the forests are alive with chirps and twitters.

Next is another historic spot where the Upper Ottawa Improvement Company used to have offices and also piled squared timber. Established in 1866, this company was a cooperative that transported logs along the river for the various pulp companies in the region. The Ottawa Valley lumbermen who founded it included A.H. Baldwin, Levi Young, J.R. Booth, and William G. Perley.

View of Pontiac Village at Chats Falls. Wood engraving by W.H. Bartlett as published in Picturesque Canada, Toronto, 1882. From author's private collection.

Continue paddling. Be continually on the lookout for shallows, which include flat shale terraces. Before long a low-lying rocky point appears ahead, on your right. Your eye will be drawn to it because of the shallow limestone terraces leading from a cluster of cottages' lawns to the water's edge. This is **Mondion's Point**, which Joseph Mondion cleared and settled in 1786. The trading depot he built here subsequently became the site of the Hudson's Bay Company's **Chats House** fur-trading post. But long before Mondion, this point provided a logical resting place for natives to camp, prior to commencing the arduous three-and-a-half mile portage that begins — or ends — here. This point of land has had many names: it also takes the name **Indian Point**, and is known (more rarely) as **Julian's Point** after a settler of that name. As if this isn't enough, some topographical maps identify it as **Hudson Point**, after the Hudson's Bay fur trading post located here in 1821.

Beyond the point, Pontiac Bay extends before you as a broad, shallowly indented bay. Continue paddling, noting the still wild-looking shoreline beyond the little row of cottages above the water's edge. Again, the water is extremely shallow around the point. Off in the distance on your left (southeast) is the channel of the Ottawa now blocked by the 1931 hydro generating station and dam.

Tim Horton Children's Camp overlooking Pontiac Bay.
Photo E. Fletcher, 2002.

Directly west across the bay, you cannot miss the beautiful lawns, outbuildings, beach, and swimming area of the **Tim Horton Children's Camp**. This is one of five such camps where children from all over Canada come to experience the outdoors. Ron Joyce started the Tim Horton Children's Foundation in 1974 to commemorate the popular Canadian hockey star. Make your way along the shore or across the bay towards the camp.

Another rocky promontory now protrudes into Pontiac Bay, but unlike the flat "beds" or terraces of shale, this is Precambrian rock. Give this rocky point a wide berth and paddle into the little bay behind it — an extension, actually, of Pontiac Bay.

As you carefully approach the north shore, look to your left. You ought to see a prominent, high point of rock jutting into the water, with several cottages on its rounded summit. Cautiously paddle as close as you can to the mainland. This is where steamships like the *Emerald* and *Ann Sisson* docked. Unbelievable as it might seem, this was once the site of a bustling wharf when the horse railway opened in 1847. Machinery hauled people's luggage, goods, and supplies uphill to the waiting horses and roughly 6-metre carriages of the horse railway. From the top of this rocky promontory, the horses pulled the coaches alongside Lac Aumond, to Union Village, a distance of nearly 6 km through bush, rock cuts, and swamp. From this time until the start of the railways in the 1870s, homes and businesses of bustling **Pontiac Village** ringed Pontiac Bay.

The Ann Sisson shown tied up at wharf at Quyon [Pontiac Village, on Pontiac Bay]. This was one of the first boats on the Ottawa River, starting her run between Aylmer and Chats Falls about 1824. Collection: Andrew Merrilees. NAC PA-207572.

Paddle around this point, keeping in mind that it is private property. In the narrow little inlet directly beyond it, look northwest to the shore to see a very narrow rim of sand and reeds, behind which is a pile of rock. Behind this "wall of rocks" is the cut of the **Grand Canal**. This cut was made between 1854 and 1856, but a block dam filled in the upper opening to the Ottawa River in 1931 when the hydro dam was built.

Part of the lower "cut" of the Grand Canal.
Photo E. Fletcher, 2002.

Now paddle along the southern edge of Pontiac Bay, always watching for rocks and shallow spots. Respect the "No Trespassing" and warning signs here on the shore. You proceed, passing a controlled outflow channel called the **Conroy Chute** (where a timber slide was built) on the western side of the **Chats Falls Dam.** The water is held back by a series of dykes and dams; the concrete structure you see to your right along the top of Mohr Island is a dyke between the dams at the top of Conroy Chute and the main power generating dam. You soon reach the main channel of the Ottawa River known as **Mohr Chute,** directly below the generating station and main dam site.

Do not even think about paddling close to the dam! Buoys indicate the danger zone, but be aware that there is turbulence and an undertow here. You don't have to get too close to be impressed by the **Chats Falls Dam and Generating Station** (built 1931-32). The dam is 152-m long, spanning the river and hence also the interprovincial boundary. There are eight turbine units housed here separated by 2.4-m thick piers. A concrete deck spans these, itself supported by a series of steel beams. A 9-m wide log slide intake is located west of the sluice gate where a 61-m long timber log slide was built.

The author in her canoe safely away from the Chats Falls Dam and Generating Station. Photo E. Fletcher, 2002.

Power development at Chats Falls, 10 July 1932.
Collection: Upper Ottawa Improvement Co. NAC C-22216.

The dam holds back an immense reservoir of water called **Lac des Chats**. Other Pontiac rivers drain into it: the Noire, Coulonge, and Dumoine. All were famous logging rivers and today offer superb whitewater canoeing and kayaking (they lie west of the National Capital Region, however).

While remaining cautious of currents here, pause in your canoe so you can read how prominent Ottawa civil engineer Thomas Coltrin Keefer described Chats Falls in 1880, prior to the dam.

> ... a crescent-like dam of primitive rock stretching across the Ottawa nearly three miles in extent — over which the river breaks at high water in more than thirty independent chutes of every conceivable form; some divided by large rocks, others arched over by the leaning forest trees under which the white foam of the rapid plays in lively contrast to the dark green foliage above, the whole presenting a scene of picturesque beauty to which the oldest voyageurs are not insensible. The Chats falls and rapids, three miles in length, unite the Chaudière [now called Deschênes] and Chats lakes, the latter fifty feet above the former.[92]

Use the current to assist you as you carefully cross Mohr Chute towards the Ontario side of the river. Before returning to Quyon via the Ontario shore, consider stopping for a visit to **Fitzroy Provincial Park**. The island at the end of Mohr Chute is **Alexandra Island**; the longer thin one closer to Fitzroy Harbour is **Grierson Island** (also called **Kedey's Island**). The channel to the boat launch at the park is between these main islands, amongst several smaller islets. The water can be as shallow as a metre or so: quite enough for your canoe or kayak, but continue to be cautious.

After exploring Fitzroy Park, where you can swim, hike, and examine the 300-year-old bur oak and 100-year-old white pine, it's probably time to return to Quyon. Although the river is relatively narrow here, take care in crossing because the wind can come up and, along with the currents, carry you downstream beyond your destination.

You need to pack your imagination along with you on a trip like this. History tells us that the rapids and falls were almost 6 km in length while the river dropped an elevation of nearly 16 m. It's quite something to consider how the dam and generating station have so dramatically altered the Ottawa River's path. Canoeing this section of Pontiac Bay as you have just done would not have been possible with the rapids as they once were.

OTHER PLACES OF INTEREST

Fitzroy Provincial Park is on the Ontario side of the river. There is a 2-km hiking trail, picnic grounds, a campsite, and boat launch. Swimming is fine from here. The 185-ha park offers a good vantage point from which to launch your canoe. Fees apply here. Note that Fitzroy is a favourite park, so if you intend to camp, you should reserve ahead. Because the Quyon beach is less known, I decided to introduce you to it as your launch site; still, it is shorter from Fitzroy's boat launch to the dam. At the mouth of the Carp River located here, there is a stand of bur oak: some are reputed to be over 300 years old. As well, some white pine are more than 100 years old.

Morris Island is also on the Ontario side of the river. To get here from Ottawa, drive along Highway 417 and exit right (north) at the Galetta Side Road. Turn left onto Logger's Way after passing through Galetta. Proceed .8 km and drive onto Morris Island via the bridge. Continue on the main road, wending around the island, alongside and through the (mostly winterized) cottage residences. There are some superb views of the river here. Proceed to the termination of the road; (5 km from the bridge) and park here in the parking lot of the **Morris Island Conservation Area**. A network of trails awaits you including an interesting one along the berm to Chats Falls Dam. As well, there is a boat launch. Canoeing or kayaking is possible here, too. Morris is the main island, though there are other small "islets" adjacent to it creating interesting backwaters and "channels." Just be cautious: currents can be tricky here because the dam creates fluctuating water levels. In winter this is an area for you to explore on skis. You can also hike along the boardwalk in summertime. There used to be a mine on Morris Island, called Kingdon Mine and a road here recalls its name.

Mississippi Mills

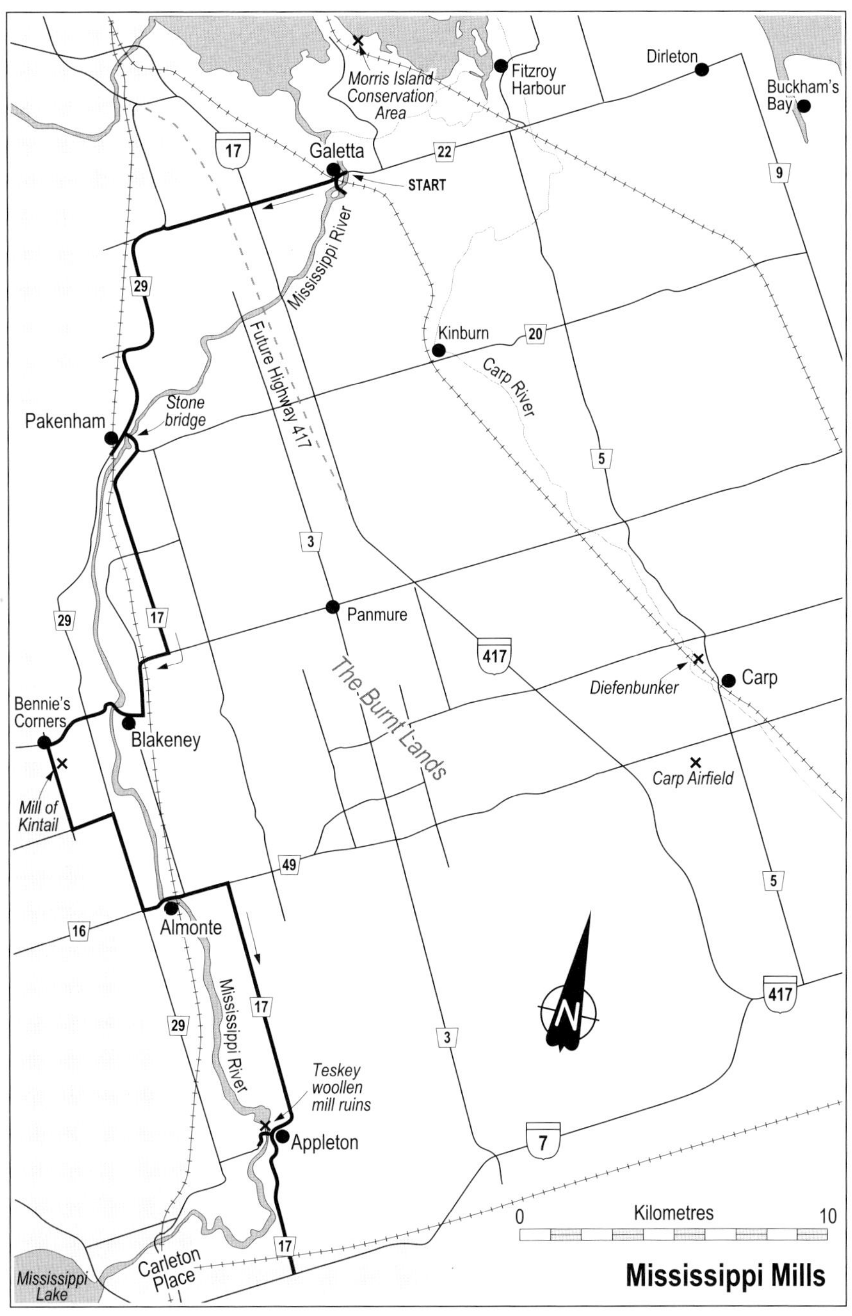

When Winter Lasted a Year

The summer of 1816 posed a desperate threat to settlers, for instead of summer's balmy breezes and relief from bitter cold, temperatures fell — as did the snow.

Crops froze in the ground and pioneers donned overcoats, scarves, gloves, and warm headgear while they saved what food they could. In his book *Pioneers of Old Ontario,* author W.L. Smith wrote:

> *Snow commenced falling in June, and the whole country was continuously covered by a wintry blanket. Practically nothing was gathered in the way of a crop. Everything rotted in the ground. There was no flour, there were no vegetables; people lived for twelve months on fish and meat — venison, porcupine, and ground-hog being varied with the thin meat of cattle, slaughtered because there was no vegetation to sustain them.*

Flour was seventy dollars per barrel at Québec, potatoes were a penny a pound, and the country was full of stories of the horrors endured during the winter of a year's duration.[93]

Fortunately, the next summer returned to normal, yielding an abundant harvest. We can imagine the heartbreak of newcomers to this country, however, as snows that fell in June of that terrible year failed to melt, and only grew deeper as "summer" progressed.

Lanark County forms the westernmost reaches of the National Capital Region in Ontario. In fact, when travelling south up the Mississippi River (Mississippi means "great river" in the Ojibwa language) in 2002, my husband Eric enquired, in Pakenham, whether we were still in the NCR. The answer was, "Oh, no. The boundary is on the east side of the river." In fact, the village of Pakenham *is* within the NCR.

While driving along this ramble, you'll travel a stretch of road forming the boundary between Fitzroy and Huntley townships (in Carleton County) to the east, and Pakenham and Ramsay townships (Lanark County) to the west. Whereas Route 17 south of Pakenham describes the westernmost extension of the amalgamated City of Ottawa as of 1 January 2001, the NCR boundary falls in a zigzag line further west of the Mississippi River. Although examining a good map that shows these boundaries will illuminate their location, it still does not reveal — by topographical or jurisdictional logic — exactly why the NCR falls where it does. In any case, it is only the easternmost sections of the three townships of Lanark (Beckwith to the south, Ramsay in the middle, and Pakenham in the north) that are within the NCR.

Teskey's wool mill, Appleton, Ontario, 1925. Photo: Colborne Powell Meredith. NAC C-7950.

But the Mississippi River flows through them all and links their histories together in this intriguing final ramble. The river's history is woven by the warp and weft of woollens made at the mills once clustered along its banks. First Galetta (in Fitzroy Township, Carleton County), followed by the mills of Lanark County's towns such as Pakenham, Blakeney, Almonte, and Appleton, were all more or less prosperous by the late 1800s. History and settlement have been kind to some of these villages, while others (Galetta, Blakeney, and Appleton), although less populated nowadays, are vestiges of their former selves.

We can just imagine, however, how rugged the shores of the Mississippi must have seemed to the earliest European settlers who came from the lowlands of Scotland. The first wave of pioneers settled Beckwith, the southernmost township of Lanark County in the vicinity of Carleton Place and Ashton between 1816 and 1818. The second wave settled Ramsay Township between 1819 and 1823. (Decades would pass, however, until in 1873, Loyalist settler Daniel Shipman built a sawmill on the Mississippi's falls at present-day Almonte. Two years after that, another group settled Pakenham.)

During the first wave settlement in the early 1800s, the Europeans encountered native people in camps along the riverside, or else see them passing through the countryside. Here is a description of such a meeting of cultures in 1816:

> In the afternoon two families of Indians in three canoes came down the river and pitched their tent upon the island in the middle of the village. They were the first I had seen since I came to the place. They had deer, muskrats and various kinds of fowls which they exposed for sale. The deer was small but they sold it at a dollar a quarter — the head with the horns at the same price.
>
> Their canoes were all of birch bark about eighteen feet long and three feet wide at the middle. They had in each canoe a capital fowling-piece and several spring traps for taking game, and all the men were armed with the tomahawk. They had all black hair, brown complexions and active well formed bodies. All of them, even the children, had silver ornaments in their ears.[94]

Four years later, settler Andrew Bell noted that the area "all about" had evidently been occupied by natives at one time. Key here is Bell's use of the past tense. By the terms of the 31 May 1819 treaty, most of these native peoples had been disenfranchised, having sold their land in phase two of the original 1783 Crawford Purchase (see Settlers on the Ottawa). Some gathered at the Golden Lake reserve in Renfrew County, west of here on the Bonnechere River system. Others stayed, but their numbers dwindled.

Between 1816 and 1820, most of the easiest land to clear and settle — typically river frontage — was granted or was intended for settlement by military officers. By 1820, Philemon Wright's community on the Chaudière was already twenty years old, and river frontages in the townships of March, Torbolton, and Fitzroy were being granted to the likes of General Lloyd, Captain John Benning Monk, and Hamnett Kirkes Pinhey (see Ottawa River Loop ramble). Military strategists knew they had to establish a secure "second line" of defence, because if the Americans successfully invaded via the St. Lawrence, additional loyal troops (a.k.a. settlers) would be required to hold the interior while more troops were massed along the Ottawa River.

Coincident to this, the Ottawa Valley pine industry was sending ships full of square timbered pine and oak downriver to Montréal, Québec City, and from there to Britain. What to do with the empty holds of ships on their return route? Use people as ballast, that's what!

The lumber industry served to supply an economical, logical means for immigration. This was hugely beneficial for the British Government, since in addition to shoring up their defences in the new colony, they could also alleviate other problems at home, such as widespread poverty in Scotland and Ireland. And what about all those loyal troops returning to Britain from overseas engagements? If they were permitted to return to their homes, they would displace others who had stayed behind to work. It made sense to ship those displaced British citizens to the new colony. Therefore, Britain had many reasons to promote emigration to the New Land.

Notwithstanding the need, tangible enticement was required. Land grants for military men were of various sizes depending on rank. The lowest rank of private was granted 100 acres, as were ordinary citizens. Other enticements included a year of army rations, tools such as an axe, and a few other supplies. Title to land was only granted, however, after three years occupation, and only after a certain amount of land was cleared and under cultivation, and a dwelling built. As well, during this settlement period, the homesteader was required to fulfil road maintenance duties.

Perth (south of the NCR) was first settled by Scottish immigrants in 1816 and was designed, as a strategic military settlement. It became a hub or landing spot, from which other military men, individuals, families, and church men began to spread out into the surrounding land. But even so, their numbers were small and the countryside vast. Who would populate the interior?

The stage was set for the weavers:

> Meanwhile in Scotland the plight of the weavers, particularly of Glasgow, was becoming acute. Discharged soldiers returning from the wars had taken up their former occupations, greatly increasing the number of weavers, and at the same time the demand for their products had dwindled. Representations were made from the Scottish counties of Lanark and Renfrew for assistance in emigrating to Upper Canada. As a result, sponsored by Scottish societies and assisted by the Government, a group of settlers sailed in 1820 on the Commerce, the Prompt, and the Broke. They travelled up the St. Lawrence from Québec to Prescott and overland to Perth. Here some remained over winter but others went on into the forests to found the third Military Settlement, Lanark.[95]

In the same year, four more ships left Britain with their holds filled with 1,883 settlers. (The journey, incidentally, could take anywhere from one to four months and the conditions were reputedly dreadful.) But still, almost no one had settled Lanark's hinterland. By this time Charles Shirreff already lived at Fitzroy on his 3,000 acres at Chats Falls. Hearing rumours of a "military settlement" in the countryside, his two sons decided to see how many "country neighbours" they really had. *Belden's Historical Atlas of Carleton County* tells the story of the brothers' journey.

> In the winter of 1821–22 [Shirreff's] two sons… procured the company of two brothers… who were half-breeds, and sons of an officer in charge of the Nor'-West Fur Co.'s trading post situated at Indians' Point, on the North Shore, and started on an exploring expedition to discover them. They traversed Fitzroy and several adjoining Townships in the County of Lanark, particularly Ramsay, without finding a solitary settler,

or any evidence of a white man ever having preceded them in any of the localities visited.[96]

(This account is particularly fascinating if you have done the Chats Falls ramble, because you will know that "Indian's Point" — a.k.a. Mondion's, Julian's and Hudson Point — is now populated by cottages, being just west of Quyon.)

Colonel William Marshall appears to have been the next person to explore Lanark. In 1822 he travelled the length of the Mississippi River, naming four of the seven falls we'll explore on this ramble: Apple Tree Falls (today's Appleton), Shepherd's Falls (Almonte, but also previously called Shipman's Mills and Ramsayville), Norway Pine Falls (Blakeney), and Little Falls (Pakenham).

The next year, Robert Harvey settled at Little Falls. Immediately he fell to clearing and settling his own land on the east bank of the Mississippi, where he also eventually erected a sawmill, gristmill, and potash works in partnership with John Powell. The largely Scottish settlement prospered, because here at Pakenham the river widens into an open area beneath the falls, which was capable of holding booms of logs. Both here and at Almonte the river could accommodate more than one enterprise. The weavers from Glasgow, Scotland, came, saw opportunity, and eventually built their wool mills and factories in these two communities.

Potash was one of the first industries. Harvey and others shipped this commodity in containers of up to 500 lbs to Montréal where there was a ready market. Although it sounds astonishing, the containers were transported on top of rafts of square timber and floated downstream. No wonder one of the first things settlers did was to build timber chutes so their cribs of timber could avoid the turbulent waterfalls!

Equally challenging was the prospect of getting along with your neighbours. This proved particularly onerous during the 1823 "emigration experiment" which saw twenty-nine families of extremely poor Irish immigrants arrive in Lanark. The first such emigration totalled thirty men, eighteen women, and thirty-eight children. It was an interesting if not somewhat flawed trial run: Britain needed more settlers and there were many poverty-stricken families in Ireland; why not help these people, at public expense, to build themselves a better life? The Irish immigrants were hand picked by Peter Robinson, who escorted them from Ireland to Upper Canada.

The families were promised 70 acres of land and although they had to work to gain title to the grants, this was one of the few similarities between the Scots and Robinson's Irish settlers. Robinson brought them to Lanark completely at public expense, from the berths on the ship through to the bateaux bringing them up the St. Lawrence and overland conveyances into Lanark itself. Moreover, Robinson had hired two Canadian guides per bateaux, and two surgeons had offered their services. And because their way was paid for, of course these Irish families brought more goods with them. The list of differences between these Irish settlers and others from Scotland and England went on and on, and was none too subtle.

The Scots, military and other settlers could hardly be blamed for looking askance at the twenty-nine families who arrived "on their doorsteps." To add insult to injury, some of the land the newcomers had been promised had already been settled by the industrious Glaswegian weavers. Robinson was able to find new lands for the Irish, but the damage was done. The newcomers were resented by earlier settlers who had had to carve their homes and settlements from the unforgiving land with their own labour and ingenuity. Verna Ross McGiffin notes that when a second boatload arrived in 1825, Robinson asked Little Falls' homesteaders

> to assist in cutting trails to the new lots, in transporting baggage and supplies, and in building the 20 by 12-foot log houses on each lot. True, they would earn welcome cash for their efforts, but they would also be in a position to see for themselves that the newcomers had been supplied with tools, bedding, food and even homes.[97]

Despite grievances real and imagined, settlement at Pakenham grew, and attracted industrious types to the turbulent falls. Because road transportation continued to pose problems, water transportation routes offered not only a source of industry for mills, but also a way of getting product to market.

One settler who made a huge difference to the development of Pakenham — and hence Lanark — was a Scotsman named Andrew Dickson. His vision and energy further highlight the human history of Lanark. Born in Elginhough, Perthshire, in 1797, Dickson emigrated to Canada in 1819. He first was occupied tending a lighthouse in Nova Scotia, but in 1821 he arrived in Perth and two years later he was farming in Fitzroy, making a name for himself as a cattleman. Ten years later he had purchased Robert Harvey and John Powell's mill at Pakenham, where he settled.

He was no slouch. His list of achievements is long: he was the village's first postmaster; in 1838 he built Pakenham's first church; in 1842 he was appointed Sheriff (succeeding John Powell); in 1844 he built a woollen carding mill. This energetic and talented soul was Sheriff for ten years, leaving the post only after being appointed Inspector of the Provincial Penitentiary in Kingston. After living there for several years, he left in July 1858 to become Warden of the Reformatory Prison of Lower Canada, and lived in Québec's Isle au Noix. He retired from that position on 19 May 1860 and returned to Pakenham where he died at age seventy-one.

It was a remarkable life, one that I relate here to indicate how well travelled people were over one hundred years ago, when getting about in this countryside was arduous. When Dickson moved to Pakenham in 1831, approximately 300 people lived at the village. But even so, this seems like amazing growth in ten years, especially when you consider that people had to clear virgin forests, build a log house, and do all manner of other things merely to survive from one year to the next.

Human history is eternally in the making. On 1 January 1998, the Townships of Pakenham and Ramsay, and the town of Almonte amalgamated, forming the town of Mississippi Mills. Along the route, you will encounter signs with this name.

NATURAL HISTORY

It is no wonder Lanark was a difficult county to settle.

Driving along the Mississippi's embankments you'll see the jagged outcrops of rock at each of its tumbling falls. You will see outcrops of 300 million year-old limestone, deposited by seas around that time. Outcrops of even more ancient Nepean Sandstone — which is between 450 and 550 million years old — can be seen south of Pakenham. But both of these sedimentary rocks are far younger than the Precambrian rock that appears as parts of the Pakenham hills. Mount Pakenham is a lofty, craggy outcrop of Canadian Shield; its rocky promontory abuts the flat St. Lawrence Lowlands more or less behind the village of Pakenham.

As if the bedrock wasn't enough of a challenge, in other fields you'll notice that large boulders are strewn about the landscape. These are remnants of glaciation that deposited boulders and moraines, and otherwise scoured and scraped the landscape. It all might appear picturesque until you try to farm it; except for pockets of land mostly to the middle or south of the county, this region proved difficult to farm. You'll be able to tell where the good land is because prosperous farms exist in these places today. As you explore, keep an eye out and see where you would prefer to have settled!

Fossils dating from the time of the Champlain Sea have been found here, as have bones from when marine mammals swam about over present-day Lanark. For example, the skull and part of the vertebrae from a beluga or white whale was discovered on a farm in Pakenham Township as a well was being dug. And at the Leray quarry, a cephalopod (resembling a trilobite) and fossilized coral was found.

While geomorphology dictates land use, other natural phenomena shape it. Fire, for example. If you've done the Ottawa River Loop ramble, you'll be familiar with the Great Fire of 1870, which apparently started in Fitzroy Township. But the fire spread, apparently at times at a terrifying 16 km an hour, with the advancing "walls of fire" extending up to 11 km or so in length. Quite apart from how terrifying this conflagration was, and how many lives, homes, buildings, livestock, and business operations were destroyed in its wake, it also had a huge impact upon the already scant topsoil. After the flames were spent, people returned to their farms, villages, and businesses. Significant numbers of them despaired and left, seeking a better, easier livelihood in the cities, while some settled in western Canada. In many cases, they drifted away, their land being impossible to sell because the soil was scorched. In some places, peat beneath the topsoil burned for years.

The Great Fire of 1870 created a swathe of land identified on maps as the "Burnt Lands," located in pockets primarily in the western sector of Carleton County, mostly in Huntley Township. Dan Brunton is a well-known Ottawa-based environmentalist and biologist who has studied the Ottawa Valley for years. He describes the Burnt Lands:

> When the land of the lower Ottawa Valley began to emerge from the frigid waters of the Champlain Sea, one of the first areas to break the surface is what we now call the Burnt Lands. A flora and fauna was established that reflected the sub-arctic climate of 11,000 years ago. Similar areas of vegetation elsewhere

in the Capital were taken over by plants more capable of coping with modern conditions but some relict species and plant communities from that time persist at the Burnt Lands. Most important are the alvars, natural spring-flooded meadows in thin soil and on bare rock flats that have been kept open by centuries of fire. Much of the plant life and many of the insects are relicts of the cold seashore habitat of long ago. Some are wildflowers like the Yellow Lady's-slipper (*Cypripedium calceolus*), while others are less visually impressive grasses and sedges. The Burnt Lands is one of the largest examples of alvar habitat in Ontario and the only large example of this rare habitat east of the Kingston area.[98]

The Mississippi Valley forms an extensive watershed of some 4,450 square kilometres. The Mississippi Valley Conservation Authority (MVC) was established in 1968 as a community-based environmental organization whose mandate it is to protect the watershed habitat. The area is prone to flooding, and so one of the principal functions of the MVC is to monitor the flood control mechanisms, including dams, along the Mississippi and its tributaries. It also owns and manages 410 ha of conservation areas including Pakenham Bridge, the Mill of Kintail, and Morris Island within the NCR. In addition, the MVC offers educational events particularly directed at children so they can learn the importance and complexity of watershed systems.

BEFORE YOU GO ON THE RAMBLE

Why go? Settlers looked for waterfalls to power their grist, saw, and woollen mills — this is how our all of our first European settlements grew. Go on this ramble, to honour our earliest immigrant's industriousness, for as we explore, we'll visit many a mill town.

Distance: As described, this ramble extends from Galetta to Highway 7, a distance of 52 km. The total circuit (from Carp Road exit on Highway 417) is 106 km.

Modes of exploration: By car, although you can certainly cycle this ramble.

Getting there: The ramble starts at Galetta. Get there from Ottawa via Highway 417 west; exit at Carp Road, Route 5, to Route 22 and Galetta. From here we explore Pakenham via Route 29, then Blakeney, the Mill of Kintail located on the Indian River, then Almonte, which we explore before turning south to Appleton, our last mill site. Return to Ottawa on Highway 7.

Facilities: There are several villages that possess shops, restaurants, and parks in which you can enjoy a picnic.

Of special note: Because we'll be travelling alongside a water route, watch for turtles on the road, particularly in May through September. Do not pick up snapping turtles: they can give you a very nasty bite. As well: do you know what poison ivy looks like? If you don't, remember this little rhyme: "leaves of three, let them be."

THE RAMBLE

The start to this exploration of the Mississippi River Valley and its heritage mill sites is at Galetta. Drive there by following a picturesque road northwest along the **Carp River Valley.** West on Highway 417 from Ottawa, take Exit 144 north onto Route 5, also known as the **Carp Road**. Immediately on your left you pass the **Ottawa Landfill** site. The pipes protruding from its manicured hillsides collect and release methane gas from the garbage pile.

You can tell by the flat valley that the Carp was once part of a broad and shallow river system; the Carp and Mississippi once would have been part of a vaster Ottawa River as the Champlain Sea started to recede.

After passing the exit to the **Carp Airport** (also home to First Air, which flies to Greenland), you reach a crossroads and the **village of Carp**. Stay straight to ascend the **Carp Ridge**, which will be the prominent geophysical feature on your right for several kilometres. Almost immediately you pass the **Carp Agricultural Fairgrounds** and then, on your left outside the village, the **Diefenbunker, Canada's Cold War Museum**. This is where Prime Minister Diefenbaker and his clutch of generals, advisers, and other VIPs would have escaped a nuclear attack, while the likes of you and I would have been vaporized! It was built in 1959 in an old gravel pit and designed to survive an atomic bomb blast. In 1994 the Department of National Defence decommissioned the shelter and the museum project was funded.

Carleton Hotel, Carp Village, Autumn 1890.
Collection: Robert F. H. Bruce. NAC PA-122498.

Beyond Carp you really start to notice the ridge's outcrops of rock, and the many homes that get grand lookouts of the old valley floor below. It more or less parallels the **Eardley Escarpment,** which forms the southern boundary of Gatineau Park (see Gatineau Park, Ottawa River and Chats Falls rambles). After a few kilometres the ridge's elevation drops. You pass by a sheltered orchard on your left, Harvest Moon Orchard, then come to the crossroad with Thomas Dolan Parkway. (It heads right (east), towards **March Township;** see Ottawa River Loop ramble.) Stay on Route 5 to cross Route 20, the Kinburn Side Road. **Kinburn** is the village to your left (west). It was founded in 1830 by Christopher Armstrong, who operated a well-known stopping place, the Swamp Tavern. It was one of two drinking holes between "The Prior" (Arnprior) and Bytown (Ottawa), the other being Frank Holmes' Hotel in March Township. Continue north on Route 20 to cross the **Carp River** before reaching a T-junction with Route 22.

Turn left (west), on Route 22 towards Galetta. After about 4 km, note the right turn to **Logger's Way,** which leads north to Morris Island (it extends south to Kinburn). This old mid-1800s roadway was cut first as the route loggers would take when hauling sticks of timber to the Ottawa River in the days of horse teams. After the forests were cut, the more established roads were used by the teamsters who spent two to three weeks hauling crops and other supplies to the lumber shanties. (There is an interesting nature trail on the island; see Other places of interest.)

Galetta Falls and Mill from below, Galetta, Ont., 17 August 1890.
NAC PA-136140.

About a kilometre past Logger's Way, you arrive at **Galetta**, located perhaps a kilometre inland from the southern branch of the Ottawa River (its southern arm creates Morris Island). Galetta was first settled in 1823 by Andrew Forbes who lived 1 km east of the river. The 1884 *Lovell's Directory* lists eighteen men of various occupations living or working here; there was a wagon maker, a cooper, carder, dyer, gristmill worker, spinner, manager of a general store, carpenter, a postmaster and mill owner, three blacksmiths, and a lighthouse keeper, who presumably must have dwelt alongside the Ottawa River. The list of occupations shows that Galetta was then a going concern. Its location took good advantage of the falls along the river: a sawmill, gristmill, and wool mill stood here. In fact, the woollen manufacturer was a man named Galetta White, which is how this little town got its unusual name.

As you cross the bridge over the Mississippi River, look to your left to see the old dam with its complex of buildings, now a small power generating station. Almost immediately turn left to follow the river. Cross the bridge onto the island and continue to the second bridge. Pause to look north to see the railroad bridge and industrial use of the waterway. There are good views here. The road continues south, climbing a hill that is a gully formed by the old watershed. Find a spot to turn around and return on the same route to Galetta and the T-junction with Route 22. At the corner on your right-hand side is the village's quaint United Church of Canada. Turn left. Immediately to your right find the model of the CN Tower on a front lawn. On your left is the **Galetta Livestock Sale Barn**. The plastic model of a Hereford bull atop its roof proclaims the barn's function as one of the Ottawa Valley's prominent stock auction halls. Beef and dairy farmers from both sides of the Ottawa River come here to sell their livestock, and after the BSE/mad cow scares of 2003, let us hope that market prices return to "normal," soon.

Cross Highway 17 next. At the time of writing, the overpass over the extension of Highway 417 was under construction; it is scheduled to open Autumn 2004. A sign here notes **Arnprior** is 7 km west (it is outside the NCR), while Ottawa is 59 km to the east. Remain on Route 22 until you reach Route 29 at the stop sign.

Turn left and follow Route 15 south to **Pakenham,** noting the five-arch stone bridge on your left as you approach the village (we'll return to it later).

The bullish market at Galetta ... hopefully prices are stable.
Photo: E. Fletcher, 2002.

The falls you see on below the bridge were named Little Falls by Colonel William Marshall in 1822. Robert Harvey and John Powell built their mills and potash processing plant along here, naming their little settlement Harvey's Mills.

Andrew Dickson moved here nine years later and it was he who named the village Pakenham Mills after erecting more mills here. Sir Edward Pakenham was a British general who died in the infamous Battle of New Orleans, which saw a British contingent of some 6,000 men decimated. Sir Pakenham was mortally wounded while urging his men forward, in the thick of battle.

Proceed along Graham Street (the continuation of Route 29). Although most of the streets in there are named for sons and daughters of Andrew Dickson, this one is named for Robert Graham who built sleighs and wagons in Dickson's day. On your left is **Stewart House**, the United Church Conference Centre. Past Renfrew Street on the left is the **Pakenham General Store**. Both façades are of cut limestone, a common building material here. Stonemasons who had completed their contract on the Rideau Canal (1826–32; see Rideau Canal ramble) were employed all along the Mississippi River Valley. The façades of Pakenham and many of the mill towns reflect their talents.

The **General Store** is worth visiting because its interior has been kept true to its earliest look and feel. Here you can purchase fresh baked goods, as well as stock up on local books and country style gifts.

Back outside, proceed down Graham to the second corner. Turn right on **Jessie Street**. At the next corner (at Isabella) note **St. Mark's Anglican Church** (1860). If you can go in, admire the vaulted and wooden ceilings inside. Turn right on Isabella then left on Elizabeth streets. At the corner, turn right onto Dalkeith. (If you continue on Elizabeth, it becomes Waba Road to White Lake and cottage country; "Waba" means white.) Immediately ahead of you on Dalkeith are the spires of **St. Peter's Celestine Church**. St. Peter's absolutely dominates this part of Pakenham and atop its steeple the cross — lit at night — is a major landmark of this part of Pakenham Township. The interior is beautiful, featuring many restored murals. If you want to pay Andrew Dickson and other early settlers your respects, continue to the end of Dalkeith where you'll find the cemetery.

Return on Dalkeith to Renfrew Street and turn east, proceeding downhill, then turn left (north) on Graham. Now you turn right to cross the **five-span stone bridge**. Although its style is common to Scotland, Pakenham's bridge is the only one of its kind in North America. Built in 1901 by Ottawa-based engineering firm O'Toole & Keating, the bridge replaced what had been a series of unsuccessful wooden affairs. The limestone was cut and hauled by horses from the Leray quarry you pass on the other side of the bridge. There are picnic areas north of the bridge on both sides of the river. Cross the bridge. If it is open, you might want to visit **Stone Bridge Shop** on the southeast side, originally Dickson's second home.

Ornate statuary grace the exterior of St. Peter's Celestine Church.
Photo: E. Fletcher, 2002.

Pakenham's unique stone bridge. Photo: E. Fletcher, 2002.

Wool mill, Blakeney, Ontario, 16 June 1925.
Photo: Colborne Powell Meredith. NAC PA-26959.

As you ascend the east side of the Mississippi on Route 20 (Kinburn Side Road), note the **Leray limestone quarry** on your left. Fossils of ancient marine life have been found in the stone here. At the abrupt right-hand turn at the top of the hill, turn right off Route 20 onto Blakeney Road. Here you travel southeast along poor farmland with scant topsoil. (East of here is the beginning of the Burnt Lands; as you travel, imagine being one of the poor residents who was trying to flee that fire of August 1870.)

At the T-intersection, turn right and cross the railway tracks, then turn left and drive through a tiny hamlet, the former mill town of **Blakeney** (also called **Snedden Mills**, and **Rose Bank**). The road curves right as it steeply descends to cross the Mississippi on a narrow bridge. It seems unbelievable today, but in 1880 some 150 people dwelt along the Mississippi here in what was then a thriving village with a wool mill. According to author Courtney Bond, Blakeney's wool factory produced almost 100,000 metres of tweed annually. There was also a store, church, hotel, and several mills. Now Blakeney is a cluster of farm houses on a stretch of road.

Immediately turn right when you reach the far side of the bridge where you can park, get out and perhaps stroll alongside the Mississippi on trails wending through the woods, taking you over pretty footbridges. Keep your eyes peeled for black (domestic) rabbits hopping about in the shrubs. Kayakers might enjoy a spring fling on the meltwaters where the river flows through the narrow rocky embankments.

It is both pretty and tranquil in this small wildlife and fish sanctuary. There are bits of hardware and ruins scattered about, reminding us of the mills once located here. In 1822, Colonel William Marshall named this **Norway Pine Falls**, but after mills were built here in 1874, the community changed the name to Blakeney in honour of **Sir Edward Blake**. Blake was an Irish-Canadian statesman, a lawyer, and after helping to defeat the Tory government of Sir John A. Macdonald in 1873, he joined the cabinet of Alexander Mackenzie's Liberal government.

Continue on the Blakeney Road to Route 29. Although you could turn south towards Almonte here, cross the main road and drive straight ahead towards **Bennie's Corners** beside the Indian River, a significant tributary of the Mississippi River. James Bennie settled here in 1821.

Take the first left onto the 8th Line. Immediately on your left is the **Andrew Toshak** house built around 1860 in a neo-classical style. The central gable over the door is flanked by two symmetrical windows on the ground floor. Cross the Indian River to the **Mill of Kintail Conservation Area,** a 154-acre site that often has special exhibits and workshops happening. The seasonally open mill (seven days a week from mid-May to mid-October) is a must-see. Fitness trails are open year round: you can use your skis or snowshoes here in wintertime, so if the Mill and Museum are closed for the season, you can still enjoy exploring. The well-preserved gristmill and miller's house were built by **John Baird** in 1830. Baird supplied flour to the Hudson Bay posts along the Ottawa River.

Dr. Robert Tait McKenzie, an internationally renowned physician and sculptor, gave the mill a new life and certain prestige when he refurbished it in 1930 as his home and studio. Born in Almonte in Ramsay Township in 1867, McKenzie actually worked in America during most of his professional career. From 1904 he was director of the Physical Education Department at the University of Pennsylvania. But he loved Canada and retired here to this mill site, where he lived from 1930 until his death eight years later. Again the mill's fortunes lapsed, but in 1952 Major and Mrs. J.F. Layes restored it, this time transforming it into their home — but also into a museum in McKenzie's honour. In it they displayed many of his maquettes for large sculptures that he made. You'll see one such sculpture called "The Volunteer," later in Almonte, appropriately located outside the museum dedicated to his good friend and neighbour, Dr. James Naismith, who invented the game of basketball.

The Long Bridge, Almonte, Ontario, 1906. NAC C-25875.

Leave the Mill of Kintail, turning left onto the 8th Line. Directly opposite the mill, on the southwest side of Indian River is the **David Snedden homestead**, a circa 1865 home constructed of bricks fabricated from clay found on-site. Snedden had a mill at Blakeney (which was once known as Snedden's Mills.) Note the carriage shed at the rear.

Proceed southeast along the 8th Line and take the next left to connect to Route 29 South. Before turning right onto it, look to your left across the road to the north to see the **Dr. James Naismith home**. It too has a neo-classical style with a highly decorative wraparound porch.

Turn right, and proceed south on Route 29 to the traffic lights where you turn left onto Highway 44, which becomes Main Street, to enter **Almonte**. This town is worth at least an entire day, if not more — there are several historic B&Bs here such as the Old Burnside, a Georgian gem complete with a walled garden — so this ramble is merely an introduction to its mills and main street. Find a parking spot as close to the **Victoria Woollen Mill** (Rosamond Mill #2) as possible. It is the tall building slightly angled fronting onto the corner of Main and Mill streets. We'll start our short walk of the city here.

Rosamond Woollen Co. Ltd., Almonte, Ont., n.d.
Photo: Hardy. NAC PA-135188.

Almonte was the first area settled in Ramsay Township, and one look at the cascading falls here at the corner of Mill and Main streets gives you a clear indication of why. Those Glasgow weavers must have thrilled to the sight of the cascading series of falls dropping 55 feet (17 m) at this point along the Mississippi. John Gemmill and David Shepherd were the first to settle here in 1821, closely followed by Loyalist Daniel Shipman, who built a sawmill in 1823 and a gristmill the following year. Meanwhile, Gemmill had built a shop. In *The Ottawa Country*, author Bond notes how far Almonte had come by 1880:

> By 1880 Almonte was an important industrial centre, with three large woollen mills, two large grist and flour mills, two foundries and machine shops, a pump factory, a "dog power" churn factory, two cabinet factories, two planing and dash mills, four wagon and carriage works, four blacksmiths, four carpenter shops and a boat-building establishment.[99]

There were so many mills here, Almonte was nicknamed "Little Manchester." The **Victoria Woollen Mill**, which overlooks the Mississippi at Main and Mill streets, was built in the 1850s by John Rosamond. Named after Queen Victoria, it is located on the second set of falls here in Almonte.

Author Gerry Wheatley explains how successful Rosamond's mills were: "Four years after arriving in Almonte, James Rosamond was using 25,000 pounds of wool, worth $2,000, and had thirty employees. The cloth the mill produced was worth $40,000 per year, a good return for his $24,000 investment."[100]

From this five-storey mill, turn left on Main Street and cross over the Mississippi River, walking to **Coleman's Island** over the **Slide Bridge**. This was erected in 1964, replacing an earlier stone single arch bridge built in the 1850s. In June 1910, a total of 3,149 sticks of white pine hurtled down the timber slide here at this waterfall into Gemmill Bay. This was the last log drive on the Mississippi.

Turn left onto Mary Street and proceed to its end, where you'll discover a National Capital Region gem: the **Mississippi Textile Museum**, in what was another Rosamond family warehouse built in 1867. Here you'll find excellent displays explaining everything about wool: from sheep to finished product. It also explains how Almonte became world-famous as a fine producer of superb woollens.

The region's success as an area of wool manufacturing did not result from the simple fact that it attracted some of Glasgow's finest weavers. The Canadian Shield geology played its part too. The thin topsoil in much of Lanark County was perfect for sheep — a creature that will thrive on almost any type of vegetation. The settlers knew how to raise sheep for both their wool and meat; consequently, they grazed their herds on the badlands, and grew crops on the fertile parts of the land.

Sheep are still raised in the Mississippi Valley. Evidently, these ones don't need to worry about sparse vegetation.
Photo: E. Fletcher, 2002.

From the museum, return to the bridge and look to your left toward the Almonte Electric Plant, built in 1925. Hydroelectricity is another important product created by the falls. Until 1940, the Almonte Electric Plant supplied all of the town's power requirements. The intake section was remodelled in 1987, but this plant still satisfies approximately 40 percent of Almonte's power needs.

Turn around and return to the first mill. Turn left at Mill Street and remain on the same side of the street as the Rosamond Mill.

Opposite you, notice **three murals** celebrating the International Year of the Older Person, 1999. They were painted by Adrian Baker. Very soon we'll see another set of murals celebrating notable Almonte residents.

Stay on the north side of Mill Street and stroll past the old Victoria Mill. Today it houses both a pub and eatery, plus an excellent gallery dedicated to showing NCR artists' and artisans' works. Continue to **Kirkland Park,** also on your left, behind the bank, to look over the falls. The park was the site of another mill that burned in 1958. Beyond the park, and still on Mill Street, is a second set of murals titled **"Windows into Our Past."** A collaboration between artists Noreen Young and Angelique Willard, the 13 portraits depict seven men (such as miller James Rosamond) and six women (such as teacher Jessie Mathews) who were key figures in Almonte's development between 1825 and 1950. As you stroll by, they appear as if they are looking down at you from windows on the third floor of the building.

Now pause to admire Thomas Fuller's design for the **Old Customs and Excise and Post Office**. Fuller (whose name is still found in today's family business in Ottawa) was the chief architect of the Department of Public Works who designed the original (1859) Centre Block on Parliament Hill, which burned on 3 February 1916. If open, step inside to view the interior, which, although much altered, still shows off its lofty ceilings. In 1967 a new post office opened but this structure still looks grand on the streets of the old milling town.

Now you are approaching the second bridge over the Mississippi and two more sites to see before returning to your car. The first is the War Memorial graced by a large bronze statue, "**The Volunteer**," sculpted by Dr. Robert Tait McKenzie. The portrait depicts a subaltern of the Canadian Expeditionary Force, 1914–18.

Adjacent to it, is the **Naismith Foundation Basketball Hall of Fame Museum**. This is particularly appropriate because Dr. Naismith and Dr. Tait McKenzie were good friends. Originally Almonte's town hall, this building was built in 1885 by George Willoughby on the site of an old brickyard. The stately and deliberately asymmetrical, two-towered building originally served as jail, fire hall, library, mayor's and clerk's office, council chamber, and an auditorium.

Return to your car, then drive back down Mill Street, connecting to Bridge Street. Pass the old Town Hall (the present-day basketball museum) and over the second, larger bridge spanning the Mississippi River. At its far side, the road becomes Queen Street. On your left is a two-and-a-half storey home, **Menzies House**, built in 1853. One of the city's oldest homes, it has a decorative porch extending the full width of the front, supported by six columns.

Opposite it is **Wylie House**, a very solid-looking, emphatically symmetrical house with two rather odd-looking front chimneys that mask a steeply pitched roof. It was built in 1882. Wylie House possesses an intriguing past. During World War II it served as the mess hall for the Princess Louise Dragoon Guards. Who would have thought that during the Cold War it also had a nuclear bomb shelter, making it a "fallout cousin" to the Diefenbunker we passed at the beginning of this ramble.

Continue down Queen Street, which becomes Highway 44 East. Just past the shopping centre on your right, turn right onto Route 17 to Appleton. After about 8 km, turn right on County Road 11 into Appleton. The small home at this corner, the **Doreen Drummond House**, is a museum and tearoom operated by the local Women's Institute.

As you descend the hill into **Appleton,** the road is first called Hill Street. Imagine the scene years back when this was the site of a native settlement. This was the last of the four falls Colonel William Marshall found while he explored the Mississippi in 1822. He named these falls Apple Tree Falls. In 1823 the Teskey family emigrated here from Rathkeale, county Limerick, in Ireland. They settled here alongside these pretty falls and, because they built a series of mills and homes, the community took the name Teskeyville. Eventually, however, the village became known as Appleton, perhaps giving a nod to the falls' first name. Author Howard Brown describes how the town evolved.

> With a population of about seventy five persons by the middle 1850s, it contained Joseph Teskey's grist mill and Robert Teskey's sawmill equipped with two upright saws and a public timber slide. Its other businesses included Albert Teskey's general store and post office, Peter and John F. Cram's tannery, two blacksmith shops, William Young's tailor shop, and a wagon shop. A foundry and machine shop were added shortly before 1860, when the village had population of three hundred. Albert Teskey, a younger brother who lived to 1887, also engaged in lumbering and became reeve of Ramsay township. A flour mill in a stone building erected in 1853 by Joseph Teskey below the east side of the Appleton Falls was operated after his death in 1865 by his son Milton.[101]

As you descend the little hill into the village, it's astonishing to think how prosperous little villages like Appleton and Blakeney once were in the mid- to late 1800s.

Now look left against the hillside: the Georgian stone house overlooking the Mississippi River is the **Joseph Teskey Home**, built around 1840 for the miller. From here he would have been able to survey his domain.

But really, as you approach the Mississippi, it will be very difficult not to stare at the evocative ruins of the **Teskey wool mill**, standing forlornly in the midst of the river. The mill used to be one of two here, both of which produced wool used for manufacturing tweeds and blankets. The Teskey mill burned in 1940 and one of its main functions today is to provide an extremely photogenic subject for amateur and professional camera buffs.

Continue over the bridge and turn left onto Wilson Street, noting the many very lovely old homes lining this side of the Mississippi. Drive down beyond the main bend in County Road 11 to find the **William Wilson House**. This is a very simple neo-classical style frame house built about 160 years ago; it is roughly the same age as the black locust tree in front of it. Turn around and return along the river. Cross the bridge again and turn right onto Church Street, which rejoins Route 17.

Follow Route 17 along the river to Highway 7, whereupon you can turn left to return to Ottawa.

The Mississippi Mills ramble has taken us through two major tributaries of the Ottawa River: the Carp and Mississippi. It seems fitting that our last picturesque village has such a picturesque ruin, evocative of a past era when mills hummed, and sheep grazed in Lanark County. Lost, but not forgotten.

OTHER PLACES OF INTEREST

Morris Island Conservation Area: Located between Fitzroy Harbour and Galetta, off the Logger's Way Road, this conservation area is on an island named after William Morris, who was given the deed of the island in the early 1800s. In the late 1800s a lead mine opened here; it operated until World War I. Here on the island's network of paths you can see granite and quartz, types of rock common to the Precambrian Shield. There is a causeway walking path and a boat launch but please, only kayak or canoe in the inland channel within the protection of the islands. Chats Falls is just downriver and turbulence can create problems for all but the most experienced paddlers. (See Chats Falls ramble.)

Fitzroy Harbour and Fitzroy Provincial Park: Instead of turning left at the first T-junction (at Routes 5 and 22), turn right. Immediately after crossing the railway tracks take a sharp left and follow this road into Fitzroy Harbour. Located on the south shore of the Ottawa River, this park provides an access point to Chats Falls because there is a boat launch here. As well, it makes a delightful summertime and early autumn destination unto itself. Register early, however, because this is a very popular campground for families. You can see three-hundred-year-old bur oak and white pine that are over one hundred years old here, and enjoy good fishing, bird watching, and hiking on a 2 km trail.

Carp Airport: Several times my husband Eric I have hired a pilot to fly us over the National Capital Region. It's great fun, and there is no better way to get an understanding of the physical features of glaciation and watersheds.

Carp Agricultural Fair is held during the last weekend in September. 2003 marked the 140th consecutive fair here. Every weekend during the summertime there is the **Carp Farmer's Market** here on the grounds.

Pakenham, **Almonte,** and the **Mill of Kintail** are all worthy of full-day visits. All offer seasonal events and there are guided walking tours in both villages (enquire at the visitors' centres).

Kayaking, canoeing, and cycling opportunities abound along this ramble, so your first drive could be a happy scouting mission.

Bibliography

SUGGESTED READING

Many authors have written books on the National Capital Region. I offer this list to you for your further enjoyment. Several of these volumes are out of print but variously available through such places as the City of Ottawa Archives, National Archives of Canada, and the Ottawa Room of the Metcalfe Street Ottawa Library.

Also note that many local historical societies have their own publications. Of particular note is the Gatineau Valley Historical Society (prior to 2003, known as the Historical Society of the Gatineau), which has published an annual collection of historical essays in its *Up the Gatineau!* booklet. This excellent resource has been published since 1975. Other notable and similar resources are the Société d'histoire de l'Outaouais, Aylmer Heritage Association, and Historical Society of Ottawa. In terms of natural history, The Canadian Field-Naturalist has published much on the region.

Aldred, Diane. *The Aylmer Road: An Illustrated History/Le Chemin D'Aylmer: Une histoire Illustrée*. Aylmer Heritage Association, 1994.

______. *Aylmer Québec Its Heritage/Aylmer Québec Son Patrimoine*. Aylmer Heritage Association, 1989.

Atherton, Jay, ed. *Echoes From the Past: Articles on the History of the Gatineau, From the Pages of The Low Down to Hull and Back News, with Pat Evans*. Historical Society of the Gatineau, 1998.

Begin, Richard M. *From Conroy's Inn to the British Hotel More than 150 Years of History in Aylmer*. Aylmer Heritage Association, 1993.

Belden, H. *Illustrated Historical Atlas of the County of Carleton (including city of Ottawa) Ont., Compiled Drawn and Published from Personal Examinations and Surveys*. H. Belden & Co., 1879.

Bond, Courtney C.J. *City on the Ottawa*. Ministry of Public Works, 1971.

_____. *The Ottawa Country*. The Queen's Printer, 1968.

Brown, Harold Morton. *Lanark Legacy: Nineteenth Century Glimpses of an Ontario County*. The Corporation of the County of Lanark, 1984.

Brunton, Daniel F. *Nature and Natural Areas in Canada's Capital. An Introductory Guide for the Ottawa-Hull Area*. The Ottawa Citizen in cooperation with the Ottawa Field-Naturalists' Club, 1988.

Burich, Alice Biehler. *Olden Days: A History of German Settlement in the Township of Mulgrave-Derry, Québec 1850–1890*. Chesley House Publications, 1990.

Champlain, Samuel de. *The Voyages and Explorations of Samuel de Champlain (1604–1616) Narrated by Himself*, Volume II, translated by Annie Nettleton Bourne, 1911.

Croft, Grace, et al. *History and Genealogy of the Milk — Milks Family*. Provo, Utah, 1956.

Cross, Stan. "The Raising." *Up the Gatineau!* vol. 21, Historical Society of the Gatineau, 1995.

Davidson, Aretha (Dale). "Reminiscences of Hartwell's Locks and Hog's Back Locks." In *Memories of the Lockstations*. Gloucester Historical Society Publication Number 1, 1982.

Davidson, Michael. *A Guide to the Gilmour and Hughson Company (1873-1930) Property*. Parc Jacques-Cartier, April 1998. Published on Ottawa University website. <http://aix1.uottawa.ca/~weinberg/gilmour.html>. Accessed February 2004.

Eggleston, Wilfrid. *The Queen's Choice: A Story of Canada's Capital*. National Capital Commission, 1961.

Evans, Pat. *The Tale of Two Chelseas*. Les Éditions J. Oscar Lemieux, 1988.

Finnigan, Joan. *Scary Tales from Canada's Ottawa Valley Witches, Ghosts & Loups-Garous*. Quarry Press, 1994.

Fletcher, Katharine. *Historical Walks: The Gatineau Park Story*. Fitzhenry & Whiteside, 3rd Edition, 2004.

_____. *Capital Walks: Walking Tours of Ottawa*. Fitzhenry & Whiteside, 2nd Edition, 2004.

Fletcher, Katharine, and Eric Fletcher. *Québec Off the Beaten Path*. The Globe Pequot Press, 3rd Edition, 2004.

Fowke, Edith Fulton, and Richard Johnston. *Folk Songs of Québec*. Waterloo Music Company Ltd., 1957.

Gaffield, Chaff, director. *History of the Outaouais*. Institut québécois de recherche sur la culture, 1997.

Gard, Anson A. *Genealogy of the Valley*. Emerson Press, 1906.

_____. *The Hub and the Spokes*. Emerson Press, 1904.

Geggie, Norma, and Stuart Geggie. *Lapêche*. The Historical Society of the Gatineau, 1980.

Geggie, Norma. *A Place Apart: A Search for the Pioneer Cemeteries of the Lower Gatineau Valley*. Chesley House Publications, 1999.

_____. *Wakefield and Its People*. Chesley House Publications, 1990.

Haldimand Papers, B115.

Hanrahan, Christine, and Stephen Darbyshire. *The Natural Values and Ecological Significance of The Petrie Islands*. Conservation Committee of the Ottawa Field-Naturalist's Club, November 1998 for submission to the Regional Municipality of Ottawa-Carleton. Quoted on Friends of Petrie Island website, <http://www.fallingbrook.com/petrieisland/index.html>. Accessed February 2004.

Hessel, Peter. *The Algonkin Tribe*. Kichesippi Books, 1987.

Hogarth, Dr. Donald. *A Guide to the Geology of the Gatineau-Lièvre District*. Reprint from *The Canadian Field-Naturalist*, vol. 76, no. 1 (January–March 1962): 1–55.

Hughson, John W., and Courtney C. J. Bond. *Hurling Down the Pine*, 2nd edition, Historical Society of the Gatineau, 1965.

Johnson, Duncan W. *Royal Visit: Ottawa Valley Tourist Guide 1939–1940*. The Ottawa Valley Tourist Bureau, 1939.

Johnston, Grace, ed. *Memories of the Lockstations*. Gloucester Historical Society Publication No. 1, 1982.

Jolicoeur, Joseph. *Histoire anecdotique de Hull*. Société Historique de l'Ouest du Québec Inc., 1977.

Keddy, Dr. Paul. *Earth, Water, Fire An Ecological Profile of Lanark County*. First Edition. Motion Creative Printing, 1999.

Kennedy, Clyde C. *The Upper Ottawa Valley: A Glimpse of Canada*. Renfrew County Council, 1970.

Laidlaw, M. *Heritage Highway — The Scenic Route to the Pontiac*. EU Editions, 2000.

Last, Rupert John. *Know Thy Neighbour: History of Poltimore and Its People*. A.F. Perrin, 1988.

Local Architectural Conservation Advisory Committee. *Cumberland Heritage: Heritage Buildings of Cumberland Township*. 1988.

MacDonald, Malcolm. *The Birds of Brewery Creek*. Oxford University Press, 1947.

March Historical Society. *Guide to a Heritage Tour of March*. 1985.

Marshall, Herbert. *History of the Ottawa Ski Club*. Private Publication, n.d. (circa 1973).

Meech, Marion. "Asa Meech." *Up the Gatineau!* vol. 7, Historical Society of the Gatineau, 1981.

McGiffin, Verna Ross. *Pakenham: Ottawa Valley Village 1823–1860*. Mississippi Publishers, 1963.

Millennium Committee of Quyon. *Quyon-Onslow 1875–2000 Souvenir of the Millennium*. ABCDezine, 2000.

Mondoux, Michelle. *Maires d'Aylmer Mayors 1847–2001 Profils Biographiques des Maires et des membres du dernier conseil/Biographic Profiles of its mayors and members of the last council*. Michelle Mondoux, 2001.

National Capital Commission. *A Capital in the Making: Reflections of the Past, Visions of the Future*. National Capital Commission. 1998.

National Geographic Magazine. "The Dawn of Humans: Peopling of the Americas," Supplement to *National Geographic*, December 2000 [Map].

Page, Enid. *Discover Aylmer's Heritage*. Aylmer Heritage Association, 1993.

Passfield, Robert W. *Building the Rideau Canal: A Pictorial History*. Fitzhenry & Whiteside in association with Parks Canada and the Canadian Government Publishing Centre, 1982.

Phillips, R.A.J. *L'Histoire de Cantley The History of Cantley*. Municipalité de Cantley, 1989.

Pilon, Jean-Luc, ed. *Ottawa Valley Prehistory/La préhistoire de l'Outaouais*. Société d'histoire de l'Outaouais, Outaouais no. 6, 1999.

Reford, Michael. "The Hetherington Farm." *Up the Gatineau!* vol. 19, Historical Society of the Gatineau, 1993.

Reid, Bertha. "Some Spring News — 1888." Letter as published in *Up the Gatineau!* vol. 17, 1991.

Reid, Richard M., ed. *The Upper Ottawa Valley to 1855*. The Publications of the Champlain Society, Ontario Series XIV, Carleton Library Series No. 157. Carleton University Press, 1990.

Rowat, Mel. "Long Island." In *Memories of the Lockstations*. Gloucester Historical Society Publication Number 1, 1982.

Sabina, Ann P. *Rocks and Minerals for the Collector. Ottawa To North Bay, Ontario; Hull to Waltham, Québec*. Department of Energy, Mines and Resources, Paper 70–50, 1975.

Sadler, Fred. *The Romance of Fitzroy Harbour*. General Store Publishing House. 1983.

Smith, William Loe. *Pioneers of Old Ontario*. 1923.

Société Historique de l'Ouest du Québec. *Asticou: Revue d'histoire de l'Outaouais*, Cahier no. 38, Juillet 1988.

Sowter, T.W. Edwin. *Highway of the Ottawa*. Ontario Historical Society. 1917.

_____. *Algonkin and Huron Occupation of the Ottawa Valley*.

_____. *29th Annual Archaeological Report*, Ontario Ministry of Education, 1917.

Vermette, Luce, and Suzanne Joubert. Le Village d'Argentine: Quelques mots d'histoire. L'Association du Patrimoine du Ruisseau, 1992.

Walker, Harry. *100 Years Ottawa and The Valley: A Backward Glance from Centennial Year*. Reprinted from *The Ottawa Journal*, January-March 1967.

Walker, Harry, and Olive Walker. *The Carleton Saga*. Carleton County Council. 1968.

Welch, Edwin. *Sights and Surveys: Two Diarists on the Rideau*. Historical Society of Ottawa, 1979.

Wheatley, Gerry. "A History of the Mills of Almonte." *Our Heritage*. Ed. Alex Hughes. vol. 1 no. 1. The Mississippi Valley Textile Museum, 1994.

Wilson, Alice E. "Geology of the Ottawa District." *The Canadian Field-Naturalist*. vol. 70, no. 1 (January–March 1956).

Wright, Philemon. *Sketch of the First Settlement of the Ottawa or Grand River*. 1824.

Acknowledgements

Capital Rambles has been on my mind for years. Bringing our region's stories and history to life, however, meant talking to a host of people who are experts on the National Capital Region, whether they be knowledgeable long-time local residents, archivists, authors, photographers, scientists, or planners. Thanks to the team at Fitzhenry & Whiteside — particularly my editor Etan Diamond — my dream of seeing *Capital Rambles* published has been realized.

My husband Eric was my companion in all my rambles whether we were paddling our cedar strip canoe, *Windigo*, as we explored our regions many waterways, or skiing, hiking, biking, horseback riding, or driving. As always, he created all my maps, read my text — and helped render all digital images included here. Special thanks to my mother, who never flags in her enthusiasm and support for my projects. She gave me three gifts: a love of the wild spaces, unbounded curiosity, and confidence to pursue my goals. Thanks, mum!

The City of Ottawa Archives possess a most helpful crew: Senior Archivist David Bullock, photographer Serge Blondin, and Archivist Serge Barbe added insight and factual corroboration along the way. Thanks, also, for the many digital images they supplied.

Eric and I have been members of the Gatineau Valley Historical Society for a long time, since the mid-1980s. The Society has always been particularly supportive of my books, and this time round was no exception. They gave me many photographs from their digital archives. Jay Atherton and Adrienne Herron: thank you so much for your time, your support. I also want to thank the members who have contributed to the *Up the Gatineau!* series of annual Society publications: their efforts are crucial contributions to the understanding of our roots.

José Lafleur, media relations at the Association Touristique de l'Outaouais, found contacts for me who are specialists on old Hull: through her, I met Raymond Jolicoeur, son of author Joseph Jolicoeur, whose books I used for research. Raymond squired me about Brewery Creek and put me in touch with the L'Association du patrimoine du Ruisseau (Brewery Creek Heritage Association). André Joyce of the Buckingham Historical Society provided historical information regarding his city, too, as did Eileen Blair from the Cumberland Heritage Village Museum.

And where would any of us be without authors who have gone before, documenting our past? Although my Bibliography lists many, I need to thank my colleagues who have assisted with interpretations and explanations when history seemed puzzling. The late author Diane Aldred was a long-time mentor and heritage friend of mine. Her painstakingly researched books on Aylmer are treasures and when she passed away in January 2003, Aylmer and the National Capital Region lost one of its tireless defenders. Norma Geggie and Alice Biehler Burich are two other extremely knowledgeable historians with whom I've had the privilege to work, when I published their books in 1990. And recognition must also go to the Quyon Millennium Committee who produced the booklet on that village's history for its 125th anniversary. Where would we be without such chroniclers? I hope they understand how valuable their legacy truly is.

We also need our biologists and scientists to help us understand and protect the biodiversity of our region. Dan Brunton is an environmental consultant, biologist, and author of countless scientific papers on species of wildlife here: thank you for your tireless contributions. I want also to thank Tony Beck, Ottawa-area birder and international wildlife tour guide — a good friend of mine — for sharing his knowledge of birds with me over the years.

I had the pleasure of interviewing the National Capital Commission's Chief Planner, Pierre Dubé for details regarding the development of the NCR. Others who patiently answered my detailed questions include "the answer lady," Director of Communications Laurie Peters, and members of her staff. As always, director of Gatineau Park Jean-Réné Doyon was a pleasure to interview.

Thanks to individual friends, too, for sharing information. George Toller is a constant source of information regarding my home region of West Quebec: thanks for all your clippings, phone calls, and support! Tony Ahearn offered information about his great-grandfather Thomas Ahearn; editor and writer Barbara Sibbald leant support when my writer's angst presented roadblocks. For those of you whom I haven't mentioned, but who have assisted in untold ways, thank you.

Finally, thanks to you, the reader. I write for you. I hope my work inspires your greater understanding of and love for our National Capital Region. As usual, I welcome your comments, updates, and stories. Please, don't hesitate to contact me at chesley@allstream.net or at the address below.

Katharine Fletcher
4316 Steele Line
Quyon, Québec, J0X 2V0
March, 2004.

Endnotes

1 Alice E. Wilson, "Geology of the Ottawa District," *The Canadian Field Naturalist* vol. 70, no. 1 (1956): 13.

2 Joseph Jolicoeur, *Histoire anecdotique de Hull* (Société Historique de l'Ouest du Québec Inc., 1977), 5–6.

3 Haldimand Papers, B115.

4 Alice Biehler Burich, *Olden Days: A History of German Settlement in the Township of Mulgrave-Derry, Québec 1850-1890* (Chesley House Publications, 1990), 14.

5 Ibid., 14.

6 Ibid., 17.

7 National Capital Commission (NCC), *A Capital in the Making: Reflections of the Past, Visions of the Future* (NCC, 1998), p. 8.

8 Mohammed Adam, *The Ottawa Citizen* (September 23, 2002), B3.

9 Quoted from Friends of Petrie Island website, <http://www.fallingbrook.com/petrieisland/index.html>. Accessed February 2004.

10 John MacTaggart, as excerpted from *Sights and Surveys: Two Diarists on the Rideau*, ed. Edwin Welch (Historical Society of Ottawa, 1979), 15-16.

11 Harry Walker, *100 Years Ottawa and The Valley: A Backward Glance from Centennial Year*, (reprinted from *The Ottawa Journal*, January–March 1967), 25–27.

12 Robert W. Passfield, *Building the Rideau Canal: A Pictorial History* (Fitzhenry & Whiteside in association with Parks Canada and the Canadian Government Publishing Centre, 1982), 17.

13 Ibid., 28.

14 Wilson, "Geology of the Ottawa District," 28.

15 Aretha (Dale) Davidson, "Reminiscences of Hartwell's Locks and Hog's Back Locks," in *Memories of the Lockstations* (Gloucester Historical Society Publication Number 1, 1982), no page numbers.

16 Passfield, *Building the Rideau Canal: A Pictorial History*, 64.

17 Davidson, "Reminiscences of Hartwell's Locks and Hog's Back Locks."

18 Mel Rowat, "Long Island," in *Memories of the Lockstations* (Gloucester Historical Society Publication Number 1, 1982), no page numbers.

19 Passfield, *Building the Rideau Canal: A Pictorial History*, 78.

20 Ibid., 78.

21 Ibid., 78.

22 Courtney C.J. Bond, *The Ottawa Country* (The Queen's Printer, 1968), 170–1.

23 Christine Hanrahan and Stephen Darbyshire, *The Natural Values and Ecological Significance of The Petrie Islands*, (Conservation Committee of the Ottawa Field-Naturalist's Club, November 1998, for submission to the Regional Municipality of Ottawa-Carleton), no page nos, quoted on Friends of Petrie Island website, <http://www.fallingbrook.com/petrieisland/index.html>. Accessed February 2004.

24 Printed chronology as supplied to me by Cumberland Historical Village Museum staff, October 2002.

25 H. Belden, *Illustrated Historical Atlas of the County of Carleton (including city of Ottawa) Ont., Compiled Drawn and Published from Personal Examinations and Surveys* (H. Belden & Co., 1879), 36.

26 Local Architectural Conservation Advisory Committee, *Cumberland Heritage* (1988).

27 Bond, *The Ottawa Country*, 182.

28 Chaff Gaffield, *History of the Outaouais* (Institut québécois de recherche sur la culture, 1997), 260.

29 Ibid., 269.

30 Ibid.

31 Ibid., 271.

32 Ibid.

33 From a map, Ville de Buckingham, Carte des rues, Édition 2000. As provided by Buckingham Historical Society.

34 Dr. Donald Hogarth, "Geology of Gatineau-Lièvre District," *The Canadian Field Naturalist*, vol. 76, no. 1 (January–March 1962): 34–35.

35 Patrick Philip Ryan, "The History Of The Town Of Buckingham Prior To 1900" (Dissertation submitted to the Faculty of Arts of St. Patrick's University), published on website on history of Buckingham, Quebec. <http://iquebec.ifrance.com/maclaren/>. Accessed February 2004.

36 Rupert Last, *Know thy Neighbour: History of Poltimore and its People* (A.F. Perrin, 1988), 21.

37 Ibid., 29.

38 Ibid., 30.

39 Grace Croft, et al., *History and Genealogy of the Milk — Milks Family*. (Provo, Utah, 1956), 85.

40 Samuel de Champlain, *The Voyages and Explorations of Samuel de Champlain (1604-1616) Narrated by Himself*, Volume II, translated by Annie Nettleton Bourne (1911), 11.

41 Claire Saint-Germain, "The End of the Pre-Contact Period in the Ottawa Valley — A Look at the Zooarchaeology of the Leamy Lake Park Sites," *Ottawa Valley Prehistory*, ed. Jean-Luc Pilon (Société d'histoire de l'Outaouais, Outaouais no. 6, 1999), 88.

42 Ibid., 91.

43 Randy Boswell, "Bones of Contention," *The Ottawa Citizen* (31 December 2002).

44 John W. Hughson and Courtney C. J. Bond, "Hurling Down the Pine" (Historical Society of the Gatineau, Second Edition, 1965), 22.

45 Quoted from the Gatineau Valley Historical Society's website. Accessed February 2003. (Note: As of February 2004 website is under reconstruction.)

46 Pat Evans, *Echoes From the Past: Articles on the History of the Gatineau, from the Pages of the Low Down to Hull and Back News*, compiled by Jay Atherton (Historical Society of the Gatineau, 1998), 14.

47 Bertha Reid, "Some Spring News — 1888" letter as published in *Up the Gatineau!* vol. 17, 1991, 19.

48 Norma Geggie, *Wakefield and Its People* (Chesley House Publications, 1990), p. 72.

49 Evans, *Echoes From the Past*, 15.

50 Norma Geggie, caption on photograph in Gatineau Valley Historical Society archival database, an archival note written by author Norma Geggie, annotating photograph #00072.

51 Geggie, *Wakefield and Its People*, 84.

52 Diane Aldred, *The Aylmer Road: An Illustrated History* (Aylmer Heritage Association, 1994), 76.

53 Ibid., 77.

54 Michael Davidson, A *Guide to the Gilmour and Hughson Company (1873-1930) Property*, (Parc Jacques-Cartier, April 1998), published on Ottawa University website. <http://aix1.uottawa.ca/~weinberg/gilmour.html>. Accessed February 2004.

55 Luce Vermette and Suzanne Joubert, "Le Village d'Argentine: Quelques mots d'histoire" (l'Association du Patrimoine du Ruisseau, 1992), 5.

56 Malcom MacDonald, *The Birds of Brewery Creek* (Oxford University Press, 1947), 99.

57 Ibid., 4.

58 Ibid., 285.

59 Chaffield, *History of the Outaouais*, 266.

60 Aldred, *The Aylmer Road*, 17.

61 Ibid., 18.

62 Enid Page, *Discover Aylmer's Heritage* (Aylmer Historical Society, 1993), 5.

63 Ibid., 30.

64 Aldred, *The Aylmer Road*, 172.

65 Bond, *The Ottawa Country*, 55.

66 Page, *Discover Aylmer's Heritage*, 27.

67 Bond, *The Ottawa Country*, 60.

68 Anson A. Gard, *Genealogy of the Valley* (Emerson Press, 1906), 38.

69 Marion Meech, "Asa Meech," *Up the Gatineau!* vol. 7 (HSG, 1981), 15.

70 Sheila C. Thomson, "Recollections of early days in the Gatineau Hills," (unpublished manuscript, collected and recorded by Sheila C. Thomson, circa 1965), 77.

71 Ibid., 163.

72 Ibid., 96.

73 Michael Reford, "The Hetherington Farm," *Up the Gatineau!* vol. 19 (HSG, 1993), 32.

74 Geggie, *Wakefield and Its People*, 69.

75 Stan Cross, "The Raising," *Up the Gatineau!* vol. 21 (HSG, 1995), 20-21.

76 Harry Walker and Olive Walker, *The Carleton Saga* (Carleton County Council, 1968), 225–6.

77 Ibid., 241.

78 T.W. Edwin Sowter, *29th Annual Archaeological Report* (Ontario Ministry of Education, 1917).

79 Clyde C. Kennedy, *The Upper Ottawa Valley: A Glimpse of Canada* (Renfrew County Council, 1970), 7-8.

80 T.W. Edwin Sowter, *Highway of the Ottawa* (Ontario Historical Society, 1915), 47-49.

81 Walker and Walker, *The Carleton Saga*, 225.

82 Ibid., 231.

83 Ibid., 237.

84 March Historical Society, *Guide to A Heritage Tour of March* (March Historical Society, 1985), 15.

85 Walker and Walker, *The Carleton Saga*, 527.

86 S.W. MacKechnie, "Early History," in *Quyon-Onslow 1875-2000 Souvenir of the Millennium* (Millennium Committee of Quyon, ABCDezine, 2000), 4.

87 M. Laidlaw, *Heritage Highway — The Scenic Route to the Pontiac* (EU Editions, 2000), 18.

88 Bond, *The Ottawa Country*, 67.

89 Kennedy, *The Upper Ottawa Valley*, 144.

90 Ibid., 133.

91 Father Basil Tanguay, "The Church of the Holy Name of Mary," in *Quyon-Onslow 1875-2000, Souvenir of the Millennium* (Millennium Committee of Quyon, ABCDezine, 2000), 16.

92 Kennedy, *The Upper Ottawa Valley*, 142.

93 William Loe Smith, *Pioneers of Old Ontario* (1923), 13.

94 Howard Morton Brown, *Lanark Legacy: Nineteenth Century Glimpses of an Ontario County* (The Corporation of the County of Lanark, 1984), 2.

95 Verna Ross McGiffin, *Pakenham, Ottawa Valley Village* (Mississippi Publishers, 1963), 13.

96 H. Belden, *Illustrated Historical Atlas of the County of Carleton, including Ottawa, 1879, H. Belden & Co.*, Wilson's Publishing Company, 1997, xiii.

97 McGiffin, *Pakenham, Ottawa Valley Village*, 37.

98 Daniel F. Brunton, *Nature and Natural Areas in Canada's Capital: An Introductory Guide for the Ottawa-Hull Area* (*The Ottawa Citizen* in cooperation with The Ottawa Field-Naturalists' Club, 1988), 144.

99 Bond, *The Ottawa Country*, 121.

100 Gerry Wheatley, "A History of the Mills of Almonte," *Our Heritage*, ed. Alex Hughes, v. 1, no. 1 (The Mississippi Valley Textile Museum, 1994), 8.

101 Brown, *Lanark Legacy*, 128.

Index

Numbers in bold indicate photograph or illustration